How to Comply with Federal Employee Laws

Sheldon I. London

Cover Design — *Eric Baker Design Associates, Inc.*

Design and Composition — *Advanced Graphics of Virginia, Ltd.*

Printing and Binding — *Peake Printers, Inc.*

HOW TO COMPLY WITH FEDERAL EMPLOYEE LAWS

ISBN 0-9613262-2-0
Library of Congress Card Catalog Number: 90-91576
Revised Edition

This publication is designed to provide accurate and authoritative information in regard the subject matter covered. It is sold with the understanding that the publisher is not engaged in rendering legal, accounting, or other professional service. If legal advice or other expert assistance is required, the service of a competent professional person should be sought. *From a Declaration of Principle jointly accepted by a Committee of the American Bar Association and Committee of Publishers.*

HOW TO COMPLY WITH FEDERAL EMPLOYEE LAWS

Table of Contents

Chapter 3 Fair Labor Standards Act—Overtime Pay

Chapter 4 Fair Labor Standards Act—Enforcement

Chapter 5 Employees/Independent Contractors

Chapter 6 Equal Pay Act

Chapter 7   Equal Opportunity and Anti-Bias Laws

Chapter 8   Americans with Disabilities Act

Chapter 9   Age Discrimination

Chapter 10   National Labor Relations Act and Union Organizing

Chapter 11   Occupational Safety and Health

Chapter 12   Employee Insurance and Pension Laws

Introduction

I admire employers and I wrote this book for them. I did so because there is a vastly expanding body of law and regulations governing their relationships with employees, and it at best can be confusing, and at worst, downright intimidating. I wanted to make some sense from this staggering array of laws and simplify compliance. If in some way my enterprise removes the doubts and concerns, I will have succeeded.

This book was written for the 1990s and can be used by the employer with a single employee or a corporation with thousands of employees. I studiously have avoided filling the text with long and involved legal explanations. This lawyer is proud of the fact that he has used no legal footnotes. The effort has been to keep it simple and understandable.

There is, however, an obvious note of caution. The various state laws and regulations governing employers and employees are outside the coverage of this text. Therefore, I recommend consulting with competent legal and accounting professionals for specific guidance on these state issues.

While I have written the book for employers, I have sought to give balanced guidance on how to build a positive work environment and employee loyalty. In this decade the emphasis must be on human resources. Your employees must be seen as assets, capable of growth and enhancement. Finding, training, and retaining quality employees will be among the significant challenges confronting employers in the 1990s.

I hope that you find this book useful and a valued reference. I enjoyed writing it for you.

Sheldon I. London

Acknowledgements

I have received the valued assistance of a number of experts, and they have immeasurably contributed to this text. I would like to express my gratitude to the following:

Gerald L. Paley, a partner in the Rochester, New York, law firm of Phillips, Lytle, Hitchcock, Blaine and Huber.

Mark A. de Bernardo, D. C. resident partner of the San Francisco, California, law firm of Littler, Mendelson, Fastiff & Tichy and Executive Director of the Institute for a Drug-Free Workplace.

John S. Satagaj, my law partner and President of the Small Business Legislative Council.

There are many anonymous regulations and public information writers in federal government agencies who have made my job easier, and I would like to extend my thanks to them.

Dedicated to Barney London, my first employer,
to honor him in his 85th year.

How to Hire and Keep Quality Employees 1

Employees as Assets

In the decade of the '90s, there is going to be a significant shortage of qualified employees. In these circumstances, wise employers will treat their employees as assets that can appreciate in value. The challenge will not only be to find the right people, but to retain them and make them loyal and productive parts of your enterprise.

In this Chapter we outline some of the effective strategies employers might consider in setting up their personnel policies. While the actual proced-ure may not be applicable to every employer, the principles are tried and tested and they can help employers create an effective workforce.

Hiring Procedures

Good personnel practice begins with the hiring process. All job applicants should be evaluated consistently as part of the interviewing process.

There are two issues that deserve additional explanation. One relates to pre-employment/ap-plication form questions, and the other, to references.

Hiring Checklist

☐ Write a job description for the vacant position or review the old one, updating the duties required.

☐ Make a skills profile which lists the precise duties of the position and the skills needed to accomplish these duties in a minimally acceptable manner.

☐ Receive applications and evaluate them. Notify unqualified candidates. Rank qualified ones.

☐ Schedule interviews. Prepare specific open-ended questions which will help to determine whether the applicant will be able to accomplish the duties of the position.

☐ Discuss the duties, responsibilities, and skills required; and describe the wages, benefits, advancement opportunities, and other aspects of the job.

☐ Summarize the interview in a written report and retain in a file.

☐ Check the candidate's references.

☐ Check the requisite documents to determine whether the new hire is a U.S. citizen or has the proper authority to work in the U.S., and complete the INS Form I-9.

☐ Federal law prohibits the use of a polygraph to prescreen prospective employees in most situations.

Pre-Employment/Application Form Inquiries — New York is among the strictest states in regard to pre-employment inquiries, and the Human Rights Agency has issued the following guidelines on what is lawful and unlawful from both a state and federal viewpoint:

Application Checklist

Subject	Lawful	Unlawful
Age	Are you 18 years of age or older? If not, state your age. Do you have a work permit?	How old are you? What is your date of birth? What are the ages of your children, if any?
Arrest Record	Have you ever been convicted of a crime? (Give details)	Have you ever been arrested?
Disability	None	Do you have a disability? Have you ever been treated for any of the following diseases . . .? Do you have now, or have you ever had, a drug or alcohol problem?
Marital Status	None	Do you wish to be addressed as Miss? Mrs.? Ms.? Are you married? Single? Divorced? Separated? Any information about one's spouse.
National Origin	None	Inquiry into applicant's lineage, ancestry, national origin, descent, parentage or nationality. Nationality of applicant's parents.
Race or Color	None	Complexion or color of skin. Coloring.
Sex	None	
Address or Duration of Residents	Applicant's place of residence. How long a resident of this state or city?	
Birthdate/ Birthplace	None	Requirements that applicant submit birth certificate, naturalization or baptismal record. Requirement that applicant produce proof of age in form of birth certificate or baptismal record.
Citizenship	Are you a citizen of the United States? If not a citizen of the United States, do you intend to become a citizen of the United States? If you are not a United States citizen, have you the legal right to remain permanently in the United States? Do you intend to remain permanently in the United States?	Of what country are you a citizen? Whether an applicant is naturalized or a native-born citizen; the date when the applicant acquired citizenship. Requirement that applicant produce naturalization papers or first papers. Whether applicant's parents are naturalized or native-born citizens of the United States; the date when such parents acquired citizenship.
Driver's License	Do you possess a valid driver's license?	Requirement that applicant produce a driver's license.
Education	Inquiry into applicant's academic, vocational, or professional education and the public and private schools attended.	
Experience	Inquiry into work experience.	
Language	Inquiry into languages applicant speaks or writes fluently.	What is your native language? Inquiry into how applicant acquired ability to read, write, or speak a foreign language.
Military Experience	Inquiry into applicant's military experience in the Armed Forces of the United States or in a State Militia. Inquiring into applicant's service in particular branch of United States Army, Navy, etc.	Inquiry into applicant's military experience other than in the Armed Forces of the United States or in a State Militia. Did you receive a discharge from the military in other than honorable circumstances?
Notice in Case of Emergency	None	Name and address of person to be notified in case of an accident or emergency.
Organizations	Inquiry into applicant's membership in organizations which the applicant considers relevant to his or her ability to perform the job.	List all clubs, societies, and lodges to which you belong.
Photograph	None	Requirement or option that applicant affix a photograph to employment form at any time before hiring.

References — There are many employers who have been counseled to give only confirming facts that relate to dates of employment and title held, but nothing more. Not even when pressed with the question, "Would the individual be eligible for rehire?", would the ex-employer answer. The possible liability from defamation of character lawsuits brought by former employees who believe that their inability to land a position stems from an adverse job reference has had a chilling effect on references.

If a reference on a potential employee is going to be important to you, as it should be, then a waiver form should be signed by the job applicant to the effect that the individual authorizes a former employer "to provide any and all information contained in my personnel file to the prospective employer." Furthermore, the applicant should release that employer from any and all claims of liability arising out of the sharing of such information. The waiver release should be signed and dated.

In seven states—California, Indiana, Kansas, Minnesota, Missouri, North Carolina, and Oklahoma—an employer can, in certain circumstances, be required to provide a letter concerning the past service of a discharged employee. In these instances, the individual state law should be consulted.

Employment Policy — Employers should give job applicants a copy of the company's employment policy statement at the time of hire and prior to their joining the work force. It also should be included in a firm's employee handbook and manual.

Employers also may wish to have employees sign a copy of this statement (sample language is provided in the Model Employee Handbook in the Appendix). The signed and dated copy should be retained in the employee's personnel file.

Immigration Control — Verification of Employment

The Immigration Reform and Control Act *affects all employers.* It contains several provisions which require employers to institute procedures for verifying that a job applicant is authorized to be employed in the United States. It also establishes civil and criminal penalties for knowingly hiring, referring, recruiting, or retaining in employment "unauthorized aliens."

All employers must verify that every new hire is either a U.S. citizen or authorized to work in the country. As a defense to a claim of violation, the employer should require of every new hire: birth or naturalization certificate, or U.S. passport or an unexpired foreign passport authorizing U.S. employment, or a resident alien card containing the new hire's identification and U.S. employment authorization (the "green card"). In the absence of any of those, the employer should require *two* documents: Social Security card and driver's license or similar state identification. The employer should photocopy any such documents and keep them on file.

The Act also requires employers to state on Immigration and Naturalization Service Form I-9 (a copy is in Appendix) that they have examined the necessary documents which show that the individual is not an unauthorized alien. The new hire must also attest on the verification form that he or she qualifies for employment. The verification forms must be retained for three years from the date of hire or one year from the date of termination, whichever is longer. There are civil penalties for violating these recordkeeping requirements.

Identity and Eligibility Documents

The law requires employers to verify *both* identity and authorization of eligibility for employment. Some documents are acceptable as evidence to fulfill both requirements, while others may fulfill only one or the other.

The following documents are acceptable evidence of both identity and employment eligibility:

1. United States passport;
2. Certificate of United States Citizenship, INS Form N-560 or N-561;
3. Certificate of Naturalization, INS Form N-550 or N-570;

4. An unexpired foreign passport which:
   (i.) contains an unexpired stamp therein which reads, "Processed for I-551. Temporary Evidence of Lawful Admission of Permanent Residence. Valid until — Employment Authorized"; or
   (ii.) has attached thereto a Form I-94 bearing the same name as the passport and contains an employment authorization stamp.
5. Alien Registration Receipt Card, INS Form I-151 or Resident Alien INS Form I-511, provided that it contains a photograph of the bearer;
6. Temporary Resident Card, INS Form I-688;
7. Employment Authorization Card, INS Form I-688A.

The following documents are acceptable to establish identity *only* for individuals 16 years of age or older:

- A state-issued driver's license or state-issued identification card containing a photograph and identifying information such as name, date of birth, sex, height, color of eyes, and address;
- School identification card with a photograph;
- Voter registration card;
- U.S. military card or draft record;
- Identification card issued by federal, state, or local government agencies or entities;
- Military dependent's identification card;
- Native American tribal documents;
- United States Coast Guard Merchant Mariner Card;
- Driver's license issued by a Canadian government authority.

Employee Handbooks

An Employee Handbook is one of the most common methods used by employers to communicate their personnel policies and benefit programs. It should set forth in detail the benefits, policies, and disciplinary rules of the company and should be updated periodically.

In recent years, there have been numerous court decisions which have held that employee handbooks constitute a contract of employment; accordingly, the common law right to dismiss at will has been carved out in certain jursidictions. It would be advisable, therefore, to check on the status of the "employment at will" doctrine in your state. An employee handbook cannot replace personal communication, but it is an effective means for informing your employees about vital information. It is safe to say that the advantages of a handbook far outweigh any potential drawbacks.

There are a number of words and phrases that employers should avoid using in their handbooks, and, for that matter, in job application forms, training manuals, letters offering employment, company policy statements, and employee evaluation forms. The following terms invite wrongful discharge claims based upon implied contract rights or an implied covenant of good faith and fair dealing (concepts which are discussed in some detail in the following Chapter):

- "just cause"
- "good cause"
- "good faith"
- "guaranteed"
- "long term"
- "secured"
- "job security"
- "permanent"
- "career path"
- "job tenure"
- "due process"
- "annual review"

There is contained in the Appendix a model Employee Handbook for the "ABC Widget Company" which illustrates what such a document should contain: a description of personnel policies, compensation, employee benefits, group insurance and retirement plans, and other provisions. The model handbook is readily adaptable for most employment situations. It contains some of the prevailing ideas for developing a personnel handbook. It is offered as an example, but one should structure a handbook with caution and have it reviewed by counsel.

Orientation for New Employees

After an individual has been hired, an orientation session with the employee should be held to discuss, in detail, the company's benefits

Some Frequently Asked
Questions About Immigration Law

1. **Q. Do these penalties apply to people who have hired illegal aliens before the new law?**

   A. No. The penalties apply only to newly hired workers. They do not apply to the continuing employment of illegal aliens who were hired prior to the law's enactment. In practice, no penalties will be imposed for at least six months after the bill is signed into law.

2. **Q. Is an employer subject to penalties if a legal alien is hired who later becomes illegal if, for example, he remains in the Untied States beyond the authorized time?**

   A. The answer is "yes" when an employer knows the alien has become illegal, but the penalties would not apply if the alien was hired before the legislation was signed into law.

3. **Q. What is the employer's responsibility?**

   A. An employer must now ask *all* job applicants for documents to verify that they are either United States citizens or aliens authorized to work in this country.

4. **Q. Does the employer have to check the authenticity of the documents?**

   A. No. An employer fulfills his responsibility if he examines the documents and each document "reasonably appears, on its face, to be genuine."

5. **Q. Do U.S. citizens have to show documents?**

   A. Yes. Note that the Immigration Act now affects each new "hire" and imposes new paperwork requirements.

6. **Q. Is there any penalty for an employer who fails to ask job applicants for identification documents?**

   A. Yes. The employer is subject to a civil penalty of $100 to $1,000 each time he fails to verify the status of a job applicant.

7. **Q. Is the employer subject to such penalties even if the person he hires is a United States citizen?**

   A. Yes.

8. **Q. How will the Government know if an employer has complied with these requirements?**

   A. Employers must sign Immigration and Naturalization Service Form I-9 certifying that they have examined the required documents. In addition, each person hired must certify, on the same form, that he is a citizen or an alien authorized to work in the United States. The employer must retain these forms for at least three years, and may not dispose of them until one year after the individual's employment ends.

9. **Q. Does an employer have to keep the paperwork for people not hired?**

   A. The bill does not require the employer to keep such paperwork. Some employers may do so voluntarily to show that they were not discriminating against Hispanic people or other groups.

10. **Q. What if an employer simply refuses to hire people who, in his eyes, appear to be foreigners?**

    A. It is already illegal for an employer to discriminate on the basis of national origin under the Civil Rights Act of 1964. The Equal Employment Opportunity Commission (EEOC) will continue to investigate these kinds of allegations of discrimination. The Immigration Reform Act also makes it illegal for employers to discriminate against legal aliens because of their citizenship status. A new special counsel's office is established in the Justice Department to investigate complaints of such discrimination. This office will investigate charges, and, if appropriate, issue complaints and prosecute the case before an administrative law judge. If there is a finding of discrimination, the Government could impose a civil penalty of $1,000 and could order the employer to hire a specific person with back pay.

and other personnel policies. If available, a copy of the company's Employee Handbook should be delivered at that time. First impressions are often lasting; therefore, a new employee's questions and concerns should be solicited and addressed, and he or she should be encouraged to discuss with the management any problems that may arise during employment with the company.

The new employee should also have a thorough orientation with his or her supervisor to become familiar with the job and working conditions. Again, the opportunity to establish effective communication channels should be stressed.

Employee Orientation Checklist

- ☐ Describe the company, its history, organization, and goals.
- ☐ Explain the duties and responsibilities of the position to the new employee and make clear what is expected. Furnish a written job description.
- ☐ Familiarize the employee with the firm's rules, compensation and benefits, frequency of employee appraisal reviews, advancement policies, and other pertinent information.
- ☐ Explain how the employee can find redress for a complaint.
- ☐ Introduce the new employee to co-workers and supervisory personnel.
- ☐ Furnish a copy of the Employee Handbook.

Communications

A company must ensure that employees are fully informed of benefits and policies as well as other matters of general interest.

The handbook could be supplemented by a regularly published company newsletter. Not only would the newsletter serve to update the handbook, it could also provide information on a variety of subjects of interest to employees and promote a sense of community. Similarly, a company bulletin board could serve as a means of communication for employees and employers. Both a bulletin board and a newsletter are useful devices for preventing misinformation or rumors from developing into crises.

Personal contact with employees is still the most simple and effective means of improving relations. Meetings with employees, both formal and informal, should be held periodically to explain policies and to listen to their concerns and suggestions. Such meetings will not only assure employees that the company cares, but also will afford management an opportunity to respond constructively to employee problems, and sympathetically to employee needs.

Communications Checklist

- ☐ Establish and maintain a communications program. Include written policies, such as an Employee Handbook, periodic newsletters, and bulletin boards available for informal notices.
- ☐ Train supervisors in methods of communicating effectively. They should serve as the link between management and workers.
- ☐ Solicit opinions from employees, and respond to questions and suggestions as soon as possible.
- ☐ Use orientation sessions and performance reviews as part of a communications program.
- ☐ Discuss the progress and goals of the firm with employees and explain any policy changes both formally and informally.

Child Care

While few employers provide child care or subsidize it, there is growing sentiment that employer-provided or employer-paid child care fosters a more productive work environment because the employee will be absent less and, when on the job, less distracted by child care problems.

For those employers who have offered the benefits, the prevailing rationale is that it provides an advantage to attract and retain quality employees, who care about the quality of their family life.

The statistics on working mothers reveal that half of them return to work before their babies are a year old. Some 10 million children under the age of six need child care during some part of the day, and as many as 7 million children under age 13 are left unsupervised for some portion of the day. It is predicted that the number of mothers in the work force will rise to 75 percent by the year 2000 from the current 60 percent level.

Bureau of Labor Statistics data establishes that mothers of preschool children have an absence rate that is nearly twice as high as all other employee groups.

The single most popular child care benefit is a spending account. Where this is used, a set amount of money is deducted from the employee's paycheck for child care, and the employee does not have to pay income tax on that amount. Neither is the FICA or FUTA tax assessed on amounts covered by employees' child care spending accounts.

Wages and Benefits

An employer must continually analyze and update the wage and benefits program. Data should be gathered concerning the wages and benefits offered locally (and nationally if relevant) for both union and nonunion employees. This data should be evaluated and the company's relative position should be determined.

If it does not have one, the company should also consider the possibility of establishing a formal wage program based on merit and longevity. The factors involved in such a program should be outlined, in detail, both to employees and supervisors. General adjustments to the program may be made when dictated by either cost-of-living and/or competitive considerations.

Apart from wages, a comprehensive benefits program should also be established. It may consist of any or all of the following:

1. Holidays
2. Vacations
3. Sick Leave
4. Excuse Absence for Emergencies
5. Insurance (life, accident, disability, medical, dental, and/or vision)
6. Pension
7. Profit Sharing
8. Bonus
9. Tuition Assistance
10. Parking or Travel Allowance
11. Maternity or Paternity Leave
12. Child Care Facility
13. Low Interest Loan Assistance
14. Jury Duty Pay

Performance Reviews

Performance reviews should be an integral part of the wage system. The review process is extremely important. It is not only a device for encouraging the employee who is doing a good

---

Performance Review Checklist

☐ Establish a date for a regular, timely, objective evaluation of the employee's performance.

☐ Document the appraisal with specific examples of acceptable or unacceptable performance by the employee.

☐ Emphasize positive comments where possible. Point out problem areas and possible solutions. Stress the attitude for achieving success and show how the employee can achieve it.

☐ Encourage the employee's comments on performance and discuss specific goals for the next review period. Outline methods of accomplishing these goals.

☐ Advise the employee of the date of the next appraisal, and place a summary of the performance review in the employee's personnel file. Employee should sign file copy.

job but also should be used to help an employee who is having difficulty. There should never be any surprises at a performance review. If the supervisor has been doing his or her job, the performance review should be only a formal confirmation of what the employee has already been told.

Job Advancement

A key ingredient to maintaining stable and effective personnel relations is assuring employees that there is real opportunity for personal advancement and growth. Thus, an employer must be continually aware of the employees' need for advancement; consequently, information concerning job openings should be publicized in the company newsletter or through some other job posting procedure.

Consistent with the desire to meet employee expectations for advancement, the company should inform its employees of its policies on promotion and transfer. The major policy considerations usually involved in any decision regarding promotion or transfer are seniority and ability. From a personnel relations standpoint, where ability is equal, seniority should be considered in making the decision as to which employee will advance. This same consideration should be used in the event of a layoff or recall.

Employee Training

If the forecasts are correct, then by the year 2000 there will be altogether too few well-educated and well-trained workers to meet the nation's economic needs. There is an enormous challenge to employers to improve the nation's job-related learning system. If you are not spending 2 to 4 percent of payroll on training you are probably making an insufficient commitment.

Training is a good deal for employers because those who train end up with productivity increases more than twice as high as the wage increases that come with training. Unfortunately, the vast majority of American employees never receive

formal training that is provided and paid for by their employers. The following is a model of high-leverage training:

Model of High-Leverage Training

Mission	Type of Training
Meeting strategic goals	Strategic training (orientation training, quality training, teamwork training)
Ensuring organizational performance	Executive development Management training and development Supervisory training and development
Implementing new technology	Technical training Scientific and engineering training Technician training Craft and apprentice training Skill training Data processing and computer training Information systems training
Engaging customers	Sales and marketing training Customer service training
Protecting employees and communities	Health and safety training Regulatory compliance (for example, meeting environmental standards)
Ensuring job readiness	Basic skills training

Source: American Society for Training and Development

In a study jointly conducted by the American Society for Training and Development and the Department of Labor, employers were urged to take the following steps:

■ Create an institutional environment that encourages the proactive use of human resource development as a tool to encourage efficiencies, quality improvements, new applications, and innovations;

■ Use selection and appraisal procedures that assess job-related training needs;

■ Use reward systems that provide compensation based on skill;

■ Build training-related performance-based requirements into management and supervisory job descriptions and work objectives;

■ Treat training as an investment with the same payoff as R&D; and

■ Work together, sharing development and delivery costs of training materials, technologies, and basic research on applied learning among adults.

Military Reservists' Rights

The major call-up of military reserve forces during the Persian Gulf crisis raised many questions for employers regarding their responsibilities to employees who have been called into active service. The Veterans' Reemployment Rights Act creates certain rights for reservists. A summary of the highlights of the law's coverage follows:

■ Every employer, regardless of the number of employees, is subject to the Act's requirements.

■ The reservist has no obligation to give notice prior to departure for duty.

■ There is no obligation to pay reservists for the time that they are on active duty. Some states, however, have laws which provide that reservists are entitled to 14 days pay while on reserve duty. In states where additional rights are conferred on reservists, the state law prevails over federal law.

■ A reservist has the right to return to a job of similar seniority, status, and pay upon one's return from active duty, so long as the application from reemployment comes within 90 days of discharge from military service. An employer has the right to request proof of satisfactory service.

■ Any employee, except for one who is deemed a "temporary" employee, is entitled to reinstatement rights. Thus, an employee, or even a probationary employee on the job for only a few days, is entitled to the full protection of the Act.

■ All benefits that would have been available

to the reservist had there not been an interruption in employment become the obligation of the employer. Thus, pay increases, vacations, pension rights based on length of service, etc., must be given to the reservists upon return from active duty. This is known as the "escalator clause," which means that the benefits that accrue from seniority continue as if the employee had never departed.

■ Where a business is sold or there is a change in ownership, the new employer succeeds to the obligations of the prior employer.

■ A reservist can elect to take paid vacation time during the period of the reserve duty.

■ If a reservist is injured or hospitalized while on active duty the law provides an additional one year beyond the 31 days to reapply for the job.

■ Where reemployment is impossible or unreasonable, the employer does not have to reemploy the reservist. However, it is clear that a person occupying the reservist's job can be bumped.

■ There are no specific penalties imposed for violations other than to offer the reservist a make-whole remedy. Once reemployed, the statute does give the employee one year protection against any kind of discharge, if not for good cause. This protection is given to assure against retaliation by employers because of the inconvenience caused by reservists' military service.

The Internal Revenue Service has ruled that COBRA coverage (for a detailed discussion see Chapter 12) must be offered unless an employer "voluntarily" maintains full coverage under a group health plan for reservists and their families. Thus, a military call-up of reserves is considered a "qualifying event" that creates COBRA rights.

Disciplinary Rules

The maintenance of a consistent disciplinary policy is absolutely essential. There are two basic alternatives which should be considered. In the first, a company can publish disciplinary rules prescribing specific penalties for violations which may occur. The advantage of this system is that, by subjecting everyone to the same punishment for the same violation, it reduces charges of unfairness. The primary drawback, however, is that it reduces a company's flexibility to take into account extenuating circumstances. Furthermore, certain acts may not be clearly covered, resulting in confusion over which penalty is appropriate.

The second alternative is to have the supervisor recommend a specific disciplinary action and then, in order to ensure consistency, have another staff member review the matter before a final decision is made.

Regardless of which approach is selected, the company should also consider the possibility of establishing a formal grievance procedure, with a designated company official responsible for resolving disputes.

Tax Reminders When Hiring

1. When Hiring New Employees
Income Tax Withholding — Ask each new employee to complete Form W-4, *Employer's Withholding Allowance Certificate.*

Federal Insurance Contributions Act (FICA) Taxes — Record each new employee's name and number from his or her Social Security card. Any employee who does not have a number should apply for one through the nearest Social Security Administration office.

Income Tax Withholding — Withhold tax from each wage payment according to the employee's Form W-4 and the correct withholding rate in Circular E, Employer's Tax Guide.

FICA Tax — Employer and employee (via payroll deduction) pay equivalent share of social security tax required to be remitted by the employer.

In 1991, the full 7.65 percent social security tax paid equally by employees and employers will be assessed on a taxable earnings base of $53,400. As the result of the 1990 budget law, the 1.45 percent hospital insurance portion of the tax will be assessed on earnings up to $125,000. For years after 1991, the $125,000 tax base will be indexed. For self-employed individuals, the social security

tax is 15.30 percent on an earnings base of $53,400 with a 2.9 percent hospital insurance tax applying on earnings up to $125,000.

Social security benefits are reduced for any individual under age 70 whose income exceeds a stated level. For those under age 65, $7,080 ($590 per month) may be earned with no diminution in benefits. Once this level is exceeded, $1 of benefits is withheld for every $2 in earnings above the limit. For those between the ages of 65 and 69, the annual earnings test level is $9,720 ($810 per month), and social security benefits are reduced by $1 for every $3 in earnings above the limit.

FUTA — The employer alone is responsible for the payment of the federal unemployment tax.

2. Recordkeeping
If one is required to report employment taxes or give tax statements to employees, an employer identification number is required. It may be obtained by using Form SS-4, *Application for Employer Identification Number,* which is available from the Internal Revenue Service or Social Security Administration offices.

Keep all records of employment taxes for at least four years. These should be available for IRS review.

3. Targeted Jobs Tax Credit
The jobs credit is 40% of the first $6,000 of wages for first year employees. For qualified summer youth employees, the jobs credit is 40% of up to $3,000 of wages.

The credit is based on a percentage of wages for each employee in the following targeted groups:
- Referrals by a vocational rehabilitation program.
- Economically disadvantaged Vietnam-era veterans.
- Economically disadvantaged youths.
- Supplemental Security Income (SSI) recipients.
- General assistance recipients.
- Youths in a cooperative education program who belong to an economically disadvantaged family.
- Economically disadvantaged ex-convicts.

■ Eligible work incentive employees.

■ Qualified summer youth employees, ages 16 or 17, who first worked for the employer between May 1 and September 15 of the calendar year.

In addition, to claim a job credit on an employee's wages:

1. More than half the wages received from the employer must be for working in your trade or business.

2. The employee must be certified. Certification is done by a local agency, generally an office of the State Employment Security Agency (Jobs Service). The agency gives the employer a form certifying that the employee is in a targeted group. The certification must be completed or the employer must request, in writing, a certification from the certifying agency by the date the employee begins work.

3. The employer may not claim a credit on wages that were repaid by a federally funded on-the-job training program.

The employee cannot be:

1. A relative or dependent, or

2. A rehired employee if he or she was not a targeted group member when employed earlier.

Under a 1990 amendment, the targeted jobs tax credit will expire on December 31, 1991, unless extended by Congress. Additionally, the revised law now requires that employers specifically identify the categories (not to exceed two) for which the individual is believed to be eligible when requesting certification. Furthermore, an employer must certify that a "good faith" effort was made to determine that the individual is eligible for the credit.

4. Obtaining Social Security Earnings Records

The Social Security Administration provides at no charge a statement of earnings credited to one's Social Security account and a projection of the expected benefits upon retirement.

To obtain this important information, there is in the Appendix at page 162 a copy of Form SSA-7004PC, Request for Statement of Earnings. We suggest that employers make copies and urge their employees to request the information.

The Social Security report has been highly praised for the way it presents an individual's retirement data in a most understandable manner.

Fair Labor Standards Act — 2 Coverage and Minimum Wage

Legislative Purpose

In 1938, Congress enacted one of the keystones of President Franklin Delano Roosevelt's New Deal, the Fair Labor Standards Act (FLSA). For the first time, it was the law of the land to permit Congress to regulate the minimum standards for hours and wages of covered employees. The legislative history reveals a Congressional intent to lessen the historic high unemployment of the depression years by shortening workweek hours and spreading available work among a greater number of workers. The principle was simple, a fair day's pay for a fair day's work. Congress wanted to discourage, if not eliminate, substandard wages by establishing a minimum wage and a premium for overtime.

In its more than five-decade existence, the FLSA has been amended numerous times by Congress, reflecting ever-expanding coverage of the work force to the extent that it is estimated that 92% of the full-time and part-time non-supervisory workers in the private sector are now covered by the law. The Wage and Hour Division, an integral part of the Employment Standards Administration of the U.S. Department of Labor, is responsible for the administration of the FLSA.

Coverage

The FLSA defines employee coverage by reference to three basic tests. Meeting any one of the following tests is sufficient for coverage.

1. Any employee engaged in interstate or foreign commerce is covered.

2. Any employee producing goods for interstate commerce is covered. By later amendment, the law specifically includes those nonproduction workers whose activities are closely related to or directly essential to production (e.g. maintenance, custodial and clerical workers). Thus, FLSA coverage would ensue in virtually all interstate manufacturing businesses, regardless of size or sales volume.

3. Any employee of an "enterprise," which is defined as an entity with a common business purpose, engaged in commerce or in the production of goods or which has employees handling, selling, or otherwise working on goods or materials is covered so long as the enterprise has annual gross sales of $500,000. [Note that tests (1) and (2) predicate coverage on the activities of the individual employee, but in test (3) employer coverage of the employees is determined by what the enterprise does; once an enterprise is covered, all employees, regardless of position, are subject to the FLSA.]

It is this "enterprise" standard that is used to cover retail and wholesale businesses. Additionally, employees of hospitals, schools, and institutional care facilities are considered to be employees of an enterprise, for which there is no sales dollar volume threshold for coverage.

Some FLSA "Coverage" Issues and Answers

1. A domestic service worker (any employee in a private home) is covered if that employee receives wages from one employer of $50 or more in a calendar quarter, or if that employee is employed for more than 8 hours in aggregate in a workweek in one or more households.

2. Both casual babysitting (less than 20 hours per week) and companionship services (not including the services of trained personnel like registered nurses) in the case of the aged or infirm are not covered.

3. To determine the applicability of the $500,000 sales volume test for a retail business, the gross receipts from all sales (excluding excise and sales tax) during a 12-month period immediately preceding the calendar quarter in question will be counted. At the beginning of each calendar quarter, volume for the preceding 12 months is determined. This is known as the "rolling quarter" method. When the statutory dollar volume levels are met, enterprise coverage applies from that time on or until such time as the dollar volume tests are not met. A new business would project annual sales based on its first quarter sales to determine whether it is covered.

4. The "enterprise" test includes all of the related activities of the employer achieved by unified operations or common control for a common business purpose. If this relationship exists, then all facets of an employer's business would be taken in aggregate to determine if the threshold dollar sales volume has been reached.

5. The 1989 FLSA amendments put in the $500,000 volume tests for laundry or dry cleaning businesses and construction or reconstruction firms. However, if as the result of this threshold test, any of these businesses would no longer be subject to the FLSA on April 1, 1990, they would have to pay no less than $3.35 an hour and be subject to the overtime provisions of the law.

6. While courts have liberally interpreted the coverage provisions of the FLSA, the burden of proving that coverage is placed on the employee in wage law suits and on the Secretary of Labor in wage recovery litigation.

7. Where there is a *bona fide* desire by individuals to volunteer and donate their time for public, charitable, religious, or humanitarian service without the expectation of compensation, there would not be an employment relationship.

8. A true, unincorporated family business which employs only family members (parent, spouse, child, or other member of the immediate family) is not a covered enterprise.

What the FLSA Does Not Regulate

While the Fair Labor Standards Act does set basic minimum wage and overtime pay standards and regulates the employment of minors, there are a number of employment practices which the Act does not regulate. For example, the Act does not require:

- vacation, holiday, severance, or sick pay;
- meal or rest periods, holidays off, or vacations;
- premium pay for weekend or holiday work;
- pay raises or fringe benefits;
- a discharge notice, reason for discharge, or immediate payment of final wages to terminated employees; and
- any limit on the number of hours of work for persons 16 years of age and over.

Minimum Wage

Congress changed the minimum wage rate in November 1989. The federal minimum wage rates are as follows:

Until March 31, 1990 - $3.35 an hour
After April 1, 1990 - $3.80 an hour
After April 1, 1991 - $4.25 an hour

Minimum Wage Rate Changes in the U.S. (1938-1991)

1938	$ .25/Hour
1939	$ .30/Hour
1945	$ .45/Hour
1950	$ .75/Hour
1956	$1.00/Hour
1961	$1.15/Hour
1963	$1.25/Hour
1967	$1.40/Hour
1968	$1.60/Hour
1974	$2.00/Hour
1975	$2.10/Hour
1976	$2.30/Hour
1978	$2.65/Hour
1979	$2.90/Hour
1980	$3.10/Hour
1981	$3.35/Hour
1990 (April)	$3.80/Hour
1991 (April)	$4.25/Hour

Hours Worked

The original FLSA contained no definition of "working time" for the purpose of computing the minimum wage. In 1944, the U.S. Supreme Court set down a rule to the effect that working hours include all time during which an employee is engaged in physical or mental effort controlled or required by his or her employer and pursued primarily for the benefit of the employer and the business. Thereafter, in 1946, the High Court ruled that any time an employee spent in a plant, after punching in, to get to the job and to get ready was a part of the hours worked, but time which the employee merely spent waiting because he or she arrived early was not compensable.

After these two decisions, many workers pressed to recover overtime pay to cover the time spent from the moment one arrived on the plant premises to the time one left. Known as the "portal-to-portal" pay litigation, the intense controversy led to Congressional enactment of the Portal-to-Portal Act (1947). This law, in part, was designed to prevent legal actions by employees to recover pay for nonproductive time. The law established the guideposts to determine what constitutes the "workday." This Act confined the employer's obligation to pay wages to the employee's principal activity, unless there is a contract, custom, or practice requiring pay for these peripheral activities.

Official Rulings On "Hours Worked" For Compensation

Activity	Yes, Paid for Compensable Hours Worked	No, Non-Compensable Hours Worked
Washing up after Work		✓
Changing Clothes		✓
Coffee Break (less than 20 minutes)	✓	
Meal Period*		✓
Staff Training/ Meeting	✓	
Voting Time		✓

*Any time the employee is required or permitted to perform any duties while eating, the time will be compensable.

As a general rule, all the time an employee is actually at work, or required to be on duty and cannot use the time for his or her own purposes, is compensable. Travel away from home is clearly work time when it cuts across the employee's workday. The employee is simply substituting travel for other duties. The table above illustrates how Department of Labor interpretations, court rulings, and legislative history have determined the status of some common workplace activities and whether they count as "hours worked." However, as with any generalization, there are exceptions. The determinations represent the prevailing rule.

Defining the "Workweek"

The workweek, seven consecutive, regular, recurring, 24-hour periods of 168 hours, is the unit of time use for determining compliance with the minimum wage. The computation and recording of hours worked is to be done on a workweek basis, and the employee must be paid, free and clear, compensation equal to at least the minimum wage for each hour worked in the workweek. It may begin on any day of the week and any hour of the day established by the employer. As long as the average hourly earnings for nonovertime hours in each workweek equal the minimum wage, the requirement is considered satisfied for that week. Average hourly earnings above the minimum in one workweek may not be used to offset earnings below the minimum wage in another workweek.

Minimum Wage Compliance

Let's examine some typical wage computations in which the minimum wage payment is the issue:

1. In the case of an employee hired on an hourly rate basis, it is required that the rate equal the statutory minimum.

2. In the case of a commission employee (e.g. commissions are the sole basis of compensation), the individual's earnings must be at least equal to the minimum wage rate for each of the hours worked, exclusive of overtime.

3. In the case of an employee who is paid an hourly rate for a portion of the workweek and a commission for the balance, earnings at the hourly rate which exceed the minimum may not be applied to make up differences in the commission earnings during the other part of the week.

4. In the case of a piece rate worker, earnings must equal at least the legal hourly minimum over the course of the workweek.

Deductions from Wages

While it is true the FLSA provides for the "free and clear" payment of the minimum wage for each workweek in cash or its equivalent each payday, the law does recognize one specific exception. Deductions are permitted for the "reasonable cost" or "fair value" of "board, lodging, or other facilities." The FLSA has been interpreted to mean that "reasonable costs" of furnishing board, lodging, or other facilities may not include any profit to the employer.

Compensation for overtime hours is disregarded in determining whether the deductions made by the employer are legal. Thus, deductions for "board, lodging, or other facilities" are legal, and so long as the cash wage and the "reasonable cost" equal the minimum wage, there is no violation. Certain taxes assessed against the employee and collected by means of a wage deduction are not "wages" under FLSA. Included in this category are an employee's contribution to Social Security (FICA), federal and state unemployment insurance, and other state and local taxes. An employee may authorize the employer to make deductions to turn over to some third party. When voluntarily assigned, these deductions are not violations of the law (e.g. union dues, purchase of savings bonds, and insurance premiums).

Deductions from an employee's wages for cash shortages are considered illegal to the extent that they reduce the wages of the employees below the required minimum or reduce the overtime compensation due under FLSA. There has been a court ruling involving deliberately misappropriated monies; in the case of repayment of these funds by an employee, there is no violation of FLSA rules as long as the criminal action has been determined in court.

In circumstances where an employee must wear a uniform, the financial burden of furnishing and maintaining (including laundry and repairing) the uniform may not be imposed upon the employee if the resulting wage would be below the minimum wage or overtime compensation required by FLSA. In cases where the employer merely pre-

Minimum Wage and Employee Uniforms
Questions and Answers

1. **Q. When is an employer required to furnish an employee with a uniform?**

   A. The FLSA does not require that employees wear uniforms. However, if the wearing of a uniform is required by some other law, the nature of a business or by an employer, the cost of the uniform is considered to be a business expense of the employer. If the employer requires the employee to bear the cost, it may not reduce the employee's wage below the minimum wage or cut into overtime compensation required by the Act.

2. **Q. May an employer require a prospective employee to purchase a uniform as a condition of employment?**

   A. The FLSA does not forbid such a requirement. However, the employee must be reimbursed, no later than the extent regular payday, to the extent that the cost of the uniform cuts into the minimum wage or overtime compensation required by the Act.

3. **Q. If an employer furnishes an employee with a required uniform, may the employer deduct the actual cost thereof from the employee's next paycheck?**

   A. The employer cannot make such a deduction, if by so doing the wages paid are reduced below the applicable minimum wage or overtime compensation required by the Act. However, a deduction which does not cut into the required minimum wage or overtime compensation is permissible.

4. **Q. If an employer is paying in excess of the applicable minimum wage, may the employer prorate deductions for uniform costs over a period of paydays?**

   A. Yes, if the prorated deductions do not reduce an employee's wages below the required minimum wage or overtime compensation in any workweek.

5. **Q. When an employee is required to purchase a uniform the cost of which cuts into minimum wage or overtime compensation by the Act, may the employer reimburse the employee periodically over the life of the uniform?**

   A. No. Reimbursement for the purchase of a uniform must be made promptly on the next regular payday, and may not be spread over the life of the uniform. In other words, to the extent that the cost of a required uniform purchased during one workweek cuts into the minimum wage or overtime wages required by the Act during that workweek, the employee must be reimbursed on the next regular payday.

6. **Q. May an employer who pays an employee more than the minimum wage deduct an hourly amount in order to recover uniform costs?**

   A. Yes. Deductions from wages for uniform costs which neither reduce the amount of pay below the applicable minimum wage rate nor reduce the amount of overtime compensation below that required by the Act do not result in a violation of the Act.

7. **Q. Sometimes an employer, instead of requiring that employees wear a uniform, instructs employees to wear dark colored trousers or skirts and dark colored shoes. Would these items be considered a uniform?**

   A. Each case of this type must be decided on the basis of all the particular facts. However, certain general guidelines apply. If an employer merely prescribes a general type of ordinary basic street clothing to be worn while working and permits variations in details of dress, the garments chosen by the employees would not be considered to be uniforms. For example, where an employer's only instructions to employees regarding their attire are that they wear dark colored trousers or skirts and dark colored shoes, such items of clothing would not constitute a uniform. On the other hand, where the employer does prescribe a specific type and style of clothing to be worn at work (e.g., where a restaurant or hotel requires a tuxedo or skirt and blouse or jacket of a specific or distinctive style, color, and quality) such clothing would be considered uniforms. Of course, any article of clothing which is associable with a specific employer, by virtue of an emblem (logo), or distinctive color scheme, would be considered a uniform.

8. **Q. Who is responsible for payment of uniform laundry costs?**

   A. Unless an employer is paying an amount sufficiently in excess of the applicable minimum wage, the employer must reimburse employees for laundry and maintenance costs in order to prevent such costs from cutting into the minimum wage or overtime pay required by the Act.

9. **Q. Is an employer responsible for payment of uniform laundry costs when uniforms are of a "wash and wear" material?**

   A. If the uniforms are of a "wash and wear" material which requires only washing and tumble or drip drying, and if they can be laundered with other personal garments, a uniform maintenance reimbursement would not be required. However, for those uniforms which require daily or special laundering due to heavy soiling or usage, or which require ironing, dry-cleaning or patching and repairs due to the nature of the work, a uniform maintenance reimbursement would be required.

scribes a general type of ordinary basic clothing and permits some diversity in details of dress, the clothing is not considered a uniform. The Wage and Hour Division has ruled that when an employee is required to purchase a uniform, that individual must be reimbursed for the cost of the uniform to the extent that the expense cuts into the required minimum wage or overtime compensation. This reimbursement must be made promptly on the immediate next payday, and may not be spread over the life of the uniform. The Department of Labor has provided a series of answers to the most commonly asked questions about employers' responsibilities for uniforms and their care.

Tip Credit

The wages paid a "tipped" employee by an employer may include a tip credit in accordance with the following schedule:

Allowable Tip Credit		
	Maximum Tip Credit	**Minimum Direct Wage Payment**
Until March 31, 1990 - 40 percent of the minimum wage ($3.35)	=$1.34/hr	$2.01/hr
April 1, 1990 - 45 percent of the minimum wage ($3.80)	=$1.71/hr	$2.09/hr
April 1, 1991 - 50 percent of the minimum wage ($4.25)	=$2.13/hr	$2.12/hr

However, in no event may the tip credit exceed the value of the tips actually received.

A "tipped employee" is any employee engaged in an occupation in which he or she customarily and regularly receives more than $30 a month in tips. The law requires that (1) the employer must inform tipped employees about this tip credit allowance before the credit is utilized; (2) the employees must be allowed to retain all tips (individually or through a pooling arrangement), and this is so regardless of whether the employer elects to take a credit for tips received; and (3) the employer must be able to show that the employee receives at least the minimum wage in the combination of direct wages and the tip credit. An employer may not take a greater tip credit in overtime hours than he does in straight time hours.

Hotel or motel employees who perform maid or custodial services must be paid not less than time and one-half their regular rates of pay for hours worked in excess of 40 per week. Employees of hotels, motels, and restaurants who are not otherwise exempt (other than maids or custodial employees) must be paid not less than time and one-half their regular rates of pay for over 40 hours per week.

Tips may include amounts designated as a "tip" by credit card customers on their charge slips. Where tips are charged on a credit card and the employer must pay the credit card company a percentage of the bill for the use of its credit plan, a practice whereby the employer reduces the amount of credit card tips paid to the employee by a percentage no greater than that charged by the credit card company will not be questioned. However, this will not be permitted where it reduces the employee's wages below the required minimum wage. Moreover, the amount due the employee must be paid no later than the regular payday and may not be held while the employer is awaiting reimbursement. The law forbids any arrangement whereby any part of the tips of a tipped employee belong to the employer or are retained by the employer. Under the Act, a tip becomes the property of the tipped employee in recognition of whose service it is presented by the customer.

The requirement that an employee must retain all tips does not preclude tip splitting or pooling arrangements among employees who customarily and regularly receive tips, such as waiters, bellhops, waitresses, countermen, busboys, and service bartenders. It is not required that the particular busboys and others who share in tips must themselves receive tips from customers. Both the amounts retained by the waiters and those given the busboys are considered the tips of the individuals who retain them. Employees who share in tips are tipped employees if they receive more than $30 a month in tips from the pool.

Tipped employees may not be required to share their tips with employees who have not customarily and regularly participated in tip pooling arrangements, such as dishwashers, chefs, and janitors. Also, waiters and waitresses cannot be required to contribute a greater percentage of their tips than is customary and reasonable. Only those tips that are in excess of those used for the tip credit, i.e., those in excess of half the minimum wage, may be taken for a pool.

A compulsory charge for service, for example, 15 percent of the bill, is not a tip. Such charges are part of the employer's gross receipts, and where service charges are imposed and the employees receive no tips, the employer must pay the entire minimum wage and overtime as required by the Act.

Learners, Apprentices, and Handicapped Workers

The FLSA provides discretion to the Wage and Hour Administration to permit the employment of learners, apprentices, and handicapped workers at hourly wages lower than the prevailing minimum wage. There is no exemption from the overtime pay provision for these workers. The subminimum may be as low as 85% of the minimum, in the case of apprentices, to 50% of the minimum, in the case of handicapped workers.

The Administration must issue a certificate to the employer before that employer can make use of the exemption. An "apprentice" is a person at least 16 years of age who is employed to learn a skilled trade requiring at least 4,000 hours to master. The agreement must be written and approved by an authorized apprenticeship council.

A "handicapped worker" is one whose earning capacity is impaired by age, physical or mental

deficiency, or injury. These workers may be engaged by commercial establishments or by "sheltered workshops." The FLSA allows for a subminimum no less than 50% of the minimum wage, but the Act requires an employer to pay wages commensurate with those paid nonhandicapped workers in the area, taking into consideration the type, quality, and quantity of work produced.

The "learner" is a beginner at a skilled occupation. In order for a certificate to be issued, there must be a showing that the lower wage is necessary to prevent the loss of employment opportunities. It was not the purpose of the FLSA to make the employment of learners more advantageous to the employer than the employment of experienced workers.

Trainees

To answer the question, "When are trainees considered 'employees' under FLSA?" it is necessary to examine all of their activities. If all of the following elements are present, then the trainees would not be considered "employees." The tests are derived from two U.S. Supreme Court cases involving the status of trainees:

1. Both the employer and trainees understand that the trainees are not entitled to compensation during the time spent for training.
2. The trainees are not necessarily entitled to a job at the conclusion of the training period.
3. The training is not unique and is merely like a vocational school's work experience period.
4. The training is primarily for the benefit of the trainee.
5. The employer derives no obvious advantage from the activities of the trainees; indeed, operations may be impeded by them.
6. The trainees neither replace regular employees nor work under their supervision.

Training Wage

The 1989 FLSA amendments provided for a training wage which may not be less than $3.35 an hour beginning April 1, 1990, and thereafter may be no less than 85 percent of the then prevailing wage; thus, after April 1, 1991, the rate may not be less than $3.62 an hour. The provision terminates on April 1, 1993, unless extended by a new law.

An employer may pay a training wage to a worker who has not attained the age of 20 years until the eligible employee has worked a cumulative total of 90 days. Migrant and seasonal agricultural workers are not eligible. The employer is not required to provide a specific training program during the first 90-Day training wage period.

To maintain "eligibility" an employer must not have laid off an employee from the position to be filled or from any substantially equivalent position; or must not have terminated the employment of any regular employee or otherwise reduced the number of employees with the intention of filling the vacancy by hiring an employee at the training wage.

During any month, the proportion of the hours worked by employees at the training wage may not exceed 25 percent of the hours worked by all employees.

An employer may not take any action to displace employees (including partial displacements such as reduction in hours, wages, or employment benefits) in order to hire individuals at the training wage. If the Department of Labor determines that an employer has taken an action to displace workers, it will issue an order disqualifying that employer from using the training wage.

Each employer shall provide any individual being paid the training wage a written notice before the employee begins work stating the requirements of the training wage program and the remedies provided by the law for violations. A copy of the Department of Labor notice is in the Appendix on page 165.

An individual who has completed 90 days at a subminimum training wage may be employed by another employer for an additional 90 days so long as on-the-job training is provided. Thus an individual under 20 years of age could work 180 days at the lower wage training wage. The individual employee is responsible for providing the requisite proof of a previous period, or periods, of employment with other employers. An employer's good faith reliance on the proof presented to the employer by an individual will constitute a complete defense to a charge that an employer has paid a worker beyond the permitted period.

Subsequent Employer Eligibility Requirements If the 90-day Training Period is Offered:

1. Post, in a conspicuous place, a notice of the types of jobs for which the employer is providing on-the-job training.
2. Annually send a copy of such notices to the Secretary of Labor. These are available to the general public upon request.
3. Annually notify the Department of Labor concerning the positions which employees are to be paid the training wage.
4. Keep a copy of the training program on file.
5. Provide a copy of the training program to employees.
6. Establish on-the-job training which meets standards issued by the Secretary of Labor.

The term "on-the-job training" means training that is offered to an individual while employed in productive work that provides training, technical and other related skills, and personal skills that are essential to the full and adequate performance of such employment. The new law does extend certain current civil penalties to willful or repeated violations of Sections 6 or 7 of the Fair Labor Standards Act.

Full-Time Students and Subminimum Wage

The FLSA provides for a minimum wage of 85% of the prevailing minimum for full-time students engaged in work at retail-service establishments, on farms, and at higher educational institutions. Certificates will be issued to employers applying for this preferential treatment so long as there is no lessening of opportunities for employment among full-time workers.

To minimize paperwork and to encourage small retail and service business, the FLSA allows these employers to engage up to six full-time students by merely notifying the Department of Labor. In this instance, only the following steps would be necessary:

1. Complete a simple application and send it to a Regional Office of the Wage Hour Division of the Department of Labor. It must contain the employer's name, address, type of business, and date the business began;

2. Affirm that no more than six full-time students will be employed on any workday, and that student employment will not reduce the full-time employment opportunities of other individuals; and

3. Post a copy of the application where employees can see it.

A full-time student must be enrolled at a *bona fide* educational institution. The student permitted to work at subminimum wage may not work more than five hours a day, nor for more than 40 hours a week when school is not in session. When school is in session, there is a 20-hour-a-week limit. An exception is when there is a school holiday and the business is open, in which case the student may work an additional 8 hours.

If more than six full-time students will be employed, then it is necessary to obtain prior approval by the Wage Hour Administration. In candor, the certification process requires an inordinate amount of paperwork. A separate application is required for each business location. Certificates are issued for periods up to one year and must be renewed annually. For these large business users of full-time students, the law will allow up to 10% of the total hours of employment of all employees. Some allowance in the summer is given for seasonal business and for firms which compete with those that employ full-time students at subminimum wage rates.

There are some special recordkeeping requirements for employers using this subminimum rate. The employee's records should contain school information, and, upon graduation, a certificate from the school next to be attended stating that the student has been accepted as a full-time student. The monthly hours of full-time students at subminimum wage and the total hours of all employees during the month should be kept for three years.

Child Labor

Congress wanted to keep the channels of commerce free from child labor, and it accomplished this with a child labor provision in the Fair Labor Standards Act. The coverage of the child labor rules embraces business involved in producing, manufacturing, mining, handling, transporting, or in any other manner working on goods shipped in commerce. In 1990, Congress stiffened the penalty for child labor violations to permit up to a $10,000 civil penalty for each employee who was the subject of such a violation.

The provisions include lists of hazardous occupation orders for both farm and nonfarm jobs declared by the Secretary of Labor as being too dangerous for minors to perform. Regulations governing youth employment in nonfarm jobs are set out in the chart on page 22.

An employer wanting to protect against unintentional violations of the child labor requirements should obtain a certificate of age for each minor employed. Age or employment certificates (work permits) are accepted as proof of age in most states and are available from state labor offices.

Permissible Nonfarm Work

AGE	JOB	HOURS OF WORK
18 years or older	Any job, hazardous or not	Unlimited
16-17 years old	Any nonhazardous job	Unlimited
14-15 years old*	Outside of school hours in various non-manufacturing, nonmining, nonhazardous jobs	No more than 3 hours on a school day, 18 hours in a week, 8 hours on a non-school day, or 40 hours in a non-school week. Work may not begin before 7 a.m. nor end after 7 p.m. except from June 1 through Labor Day, when evening hours extend until 9 p.m.

*Under a special provision, 14- and 15-year-olds enrolled in an approved Work Experience and Career Exploration Program may be employed for up to 23 hours in school weeks and 3 hours on school days (including work during school hours).

**Fourteen is the minimum age for most nonfarm work. However, at any age, youths may deliver newspapers; perform in radio, television, movie, or theatrical productions; or work for parents in their solely owned nonfarm business (except in manufacturing or hazardous jobs).

Fair Labor Standards Act — Overtime Pay **3**

Overtime Pay

Compared to the relatively straightforward rules governing minimum wage, the rules governing overtime pay are complicated and confusing. The overtime pay premium (one and one-half times the regular rate) applies to all hours worked above *40* in a workweek.

Each workweek is a separate unit for overtime purposes; hours may not be averaged over two or more weeks. There is no absolute limit on the number of hours an employee may work in any workweek. The FLSA does not require that an employee be paid overtime compensation for working more than eight hours in a day, or for work on Saturday or Sunday, holidays, or regular days of rest.

Overtime compensation need not be paid weekly; instead, it must be paid on the regular pay date for the periods in which such workweeks end. If there is a problem in completing the overtime computations by the end of the pay period, the FLSA will be satisfied if the employer pays the excess overtime compensation as soon as possible. In no event may payment be delayed beyond the next payday.

The Regular Rate

The "regular rate" of pay has been declared by the U.S. Supreme Court as the hourly rate actually paid the employee for the normal, nonovertime workweek. The "regular rate" is a rate per hour. Yet, the FLSA does not require employers to compensate on an hourly basis; accordingly, piece-rate, salaried, and commission workers must have their compensation converted to an hourly rate. The regular hourly rate of pay is determined by dividing an employee's total remuneration (less the statutory exclusions discussed later) in any workweek by the total number of hours worked. The following examples illustrate the determination of the regular rate.

1. Hourly Rate Employees — If an employee is employed solely on the basis of a single hourly rate, the hourly rate is the "regular rate." For overtime hours the employee must be paid, in addition to the straight-time for hourly earnings, a sum determined by multiplying one-half the hourly rate by the number of hours worked over 40 in the week. If, for example, the hourly rate is $5.00 and one works 46 in a week, the employee would be entitled to receive $245 (46 hours at $5.00 and 6 at $2.50). Stated another way, 40 hours times $5.00 plus 6 hours times $7.50 (time and one-half).

2. Hourly Rate and Bonus — If the employee in the above example received in addition to the earnings at the hourly rate, a bonus of $20.00, the regular rate of pay would be $5.43 an hour (46 hours at $5.00 equals $230.00 plus the $20.00 bonus, making a total of $250.00); this total divided by 46 hours yields a rate of $5.43. The employee would then be entitled to receive a total wage of $266. (46 hours at $5.43 plus 6 hours at $2.72).

3. Piece Rate — The regular rate of pay for an employee paid on a piecework basis is obtained by dividing the total weekly earnings for the week in which he or she worked more than 40 hours by the total number of hours worked in the same week. The employee is entitled to an additional 1½ times this regular rate for each hour over 40, in addition to the full piecework earnings.

Example: An employee paid on a piecework basis works 45 hours in a week and earns $230.00. The regular pay rate for that week is $230.00 divided by 45, or $5.11 an hour. In addition to the straight time pay, the employee is entitled to $2.56 (half the regular rate) for each hour over 40. Another way to compensate pieceworkers for overtime, if agreed to before the work is performed, is to pay 1 1/2 times the piece rate for each piece produced during overtime hours. The piece rate must be the one actually paid during nonovertime hours and must be enough to yield at least the minimum wage per hour.

4. Day Rates and Job Rates — An employee may be paid a flat sum for a day's work or for doing a particular job, without regard to the number of hours worked in the day or at the job, and receive no other form of compensation. In such a case the employee's regular rate is found by totaling all the sums received at such day rates or job rates in the workweek and dividing by the total hours actually worked. The employee is then entitled to extra half-time pay at this rate for all hours worked over 40 in the workweek.

5. Employee Paid on a Salary Basis — If an employee is employed solely on a weekly salary basis, the regular hourly rate of pay is computed by dividing the salary by the number of hours which the salary is intended to compensate. For example, if an employee is hired at a salary of $200.00 and if it is understood that this salary is compensation for a regular workweek of 35 hours, or $5.71 an hour, when overtime is worked, the employee is entitled to receive $5.71 for each of the first 40 hours and $8.57 (time and one-

half) for each hour thereafter. If an employee is hired at a salary of $200.00 for a 40-hour week, the regular rate is $5.00 an hour.

6. Salary for Periods Other Than a Workweek — Where the salary covers a period longer than a workweek, such as a month, it must be reduced to its workweek equivalent. A monthly salary can be converted into its equivalent weekly wage by multiplying by 12 (the number of months) and dividing by 52 (the number of weeks). A semi-monthly salary is converted into its equivalent weekly wage by multiplying by 24 and dividing by 52.

7. Fixed Salary for Fluctuating Hours — The regular rate of an employee whose hours of work fluctuate from week to week, who is paid a stipulated salary with the clear understanding that it constitutes straight-time pay for all hours worked (whatever their number and whether few or many), will vary from week to week. The regular rate is obtained for each week by dividing the salary by the number of hours worked in the week. It cannot, of course, be less than the applicable minimum wage in any week. Since straight-time compensation has already been paid, the employee must receive additional overtime pay for each overtime hour worked in the week at not less than one-half this regular rate. Take the example of an employee who works no more than 50 hours and is compensated on a fluctuating workweek basis at a weekly salary of $250.00. If during the course of four weeks the employee works 40, 44, 50, and 48 hours, the regular hourly rate of pay in each of these weeks is $6.25, $5.68, $5.00 and $5.21, respectively. Since straight-time pay for all hours worked has already been paid, only additional half-time pay is due. For the first week the employee is due $250.00; for the second week $261.36 ($250.00 plus 4 hours at $2.84); for the third week $275.00 ($250.00 plus 10 hours at $2.50); for the fourth week $270.80 ($250.00 plus 8 hours at $2.60).

8. Employees Working at Two or More Rates — Where an employee in a single workweek works at two or more different types of work for which different straight-time rates have been established, the regular rate for that week is the weighted average of such rates. That is, the earnings from all such rates are added together and this is then divided by the total number of hours worked at all jobs.

9. Payments Other Than Cash — Where payments are made to employees in the form of goods or facilities which are regarded as part of wages, the reasonable cost to the employer or the fair value of such goods or facilities must be included in the regular rate. Where, for example, an employer furnishes lodging to employees in addition to cash wages, the reasonable cost or the fair value of the lodging (per week) must be added to the cash wages before the regular rate is determined.

10. Commission Payments — Commissions (whether based on a percentage of total sales or sales in excess of a specified amount or on some other formula) are payments for hours worked and must be included in the regular rate. This is so, regardless of whether the commission is the sole source of the employee's compensation or is paid in addition to a salary or hourly rate. It does not matter whether the commission earnings are computed daily, weekly, monthly, or at some other interval.

11. Commission Paid on a Workweek Basis — When a commission is paid on a workweek basis, it is added to the employee's other earnings for that workweek, and the total is divided by the total number of hours worked in the workweek to obtain the employee's regular rate for the particular workweek. The employee must then be paid extra compensation at one-half of that rate for each overtime hour worked.

12. Deferred Commission Payments — If the calculation and payment of the commission cannot be completed until some time after the regular payday for the workweek, the employer may disregard it until the amount of commission can be determined. When the commission is computed, the additional overtime compensation must be paid.

To compute this additional overtime compen-

sation, the commission is apportioned back over the workweeks of the period during which it was earned. The employee must then receive additional overtime pay for each week during the period in which overtime was worked. If it is not possible or practical to allocate the commission on the basis of the amount of commission actually earned each week, some other reasonable and equitable method must be adopted. One such method is to allocate an equal amount of commission earnings to each workweek in the period in which the commission was earned; another is to allocate equal amounts to each hour worked in that period.

For the weekly basis:

(1) If the commission computation period is one month, multiply the commission payment by 12 and divide by 52 to get the amount of commission allocable to a single week.

(2) To figure the increase in the hourly rate, divide the commission for each week by the total number of hours worked in that week. Additional overtime due is computed by multiplying one-half of this figure by the number of overtime hours worked in the week.

For example, if there is a monthly commission payment of $120.00, the amount of commission allocable to a single week is $27.69 ($120.00 times 12 equals $1,440.00 divided by 52 equals $27.69). In a week in which an employee works 48 hours, dividing $27.69 by 48 yields an increase to the regular rate of 58 cents. Multiplying one-half of this figure by 8 overtime hours gives the additional overtime pay due of $2.32.

Exclusions From the "Regular Rate"

The FLSA specifically excludes a number of categories of payments from the computation of the "regular rate." It is important to qualify each exclusion payment since any amount paid to an employee not specifically covered by these seven exclusions must be added to the total compensation received by the employee before the regular rate of pay is computed.

■ **Overtime pay for hours in excess of a daily or weekly standard** — Many employment contracts provide overtime pay for hours worked over 8 per day or 40 per week. Such extra compensation paid for the excess hours, whether or not at time and one-half, is excludable from the regular rate and may be credited toward statutory overtime payments.

■ **Premium pay for work on Saturdays, Sundays, and other special days** — Extra compensation provided by a premium rate of at least time and one-half which is paid for work on Saturdays, Sundays, holidays, or regular days of rest, or on the sixth or seventh day of the workweek as such, may be treated as overtime pay. If the premium rate is less than time and one-half, the extra compensation paid must be included in determining the regular rate of pay and cannot be credited toward statutory overtime due.

■ **"Clock Pattern" premium pay** — A collective bargaining agreement or other employment contract may, in good faith, establish certain hours of the day as the basic, normal or regular workday (not exceeding 8 hours) or workweek (not exceeding 40 hours) and provide for the payment of a premium for work outside such hours. The extra pay will be treated as an overtime premium as long as the premium rate is not less than one and one-half times the rate established in good faith by the contract or agreement for like work performed during the basic, normal or regular workday or workweek.

■ **Non-overtime premium** — Lump sum payments which are paid without regard to the number of hours worked are not overtime premiums and must be included in the regular rate. For example, where an employer gives 8 hours pay for a particular job whether it is performed in 8 hours or in less time, the extra premium of 2 hours pay received by an employee who completes the job in 6 hours must be included in the regular rate.

■ **Discretionary bonuses** — A bonus need not be included in the regular rate if the employer retains discretion both (1) that a bonus will be paid and (2) that the amount is not determined until the end, or near the end, of the bonus period.

■ **Gifts, Christmas and special occasion bonuses** — If a bonus paid at Christmas or on other special occasions is a gift, it may be excluded from the regular rate even though it is paid with regularity so that the employees are led to expect it. It may be excluded even though the amounts paid to different employees or groups of employees vary with the amount of the salary or regular hourly rate.

■ **Reimbursement for expenses** — When an employee incurs expenses on the employer's behalf or where the employee is required to spend sums solely for the convenience of the employer, payments to cover such expenses are not included in the employee's regular rate of pay.

■ **Pay for certain idle hours** — Payments that are made for occasional periods when the employee is not at work due to vacation, holiday, illness, failure of the employer to provide sufficient work (for example, because of machinery breakdown or materials shortage), or other similar causes, where the payments are in amounts approximately equivalent to the employee's normal earnings for a similar period of time, are not made as compensation for the hours of employment and may be excluded from the regular rate of pay.

■ **Pay for foregoing holidays and vacations** — In some instances employees are entitled to holiday or vacation pay but forego the holiday or vacation and work on that day or period. If they receive their customary rate (or higher) for their work on the holiday or vacation day, the additional sum given as holiday or vacation pay is excluded from the regular rates of pay.

■ **Profit-sharing and thrift or savings plans** — Payments made by an employer on behalf of an employee to a *bona fide* profit-sharing plan or trust, or *bona fide* thrift or saving plan, may be excluded from the regular rate of pay.

■ **Benefit plans** — Contributions irrevocably made by an employer to a trustee or third person pursuant to a *bona fide* plan for providing old-age, retirement, life, accident, or health insurance or similar benefits, such as Supplemental Unemployment Benefits, may be excluded from the regular rate of pay for purposes of computing overtime pay.

Overtime Calculations in Special Situations

How Deductions Affect the Regular Rate — Deductions made for such items as "board, lodging, or other facilities" furnished employees, union dues, savings bonds, and charitable contributions do not affect the regular rate. The employee's regular rate is computed before the deductions are made.

Fixed Sum for Varying Amounts of Overtime — A lump sum paid for work performed during overtime hours, without regard to the number of overtime hours worked, does not qualify as an overtime premium even though the amount of money paid is equal to or greater than the sum owed on a per-hour basis. For example, no part of a flat sum of $60, to employees who work overtime on Sunday, will qualify as an overtime premium, even though the employees' straight-time rate is $5.00 an hour and the employees always work less than 8 hours on Sunday. Similarly, where an agreement provides for 6 hours pay at $6.00 an hour, regardless of the time actually spent for work on a job performed during overtime hours, the entire $36.00 must be included in the employees' regular rate. The reason for this is clear. If the rule were otherwise, an employer desiring to pay a fixed salary regardless of the number of overtime hours worked could merely label as overtime pay a fixed portion of such salary, sufficient to take care of compensation for the maximum number of hours that would be worked. The same reasoning applies to payment of a flat sum for a special job performed during overtime hours. Extra compensation paid in the form of a lump sum for varying amounts of overtime hours must be included in the regular rate and may not be credited against statutory overtime compensation due.

Salary for Workweek Exceeding 40 Hours — A fixed salary for a regular workweek longer than 40 hours does not discharge the statutory obligation. For example, an employee may be hired to work a 44-hour workweek for a weekly salary of $200.00. In this instance the regular rate is obtained by dividing the $200.00 straight-time salary by 44 hours, which results in a regular rate of pay, $4.55. The employee is then due additional overtime computed by multiplying the 4 overtime hours by one-half the regular rate of pay ($2.28) or $9.12.

Overtime Pay May Not Be Waived — The requirement that overtime must be paid after 40 hours a week may not be waived by agreement between the employer and employees. Similarly, an agreement that only 8 hours a day or only 40 hours a week will be counted as working time will clearly fail. An announcement by the employer that no overtime work will be permitted, or that overtime work will not be paid for unless authorized in advance, also will not impair the employee's right to compensation for the overtime work.

Computing Overtime Pay on the Rate Applicable to the Type of Work Performed in Overtime Hours — A simpler method of computing overtime pay for employees paid piece rates or at a variety of hourly rates is provided in section 7(g)(1) and (2) of the FLSA. The regular rate may be computed at a piece rate not less than one and one-half times the *bona fide* piece rate applicable to the same work when performed during non-overtime hours. In the case of an employee performing two or more kinds of work, for which different hourly rates have been established, the regular rate may be computed at rates not less than one and one-half times the *bona fide* rate for the same work when performed during non-overtime hours. Under these methods, there must be an agreement or understanding with the employees before performance of the work.

Special Overtime Provision for Hospital Employees — Under Section 7(j) of the FLSA, hospitals and residential care establishments may, pursuant to a prior agreement or understanding with their employees, utilize a fixed work period of fourteen consecutive days in lieu of the workweek for the purpose of computing overtime, if they pay time and one-half the regular rate for hours worked over eight in any workday or eighty in the fourteen-day period, whichever is the greater number of hours.

Guaranty Wage Contracts

The FLSA does permit a wage plan that provides for a constant wage, even though overtime is worked. It is known as the "Belo Plan," named after the company that successfully argued its merits to the U.S. Supreme Court. Later, Congress amended the FLSA to provide specifically for this type of plan.

The Belo Plan is designed for salaried employees who work irregular hours, but there are a number of restrictions. Under a Belo Plan, the employer and the employee agree on an hourly rate of pay which is substantially less than the employee's average hourly earnings in an ordinary week. The employee is promised this hourly rate for the first 40 hours each week, not less than time and one-half this rate for overtime hours, with a guarantee of a certain weekly salary regardless of the number of hours the employee works.

A Belo Plan is appropriate when the employee's job demands irregular hours of work. It requires:

1. A written agreement between the employer and the employee.
2. The specification of the employee's regular hourly rate.
3. A guarantee of time and one-half the regular rate for hours worked over 40.
4. A guaranteed weekly salary, regardless of the hours worked.
5. The guaranteed weekly salary may not cover more than 60 hours per week.
6. When the employee's earnings at the regular rate for 40 hours and time and one-half for additional hours exceed the amount of the guarantee, the employee must be paid the excess over the guarantee.

Retail/Service Commission-Paid Employees

There is a special provision of the FLSA that allows an employee of a "retail or service establishment" paid on a commission basis or whose compensation includes commissions to be exempt from the payment of overtime providing two conditions are met:

1. The regular rate of pay of this employee must be more than one and one-half times the prevailing minimum wage, and

2. More than half of the compensation for a "representative period" (not less than one month) must represent commissions on goods or services.

Exemptions From FLSA Overtime Provisions

Industry/Occupation of Employees	
Administrative, Executive and Professional	Exempt
Commission Salespersons of Retail or Service Establishments	Exempt
Domestic Service Workers Residing in the Employer's Residence	Exempt
Farm Workers	Exempt
Hospitals/Nursing Homes	Limited
Railroad and Airline Workers	Exempt
Seamen	Exempt
Auto, Truck, Trailer, Farm Implement, Boat or Aircraft Salespersons, Partsmen, and Mechanics Employed by Non-Manufacturing Dealers	Exempt
Outside Salespersons	Exempt
Retail-Service Establishments (Laundry-Dry Cleaning Businesses Not Included)	Limited Exemptions

The term "retail or service establishment" means that a business must engage in the selling of goods or services and 75% of its sales of goods or services must be recognized as traditionally in a "retail" concept. Further, not over 25% of its sales of goods or services may be for resale.

The purpose of this exemption was to relieve a retail employer from the obligation of paying overtime compensation to employees who typically sell "big ticket" items, such as home furnishings, floor covering, and major appliances. It is a good policy to have a written agreement with commission salespersons acknowledging that the compensation plan is based upon Section 7(i) of the FLSA; and, therefore, no overtime will be paid. The "representative period" to test an employee's compensation may not be shorter than a month and should be of sufficient length to reflect fairly as many factors as possible. The period chosen should be long enough to stabilize the measure of the balance between the portions of the employee's compensation which respectively represent commissions and other earnings (bonuses and contest prizes) against purely seasonal or plainly temporary changes. The exemption is given to individuals and not to commission salespersons as a category of employees. A written agreement between a commission salesperson and an employer should at least contain these elements:

1. Definition of the pay period (e.g. a calendar month);
2. The pay date for each pay period;
3. The hourly rate for every hour worked (e.g. may not be less than 1½ times prevailing minimum wage);
4. Definition of the representative period, and statement of the basis of the Section 7(i) exemption from the overtime provisions; and
5. Both parties should sign and date the agreement.

Overtime Exception for State and Local Government Employees

In February 1985, the United States Supreme Court ruled that the minimum wage and overtime pay provisions of the Fair Labor Standards Act apply to public employees. The ruling expressly overruled an earlier decision that the minimum wage and overtime pay provisions could not constitutionally be applied to state and local government employees who are engaged in traditional government functions.

In November 1985, Congress addressed the significant concerns of state and local governments and their employees by amending the overtime pay provision of the FLSA as they apply to public employees.

The amendments permit state and local governments to compensate their employees for overtime hours worked with compensatory time off in lieu of overtime pay, at a rate of one and one-half hours for each hour of overtime worked. The amendments provide that the use of compensatory time in lieu of overtime pay must be pursuant to some form of collective bargaining agreement or other agreement or understanding between the employer and the employee prior to the performance of work and that compensatory time may be accrued up to a maximum of 240 hours for most public employees. This does not include those employees engaged in public safety, emergency response, and seasonal activities, who may accrue compensatory time up to 480 hours. For hours worked in excess of the accrued maximum amounts, an employee would receive overtime pay. The amendments also exclude, from the definition of "employee," individuals who volunteer their services to state and local governments without compensation but receive a nominal fee, reasonable benefits, or reimbursement for expenses. The amendments became effective April 15, 1986.

An employee is permitted to use accrued compensatory time within a reasonable period after it is requested if to do so would not unduly disrupt the operations of the employing public agency.

Payment for accrued compensatory time upon termination of employment is to be calculated at the average regular rate of pay for the final 3 years of employment, or the final regular rate received by the employee, whichever is the higher.

"Compensatory time" and "compensatory time off" are defined as hours when an employee is not working and which are paid for at the employee's regular rate of pay. These hours are not counted as hours worked in the week in which they are paid.

"White Collar" Employees

The FLSA provides for an exemption from both the minimum wage and overtime pay provisions for employees engaged in an executive, administrative, or professional capacity, or for the position of an outside salesperson. The Department of Labor established the criteria which designates these individuals. The last significant revision occurred in 1975. It is a near certainty that the Department of Labor will seek a significant upward revision of the dollar earnings threshold as well as a clarification of the "duties and responsibilities" test used for the purposes of applying these so-called "white collar" exemptions sometime soon. (Author's note: For this reason, I have deliberately avoided setting out the existing minimum salary amounts in this text, as they are likely to be changed at any time.)

The determination of an individual's exemption is dependent upon one's duties and is largely a question of fact. A federal court has ruled that the Department of Labor may disregard an employee's title as irrelevant; the exemption is based on job duties and not titles.

There is a requirement that the white collar employee be paid on a salary basis; that is, the individual must receive full salary for any week in which he or she performs any work, without regard to the number of days or hours worked.

There is both a standard test and a so-called shortform or "upset test" for every category but the commission salesperson. To qualify for an exemption, all elements of the applicable test must be present.

Exemption Rules
For Executive Employees

1. Primary duty is management, e.g. overall head of operations or a department.

2. Directs on a regular basis the work of two or more employees.
3. Hires and discharges employees and is responsible for recommending promotions and employee review.
4. In the normal course of work exercises discretionary powers.
5. Receives a minimum salary as established by the Department of Labor.
6. Devotes no more than 20% of the hours worked to nonexecutive work. In the case of a retail or service business, the nonexempt work ratio may not exceed 40% of the hours worked. The 40% limit also applies to any employer in any line of business who has a 20% ownership interest or is in sole charge of a branch operation of that business.

Short Test For
Executive Exemption

If an executive earns a minimum salary as established by the Department of Labor, he or she may qualify for exemption if these tests are met:
1. Primary duty is management, e.g. overall head of operations or a department.
2. Directs on a regular basis the work of two or more employees.

Exemption Rules For
Administrative Employees

1. Primary duty is the performance of office or nonmanual work directly related to management policies or business operations.
2. Exercises discretion and independent judgment.
3. Regularly assists a proprietor, or an employee, in an executive administrative capacity, or performs under general supervision work requiring special training, experience, or knowledge, or executes special assignments and tasks. (Note: only one of these tests must be met).
4. Devotes no more than 20% of the hours worked to nonadministrative work. In the case of a

retail or service business, the non-exempt work ratio may not exceed 40% of the hours worked per week.
5. Receives a minimum weekly salary as established by the Department of Labor.

Short Test For Administrative Exemption

If administrative employees earn a minimum weekly salary as established by the Department of Labor, they may qualify for exemption if they meet these tests:
1. Primary duty is the performance of office or nonmanual work directly related to management policies or business.
2. Exercises discretion and independent judgment.

Exemption Rules For Professional Employees

1. Primary duty must be in work requiring knowledge of advanced type of science or learning, original work in an artistic field, or teaching. (Note: only one of the tests must be met.)
2. Exercises discretion and independent judgment.
3. The work must require intellectual abilities and be so nonroutine that the output cannot be standardized in relation to a given period of time.
4. Devotes no more than 20% of the hours worked to nonprofessional duties.
5. Receives a minimum weekly salary as established by the Department of Labor.

Short Test For Professional Employees

If professional employees earn a minimum weekly salary as established by the Department of Labor, they may qualify for exemption if they meet either of these tests:
1. Primary duty consists of work requiring exercise of discretion and judgment and knowledge of an advanced type in a field of science, learning, or teaching.
2. Primary duty consists of the performance of work in an artistic endeavor which requires imagination and talent.

Exemption Rules For Outside Salespersons

1. Customarily and regularly works away from the employer's place of business in making sales or obtaining orders or contracts.
2. Devotes no more than 20% of the hours worked to nonexempt activities.

Remedial Education Exemption

The 1989 FLSA Amendments provided a limited, special exemption for up to 10 hours in any workweek from the overtime provisions of the FLSA for remedial education. The latter term is limited to individuals who lack a high school diploma or educational attainment at the eighth grade level. The program must be designed to provide reading and other basic skills at an eighth grade level or below and does not include job specific training.

Computer Industry Exemption

Congress, in 1990, enacted an amendment that permits computer systems analysts, computer programmers, software engineers, and other similarly skilled professional workers to qualify as exempt executive, administrative, or professional workers so long as their hourly rate of pay is at least 6 1/2 times greater than the federal minimum wage rate. Thus, anyone earning $27.63 an hour in the covered occupations would not be eligible for overtime pay. For the first time since the passage of the FLSA an individual has become exempt from overtime payment simply by the level of their earnings in a specific occupation.

Fair Labor Standards Act — Enforcement 4

FLSA Recordkeeping

Employers are required to keep records on wages, hours, and other items for at least three years. Most of the information is of the kind generally maintained by employers in ordinary business practice and in compliance with other laws and regulations. The records may be kept in any particular form including microfilm and other source documents such as an automatic word or data processing memory. With respect to an employee subject to both minimum wage and overtime pay provisions, the following records must be kept:

1. Personal information, including employee's name, home address, including zip code, occupation, sex and birth date (if under 19 years of age).
2. Hour and day when workweek begins.
3. Total hours worked each workday and each workweek.
4. Total daily or weekly straight-time earning.
5. Regular hourly pay rate for any week when overtime is worked.
6. Total overtime pay for the workweek.
7. Deductions from or additions to wages.
8. Total wages paid each pay period.
9. Date of payment and pay period covered.

Records required for exempt employees differ from those for nonexempt employees, and special information is required about employees working under uncommon pay arrangement or to whom lodging or other facilities are furnished.

In addition to these general recordkeeping requirements, the FLSA imposes additional recordkeeping requirements for employees subject to miscellaneous exemptions under the law. The specific terms of each such exemption covering these workers must be documented. They include:

1. Employees exempt from both overtime pay requirements and minimum wage.
2. Employees exempt from overtime pay requirements.
3. Employees of hospitals and residential care facilities compensated for overtime work on the basis of a 14-day work period.
4. Employees working under a "Belo" contract.
5. Board, lodging or other facilities.
6. Tipped employees.
7. Learners, apprentices, messengers, students, or handicapped workers.
8. Individual homeworkers.
9. Agricultural employees.

Timeclocks are a good means of recording work hours, but they are not required. If there is a timeclock, note that in addition to the timecard punches, *the number of hours worked and the workweek should be written down.* These figures may be noted on the timecard itself or on another record.

Timecard punches often do not show the true hours of an employee's work. Often, workers arrive early at the plant for personal reasons and punch in right away, but they don't start work until their shifts begin. This kind of early punching may be disregarded in counting hours worked.

On the other hand, workers who punch in and out with their shifts may be engaged in set-up work before or after punching. In that case, the time doing the make-ready work should also be counted. This also would be true of work done during lunch hours. If an employee works but doesn't punch a card, the time spent on the job still must be counted as hours worked. As far as the law is concerned, the important thing is whether the employee actually worked, not whether a time record device has been correctly used.

When workers are credited with more or fewer hours of work than the timecard punches show, and when there is a discrepancy of more than a few minutes, a brief note should be made on the timecard to explain the difference. This will avoid disputes about the time actually worked. Basic employment and earning records (i.e., timecards) must be preserved for two years.

The Wage and Hour Division of the Department of Labor requires that its poster must be displayed in a conspicuous place at each business location so employees may readily observe it. (A pull-out poster is provided on page 171.)

Enforcement

The Wage and Hour Division administers and enforces the law with respect to private employment. The Wage and Hour Division's enforcement of the FLSA is carried out by compliance officers stationed across the United States. As the Division's authorized representatives, they have the authority to conduct investigations and gather data on wages, hours, and other employment conditions or practices in order to determine compliance with the Act. Where violations are found, they also may recommend changes in employment practices in order to bring an employer into compliance with the law.

It is a violation of the FLSA to fire, or in any other manner discriminate against an employee for filing a complaint or participating in a legal proceeding under the law.

Wage and Hour inspectors carry an official identity card with their photograph and the signature of the Wage and Hour administrator. Upon arrival, they will ask for the person "in authority" and upon meeting that person will show identification and state that they are there to make an inspection.

Inspections may be made on the initiative of the Department of Labor as part of a random pattern of inspection or upon complaints from any source. If made upon the complaint of an individual or individuals, the names of the complainants (e.g. employees, competitors) will not be revealed. The courts have ruled that any benefit to the employer does not equal the need and right of government informers to remain anonymous. Inspectors may not only examine payroll records but, in addition, may ask to interview employees.

An employer under investigation for violation is entitled to see those passages in the Wage and Hour Division's *Field Operations Handbook* which may inform the employer as to the government's interpretation of the law. Certain portions of that handbook which deal with the Department's enforcement strategies and methodology are not available even under the provisions of the Freedom of Information Act. In any case, where there are alleged violations, it is strongly advised that the inspection be made with the employer's accountant or attorney present.

Where no violations are found, the field investigator will advise the employer and that is the end of the matter. On the other hand, where violations are found, the employer is entitled to a complete written report detailing the violations, the back-wage liability, if any, and other remedial actions necessary to bring the employer into compliance.

Confronted with a report of violation of the FLSA, it is appropriate to have a conference with counsel present, if desired, to discuss the matter with the investigator. The employer will be given a "Summary of Unpaid Wages" owed employees. At this point, the investigative conclusions should be carefully checked for accuracy. There are so many special situations in the law that can be inadvertently overlooked to the employer's disadvantage. If the matter is settled at this point by the payment of back wages, then the case will be closed.

Let us assume that a substantial difference of opinion between the investigator and the employer remains. The employer can then request a conference with the investigator's immediate supervisors or even an official at the regional office level.

When the dispute remains unresolved, there is recourse available at the national office of the Wage and Hour Division of the Department of Labor in Washington. While it is a time consuming process, one finds the greatest amount of latitude at this administrative level. In the absence of any resolution, the Department of Labor will instruct the Solicitor of Labor to bring an appropriate type of action which will often include injunctive relief to prevent future violations.

Penalties and Other Relief Measures

The FLSA provides for the following methods of recovering unpaid minimum and/or overtime wages:

1. The Secretary of Labor may bring suit for back wages and an equal amount as liquidated damages.
2. An employee may file a private suit for back pay and an equal amount as liquidated damages, plus attorney's fees and court costs.
3. The Secretary may obtain an injunction to restrain any person from violating the law, including the unlawful withholding of proper minimum wage and overtime compensation.

An employee may not bring suit if he or she has been paid back wages under the supervision of the Division or if the Secretary has already filed suit to recover the wages.

A two-year statute of limitations applies to the recovery of back pay, except in the case of willful violation, in which case a three-year statute applies.

Willful violations may be prosecuted criminally and the violator fined up to $10,000. A second conviction may result in imprisonment. Violators of the minimum wage and overtime provisions are subject to a civil money penalty of up to $1,000 for each violation.

Wage Garnishments

The Consumer Credit Protection Act limits the amount of an employee's disposable earnings which may be garnished in any one week, as well as protects the employee's job so long as the garnishment results from a single indebtedness. Garnishment is the court procedure through which earnings of an individual are required to be withheld for the payment of any debt.

The employee's disposable earnings (i.e. that part of a person's pay remaining after the deduction from those earnings of any amounts required by law to be withheld) are that portion of his or her pay after deduction for any amount required by law. The maximum subject to garnishment in any workweek may not exceed the lesser of:
(a) 25% of the disposable earnings for that week; or
(b) the amount by which disposable earnings exceed 30 times the prevailing federal minimum wage.

The Consumer Credit Protection Act is enforced by the Department of Labor's Wage and Hour Division, unless a state by prior agreement has been specifically granted this responsibility. The Federal government alone enforces the restrictions on job dismissal. Anyone who violates the discharge provision is subject to criminal prosecution.

Child Support Enforcement

In 1975, Congress passed major legislation that established the Federal/State Child Support Enforcement program. Its purposes are:
- to ensure that children are supported by their parents,
- to foster family responsibility, and
- to reduce the costs of welfare to the taxpayer.

To continue to deal with the national problem of financially abandoned children, a new federal

---

Typical Employer Compliance Questions
About Child Support

1. Q. How will I be informed that I have to start withholding child support from an employee's wages?

A. You will receive a notice from the State Child Support Enforcement (CSE) withholding agency that tells you when to begin, how much to deduct, and where to send the money.

2. Q. Will I have to tell the employee?

A. The employee will already have received notice of the forthcoming withholding action containing all the pertinent information, and will have been given a chance to contest any mistakes of a fact believed to be in the notice.

3. Q. How long after I receive the notice do I begin the withholding?

A. Withholding is to begin no later than the first pay period that occurs 14 days after the mailing date of the notice, or on the date specified in the notice, whichever is earlier.

4. Q. Can I combine all the deductions I make in a pay period and send one check to the withholding agency?

A. Yes. For each withholding agency you send payments to, one check can be written for the total amount as long as you include an itemization of the amount withheld from each person and the date it was withheld.

5. Q. I pay my employees every two weeks. When do I send the payments to the withholding agency?

A. While you may wish to send the funds immediately, you may wait for ten days and send all amounts to the withholding agency at that time.

6. Q. I would rather not get involved in withholding for child support. Can't I just refuse to hire someone who has a withholding against his wages?

A. No. If you refuse to hire or if you discipline or discharge an employee because of a wage withholding for child support, you will be subject to a fine under your State law.

7. Q. And if I don't carry out the withholding?

A. If you fail to withhold wages as specified in the notice, you will be liable for the full amount, as it accumulates from the date of the notice.

8. Q. How do I know when to stop the withholding?

A. The withholding remains in effect until you are notified by the withholding agency of any changes to the order.

Typical Employer Compliance Questions About Child Support (continued)

9. Q. In addition to wages, my employees are periodically paid a sales commission. Do I have to withhold child support from the commission?

A. Federal law requires that child support be withheld only from wages. The State is given the option, however, of applying withholding to other forms of income such as commissions, dividends, retirement benefits, and other types of compensation. If you need further clarification, ask your State Child Support Enforcement agency.

10. Q. Is there any limit to the amount that can be withheld?

A. The total amount allowed to be withheld from any employee's paycheck is limited to the amounts in the Consumer Credit Protection Act (CCPA) unless otherwise specified by State law. The limits provided in the CCPA are 50 percent of disposable earnings in the case of an absent parent who has a second family, and 60 percent if there is no second family. These limits are each increased by 5 percent (to 55 and 65) if payments are in arrears for a period equal to twelve weeks or more.

11. Q. Several of my employees already have wage attachments against their paychecks and if I deduct for child support, the total deducted will be more than allowed under the law. How do I handle the situation?

A. By Federal law, withholding for child support takes priority over any other legal process carried out under State law against the same wages. This means that the child support withholding must be done first, then the deductions for other withholding orders can be made.

12. Q. If I receive a withholding notice from another State, am I required to honor it?

A. Some States have long arm statues that allow them to request withholding directly from employers in other States. You should honor that request, just as you do one from your State. If you have questions, your State withholding agency will be able to assist you.

13. Q. What do I do when the employee leaves my employ?

A. You must notify the State Child Support Enforcement withholding agency promptly when the employee leaves, giving the employee's last known home address and new employer's name and address, if known.

---

law, the Child Support Enforcement Amendments of 1984, P.L. 98-378, was enacted to strengthen state laws and put strong enforcement techniques in place that get the support money to the children for whom it is destined, regularly and reliably.

The cornerstone of the new law is automatic, mandatory wage withholding (i.e. withholding support payments without modification to the support order or a return to court). This process goes into effect automatically for all child support cases being enforced through the State Child Support Enforcement (CSE) program when the amount of past-due support equals one month's support payments (or earlier at state option). All child support orders issued in a state must include a provision for wage withholding regardless of whether the petition for support was made by the state CSE agency or through a private attorney.

Employees/ Independent Contractors 5

Critical Classification

Whether an individual is classified as an employee or an independent contractor has far-reaching consequences for determining a business's responsibility for the individual under the Fair Labor Standards Act, for determining liability under the Federal Insurance Contribution Act (FICA) and the Federal Unemployment Tax Act (FUTA), determining income tax withholding responsibilities, and for determining liability for providing benefits to an individual under evolving sections of the Internal Revenue Code such as those applicable to employee leasing.

While similar, the definitions of, and the procedures for, determining whether an individual is an independent contractor or employee, are different for the purposes of FLSA and for most tax purposes. The remainder of this chapter is divided into a discussion of each process.

FLSA Determinations

It is no easy matter to determine when an individual is an independent contractor. There have been many legal challenges over the years by employers, and the Supreme Court has been asked on a number of occasions to resolve controversies arising out of the dilemma to define who is an "independent contractor" and who is an "employee."

The U.S. Supreme Court has been careful to point out that there is no rule or test which can determine whether an individual is an independent contractor or an employee for purposes of the FLSA. It is the totality of the activities which is the controlling factor. Among the circumstances that the Supreme Court has considered significant have been the following:

1. The nature of the relationship of the services to the principal's business. In this connection, it has been judicially commented upon that routine work which requires industry and efficiency is not indicative of independence and nonemployee status.

2. The permanency of the relationship. The less permanent, the more persuasive it is that it is not an employer-employee relationship. The courts have stated, "It is not significant how one could have acted under the contract terms. The controlling economic realities are reflected by the way one actually acts."

3. The amount of individual investment in facilities and equipment. Obviously, the greater the dollar commitment of the individual, the more likely there will be a determination of independent contractor status.

4. The opportunities for profit and loss. There must be more than mere compensation for time spent at work. At the very least, there must be opportunities of profit or loss flowing from the operations of independent business people in open market competition.

5. The degree of independent business organization and operation. This is a crucial test and

goes to the heart of the question whether there is the requisite degree of independence. The employer does not have to actually control the details and ways of accomplishing tasks in order for individuals to be considered "employees." There need only be the right to exercise that control.

6. The degree of independent initiative or judgment. If the task performed is identical to one performed by an employee, and no amount of personal initiative would change the condition of work or the job to other than an employee's, then there is no basis to find an independent contractor relationship.

Questions to Determine Who Is an Independent Contractor

(Answer "Yes" or "No")

☐ Does the enterprise set the hours of work?

☐ Does the enterprise dictate the methods by which the task is to be implemented?

☐ Does the enterprise pay an hourly wage?

☐ Does the enterprise supply material and tools?

☐ Does the enterprise furnish space, telephone, or secretarial services?

☐ Does the enterprise set fixed, geographical limits on work?

The courts have held that "yes" answers to these questions would indicate an employer-employee relationship. Each case will be determined by its own facts, but each "yes" answer to the above questions lessens the likelihood of a finding of independent contractor status. The employer-employee relationship is tested by economic reality rather than technical concepts.

Internal Revenue Service Determinations

In the Tax Equity and Fiscal Responsibility Act of 1982, Congress provided for two categories of statutory nonemployees — qualified real estate agents and direct sellers. (A "direct seller" is any salesperson who sells consumer products in the home or in a place other than in a permanent retail establishment.) In other employment situations the Internal Revenue Service uses common law principals.

Under the common law test, an individual generally is an employee if the person for whom the individual performs services has the right to control and direct that individual, both as to the result to be accomplished by the work and to the details and means by which that result is accomplished. Thus, the most important factor under the common law is the degree of control, or rights of control, which the employer has over the manner in which the particular work is to be performed.

In determining whether the necessary degree of control exists in order to find that an individual has common law employee status, the courts and the Internal Revenue Service ordinarily consider all of the facts of a particular situation, which are evaluated and weighed in light of the presence or absence of the various pertinent characteristics. The decision as to the weight to be accorded to any single factor necessarily depends upon both the activity under consideration and the purpose underlying the use of the factor as an element of the classification decision.

Because of the particular attributes of a specific occupation, any single factor may be inapplicable. The Internal Revenue Service does have a form to request a determination on the status of a particular individual, known as FORM SS-8.

The 20 common law factors generally considered by the Internal Revenue Service in determining whether an employer-employee relationship exists center around the questions on the opposite page.

IRS — Common Law Factors

1. Is the individual providing services required to comply with instructions concerning when, where, and how the work is to be done?

2. Is the individual provided with training to enable him or her to perform a job in a particular manner?

3. Are the services performed by the individual integrated into the business's operations?

4. Must the services be rendered personally?

5. Does the business hire, supervise, or pay assistants to help the individual performing the services under contract?

6. Is the relationship between the individual and the person for whom he or she performs services a continuing relationship?

7. Who sets the hours of work?

8. Is the individual required to devote full time to the person for whom he or she performs services?

9. Does the individual perform work on another's business premises?

10. Who directs the order or sequence in which the work must be done?

11. Are regular oral or written reports required?

12. What is the method of payment — hourly, weekly, commission, or by the job?

13. Are business or traveling expenses reimbursed?

14. Who furnishes tools and materials necessary for the provision of services?

15. Does the individual performing services have a significant investment in facilities used to perform services?

16. Can the individual providing services realize a profit or loss?

17. Can the individual providing services work for a number of firms at the same time?

18. Does the individual make his or her services available to the general public?

19. Is the individual providing services subject to dismissal for reasons other than nonperformance of contract specifications?

20. Can the individual providing services terminate his or her relationship at any time without incurring a liability for failure to complete a job?

Employment Tax "Safe Haven" For Independent Contractors

Section 530 of the Revenue Act of 1978 was enacted in response to complaints by a number of industries regarding increased enforcement and allegedly aggressive application of the employment tax laws by the Internal Revenue Service. Beginning in the late 1960's the IRS increased its audit activity in this area and proposed changing the employment tax status of many individuals who had historically been treated as independent contractors. Section 530 was intended as a temporary relief measure to foreclose the IRS's actions, while Congress studied the problem and developed a legislative solution. In 1982, with no legislative proposal in sight, the relief provisions of Section 530 were extended indefinitely. They are still in effect today. In 1986, Congress enacted an amendment that prohibits companies from using Section 530 as justification for treating technical service personnel such as an engineer, designer, drafter, computer programmer, or similar skilled worker, as an independent contractor.

The basic approach of Section 530 is to grandfather those workers who have been treated as independent contractors for employment tax purposes on the basis of industry practice, legal authority, prior audits or rulings by the Internal Revenue Service, or any other reasonable grounds. If a worker qualifies under Section 530, the taxpayer, or person for whom he provides services, will be entitled to treat him as an independent contractor for purposes of income tax withholding as well as FICA and FUTA taxes — regardless of the worker's status under the common law control test. However, in order to qualify, the taxpayer must have (1) consistently treated the worker, as well as others performing substantially similar work, as an independent contractor for all years after 1977, (2) timely filed annual information returns (Form 1099-NEC) covering all amounts paid to the worker, and (3) has a reasonable basis for not treating the individual as an employee. If a taxpayer fails to satisfy the

41

requirements of Section 530, he may still be entitled to treat the individuals in question as independent contractors under the common law control test.

Consistent Treatment Requirement. A taxpayer is not entitled to relief under Section 530 if for any period after December 31, 1977, the taxpayer or a predecessor treated, for employment tax purposes, an employee as any individual holding a position which is substantially similar to the position of the individual whose status is in question. According to the legislative history, the purpose of this "consistency" requirement is to prevent taxpayers from changing the way they treat workers solely to take advantage of Section 530. Application of the requirement to predecessors is designed to prevent avoidance through, for example, reincorporations.

The IRS has used the consistency requirement on a number of occasions to deny relief to taxpayers under Section 530. For example, a trucking company was denied relief because it changed the treatment of its drivers for employment tax purposes from employee to independent contractor status "with no change in the working relationship between the company and the drivers."

In contrast, where there has been no attempt to change a worker's status, the IRS appears to take a more liberal approach to the "consistency rule." In a recent technical advice memorandum, the IRS considered the status of *per diem* accountants who were hired during the tax season to prepare returns. Although the taxpayer treated their full time accountants (who prepared returns and also performed audit work) as employees, they treated the *per diem* accountants as independent contractors in accordance with industry practice. The memorandum points out that "although it is not completely clear whether positions held by employees are substantially similar to those held by the *per diem* accountants, it is clear that the taxpayer did not change the status of these individuals to take advantage of the relief positions." The memorandum concludes that "since the services performed by the *per diem*

accountants are somewhat different [from the services performed by the employees] and since there appears to be an industry practice . . . a liberal construction should be given in this case."

In determining whether a taxpayer has "treated" the individual whose status is in question, or any worker who holds a substantially similar position, as an employee for any period, the following guidelines are provided by the IRS:

(1) The withholding of income tax or FICA tax from an individual's wage is treatment of the individual as an employee, whether or not the tax is paid over to the IRS.

(2) The filing of an employment tax return — including Form 940 (Employer's Annual Federal Unemployment Tax Return), Form 941 (Employer's Quarterly Federal Tax Return), and Form W-2 (Wage and Tax Statement) — for a period with respect to an individual, whether or not tax was withheld from the individual, is treatment of the individual as an employee for that period.

(3) The filing for a particular period of a delinquent or amended employment tax return with respect to an individual as the result of an IRS audit of that period, or the execution for a particular period of an Agreement to Assessment and Collection of Additional (Employment) Tax is not treatment of the individual as an employee for that period. However, if the taxpayer withholds employment taxes or files employment tax returns with respect to the individual for periods following the period under audit, the action is treatment of the individual as an employee for the later periods.

Reporting Requirement. To satisfy the reporting requirement, a taxpayer must have *timely* filed Form 1099-NEC, accompanied by Summary and Transmittal Form 1096, with respect to the individuals in question for all taxable years after December 31, 1978.

A Form 1099-NEC must be prepared with respect to each worker who was paid compensation in the amount of $600 or more and, together with Form 1096, must be filed by February 28 of the year following the calendar year in which the compensation is paid. Reasonable extensions of time for filing these forms may be granted by the IRS if requested on or before the due date. In addition, the IRS has announced that it will not deny relief under Section 530 to taxpayers who mistakenly, but in good faith, timely file Form 1099-Misc (Statements for Recipients of Miscellaneous Income) instead of Form 1099-NEC.

Reasonable Basis Requirement. Section 530 provides three alternative standards which constitute "safe havens" in determining whether a taxpayer has a reasonable basis for not treating an individual as an employee. As explained in IRS official publications, reasonable reliance on *any one* of the following is sufficient:

a. Legal authority — This includes judicial precedent or published rulings, whether or not relating to the particular industry or business in which the taxpayer is engaged. It also includes technical advice, a letter ruling, or a determination letter issued by the IRS National Office to the particular taxpayer.

b. Prior IRS audit — This standard is satisfied if there was a prior examination of the taxpayer by the Internal Revenue Service which was concluded without any assessment attributable to the taxpayer's treatment concerning employment tax purposes, of individuals holding positions substantially similar to the position held by the individual whose status is in question. A taxpayer may rely on their audit history even if the previous audit or audits did not involve an examination of the taxpayer's employment tax returns.

c. Industry practice — A taxpayer is entitled to rely on the long-standing recognized practice of a significant segment of their industry. The practice need not be uniform throughout the entire industry. Thus, if a significant portion of the companies in the industry have historically treated the individuals in question as independent contractors, the taxpayer is entitled to rely on this practice, even though other members of the industry have historically treated the same class of individuals as employees.

A taxpayer who fails to meet any of these tests may still be entitled to relief if one can demonstrate, in some other manner, a reasonable basis for not treating the individual in question as an employee. In this connection, the legislative history makes it clear that the "reasonable basis" requirement should be construed liberally in favor of the taxpayer.

Conclusion. Taxpayers who have continuously treated their workers as independent contractors in reliance on any of the grounds outlined above and have filed the required IRS information returns should be able to qualify for relief under Section 530. It should be noted, however, that even if a taxpayer fails to satisfy the requirements of Section 530, he may still be entitled to treat the individuals in question as independent contractors under the common law control test.

Finally, the IRS has stepped up its effort to reclassify independent contractors as employees. A matter of contention for the Service and business has been the "industry practice" basis for treating an individual as an independent contractor under Section 530. The nature of the evidence and the manner in which it should be collected are open issues at this time.

A Congressional committee has completed a review of Section 530 and is proposing major modifications. In a related development, the General Accounting Office has called for the repeal of Section 530.

Contingent Workforce Growth

While independent contractors by definition remain outside the scope of employer-employee relationships, there has been an enormous increase in the use of part-time, temporary, and leased personnel who have become part of the contingent workforce. Indeed, government data confirm that the contingent workforce is growing at a faster rate than the entire labor force. Approximately 25 percent of the workforce is contingent.

1. Temporary Employees — Known by a variety of names, ("temporaries," "part-timers," "casuals," "non-regulars") these individuals may be on the payroll or working for a temporary service, in which case they become the employees of that company. Temporary service employees receive their entire compensation and benefit package from their employers. The question of who actually employs temporary employees is important in circumstances where the employee files a discrimination complaint, or if the employee is discharged or is the subject of any disciplinary action.

2. Leased Employees — It is estimated that there are now between 200 and 300 employee leasing companies in business with some 500,000 workers under lease. Rapid future growth is predicted because of the myriad of federal laws and regulations. Small employers, especially, like the fact that leasing allows them to obtain for their workers the kinds of benefits that a large company can provide because of the greater leverage the leasing company has.

Employee leasing was spurred initially by professionals in the early 1970s as a way to avoid providing benefits. For example, at that time it was possible for a professional to provide the most generous insurance and retirement benefits for himself, while offering his leased employees nothing. Changes in the tax laws have since corrected these abuses.

A recent book by David Nye, *Alternative Staffing Strategies,* suggested these advantages to leasing:

- *Responsibilities can be delegated to the leasing company.* Because the leasing company becomes the "employer of record," the leasing firm can be assigned functions such as hiring, firing, performance evaluation, payroll, personnel administration and recordkeeping, and employee benefits plan administration. The leasing company also makes all legally required withholdings of income taxes and pays workers' compensation and unemployment insurance premiums.

- *Improved employee benefits.* Leasing firms can purchase employee benefits at a lower cost than most small employers. Thus, they can provide a better benefit package to employees than the individual employer would be able to afford. In addition, leasing firms may offer services such as a credit union and employee awards programs.

- *Time savings.* It is estimated that the average

manager spends anywhere from 7-23 percent of his time on non-productive, employee-related paperwork. Turning this paperwork over to the leasing company would enable managers to be more productive.

- *Wage cost and administration.* Although wage and salary rates would not necessarily change with an employee leasing arrangement, leasing firms can increase the effectiveness of the compensation dollar. They keep abreast of compensation rates and trends, and may even conduct area salary surveys for their client companies.

- *Three-tiered personnel services.* Employee leasing firms can offer structure, consultation, and intervention to client companies. Structure is provided through employee handbooks that spell out personnel policies and benefits. They also use formal grievance procedures, and performance appraisal systems and may develop job descriptions for client companies. Consultation is provided through a staff of field supervisors to monitor the service provided and deal with employee-related problems. And intervention in work-related conflicts between employees and the client company can also be provided.

- *Quality and continuity of staff.* Employee leasing firms generally act promptly to fill vacancies—they usually have an existing pool of qualified applicants. The ability to offer comprehensive benefits enables the leasing company to compete with larger companies for skilled personnel. This helps to reduce turnover because employees are less inclined to leave for the larger companies.

- *Positive employer attitudes.* Although employees may be initially apprehensive about the leasing arrangement, employees are positive about leasing once they are accustomed to it. In fact, leasing may provide greater job security for employees because if they don't work out at one client company, they may be able to transfer to another client company. Even if they can't transfer, many leasing companies offer outplacement services to their employees.

Equal Pay Act 6

Legislative Purpose

A significant amendment to the FLSA occurred in 1963. Congress passed the Equal Pay Act prohibiting unequal wages for women and men who work in the *same establishment* for equal work on jobs which require *equal skill, effort,* and *responsibility* and which are performed under similar working conditions. [Emphasis added to indicate further explanation of these key terms.]

Initially, the Act was enforced by the Department of Labor; however, on July 1, 1979, by Executive Order, the enforcement responsibilities were transferred to the U.S. Equal Employment Opportunity Commission (EEOC). In October, 1986, the EEOC published its own regulations which no longer followed those filed earlier by the Department of Labor.

Coverage

With a few inconsequential exceptions, the Equal Pay Act now covers most employees, including executive, administrative, and professional employees as well as U.S. government employees who had initially been exempted from coverage. The Equal Pay Act is designed to eliminate any wage rate differential based on sex; nothing in the law is intended to prohibit differences in wage rates that are based not at all on sex, but wholly on other factors. The equal pay standards does not rely upon job classifications or titles, but depends rather on actual job requirements and performance. The focus of any equal pay inquiry is the job itself and the worker's hour-by-hour duties and responsibilities. Men are protected under the law equally with women. While the Equal Pay Act was motivated by concern for the weaker bargaining position of women, the law by its expressed terms applies to both sexes.

Establishment

The law uses "establishment" to mean a distinct place where employees work. Therefore, the obligation to comply with the equal pay provisions must be determined separately with reference to those employees at that particular location. Thus, where there are disparities in wage rates among various branch operations of a business, it is not relevant as the EEOC inquiry will be limited to a single location. Further, the "establishment" limit in the law does not preclude protection for employees whose employment is outside a "fixed location" (e.g., outside salespersons).

Wages

Wages paid an employee include all payments made to the employee as remuneration for employment. Vacation and holiday pay, premium payments of any kind, and fringe benefits are also included. [Note, however, that payments which do not constitute remuneration for employment are not "wages" (e.g., expense reimbursements).]

Fringe Benefits

Fringe benefits are considered to be remuneration for employment; therefore, it is unlawful for an employer to discriminate between men and women performing equal work with regard to fringe benefits. Fringes include medical, hospital, accident, and life insurance, retirement benefits, profit sharing, bonus plans, leave, etc. Among the key points in the EEOC regulations are the following:

1. Where an employer conditions benefits to employees and their spouses and families on whether the employee is the "head of the household" or "principal wage earner" in the family unit, the overall implementation of the plan will be closely scrutinized.

2. It is unlawful for an employer to make available benefits for the spouses or the families of employees of one gender when the same benefits are not made available for the spouses or families of the opposite gender employees.

3. It shall not be a defense to a charge of sex discrimination in benefits, under the Equal Pay Act, that the cost of such benefits is greater with respect to one sex than the other.

4. It is unlawful to have a pension or retirement plan which establishes different optional or compulsory retirement ages based on sex, or which otherwise differentiates benefits on the basis of sex.

In the intervening years since the Equal Employment Opportunity Commission has taken over the enforcement of the Equal Pay Act, the Supreme Court has ruled in two decisions that retirement benefits constitute "wages." In these new rules, the EEOC makes clear that wages have been consistently defined for Equal Pay Act purposes as "all payments made to an employee as remuneration for employment." Therefore, the specific references to "fringe benefits" in the new regulations is intended simply to resolve any lingering doubts that they are covered by the Equal Pay Act.

Determining "Equal Work"

Congress intended that jobs requiring equal pay should be substantially equal with respect to skill, effort, and responsibility and performed under similar working conditions.

In determining whether employees are performing equal work within the meaning of the Equal Pay Act, the amounts of time which employees spend in the performance of different duties are not the sole criteria. It is also necessary to consider the degree of difference in terms of skill, effort, and responsibility. These factors are related in such a manner that a general standard to determine equality of jobs cannot be set up solely on the basis of a percentage of time. Consequently, a finding that one job requires employees to expend greater effort for a certain percentage of their working time than employees performing another job, would not in itself establish that the two jobs do not constitute equal work.

Similarly, the performance of jobs on different machines or equipment would not necessarily result in a determination that the work so performed is unequal within the meaning of the statute if the equal pay provisions otherwise apply. If the difference in skill or effort required for the operation of such equipment is inconsequential, payment of a higher wage rate to employees of one sex because of a difference in machines or equipment would constitute a prohibited wage rate differential.

Where greater skill or effort is required from the lower paid sex, the fact that the machinery or equipment, used to perform substantially equal work, is different does not defeat a finding that the Equal Pay Act has been violated. Likewise, the fact that jobs are performed in different departments or locations within the establishment would not necessarily be sufficient to demonstrate that unequal work is involved where the equal pay standard otherwise applies. This is particularly true in the case of retail establishments. Unless a showing can be made by the employer that the sale of one article requires such a higher degree of skill or effort than the sale of another article as to render the equal pay standard inapplicable, it will be assumed that the salesmen and saleswomen concerned are performing equal work.

Although the equal pay provisions apply on

an establishment basis (the jobs to be compared are those in the particular establishment), all relevant evidence that may demonstrate whether the skill, effort, and responsibility required for the jobs in the particular establishment are equal should be considered, whether this relates to the performance of like jobs in other establishments or not.

The law uses three tests: equal skill, effort, and responsibility; these terms are considered to constitute three separate tests. Each of them, however, must be present in order for the equal pay law to apply.

1. *Equal Skill.* Here, the analysis includes experience, training, education, and ability. Skill should be measured in terms of the performance of the job. Possession of a skill not needed to meet the requirement of the job cannot be a relevant factor in determining the quality of skill. It is, after all, the job that is being scrutinized and not the worker. Similarly, the efficiency of the employee's performance on the job is not itself an appropriate factor to consider in evaluating an individual's skill.

2. *Equal Effort.* The measure of the physical or mental exertion needed for the performance of a job is the key here. Jobs may require equal effort in performing them even though the effort may be displayed in different ways in two otherwise similar jobs. Differences only in the kind of effort required of the job in such a situation will not justify wage differentials among employees.

The occasional or sporadic performance of an activity which may require extra physical or mental exertion is not alone sufficient to justify a finding of unequal effort. Suppose, however, that men and women are working side by side in a factory line assembling parts. Suppose further that one of the men who performs the operations at the end of the line must also lift the assembly, as he completes his part of it, and place it on a waiting pallet. In such a situation, a wage rate differential might be justified for the person (but only for that person) who is required to expend the extra effort in the performance of the job, provided that the extra effort is substantial and

is performed over a considerable portion of the work cycle.

3. *Equal Responsibility.* For this test, the degree of accountability in the performance of the job with the emphasis on the importance of the job obligation is paramount. To illustrate this test, let us say that there are sales clerks, engaged primarily in selling identical or similar merchandise, who are given different responsibilities. Suppose that one employee of such a group is authorized and required to determine whether to accept payment for purchases by personal checks from customers. The person having the authority to accept personal checks may have a considerable additional degree of responsibility which may materially affect the business operations of the employer. In this situation, payment of a higher wage rate to this employee would be permissible.

Similar Working Conditions

Employees performing jobs requiring equal skill, effort, and responsibility are likely to be performing them under similar working conditions. However, in situations where some employees whose work meets these standards have working conditions substantially different from those required for the performance of other jobs, the equal pay principal would not apply. For example, if some salespersons are engaged in selling a product exclusively inside a store and others employed by the same establishment spend a large part of their time selling the same product away from the establishment, the working conditions would be dissimilar.

Also, where some employees do repair work exclusively inside the shop and others spend most of their time doing similar repair work in customer's homes, there would not be a similarity in working conditions. On the other hand, slight or inconsequential differences in working conditions that are essentially similar would not justify a differential in pay. Such differences are not usually taken into consideration by employers or in collective bargaining in setting wage rates.

Exceptions to Equal Pay Standard

The Equal Pay Act provides three specific exceptions and one broad exception to its general standard requiring that employees doing equal work be paid equal wages, regardless of sex. Under these exceptions, where it can be established that a differential in pay is the result of a wage payment made under a *seniority system, a merit system, a system measuring earnings by quantity or quality of production, or that the differential is based on any other factor other than sex,* the differential is expressly excluded from the statutory prohibition of wage discrimination based on sex. *The legislative intent was stated to be that any discrimination based upon any of these exceptions shall be exempted from the operation of the statute.* These exceptions recognize that there are factors other than sex that can be used to justify a wage differential, even as between employees of opposite sexes performing equal work on jobs which meet the statutory tests of equal skill, effort, and responsibility and similar working conditions. An employer who asserts an exception to equal pay has the burden to provide the facts establishing this affirmative defense.

Additional duties may not be a defense to the payment of higher wages to one sex where the higher pay is not related to the extra duties. The Commission will scrutinize such a defense to determine whether it is *bona fide.* For example, an employer cannot successfully assert an extra duties defense where:

1. Employees of the higher paid sex receive the higher pay without doing extra work;
2. Members of the lower paid sex also perform extra duties requiring equal skill, effort, and responsibility;
3. The extra duties do not in fact exist;
4. The extra task consumes a minimal amount of time and is of peripheral importance; or
5. Third persons (i.e., individuals who are not in the two groups of employees being compared) who do the extra task as their primary job are paid less than the members of the higher paid sex for whom there is an attempt to justify the pay differential.

The term "red circle" rate is used to describe certain unusually higher wage rates which are maintained for reasons unrelated to sex. An example of *bona fide* use of a "red circle" rate might arise in a situation where a company wishes to transfer a long-service employee, who can no longer perform his or her regular job because of ill health, to different work which is now being performed by opposite gender employees.

Under the "red circle" principle the employer may continue to pay the employee his or her present salary, which is greater than that paid to the opposite gender employees, for the work both will be doing.

Under such circumstances, maintaining an employee's established wage rate, despite a reassignment to a less demanding job, is a valid reason for the differential even though other employees performing the less demanding work would be paid at a lower rate. Here the differential is based on a factor other than sex. However, where wage rate differentials have been or are being paid on the basis of sex to employees performing equal work, rates of the higher paid employees may not be "red circled" in order to comply with the Equal Pay Act. To allow this would only continue the inequities which the Equal Pay Act was intended to cure.

Equal Pay Recordkeeping

All records required by the FLSA described in Chapter 3 must also be made available to EEOC representatives. In addition, every employer subject to the Equal Pay Act shall maintain and preserve, for at least two years, any records relating to the payment of wages, wage rates, job evaluations, job descriptions, merit systems, seniority systems, collective bargaining agreements, and any description of a wage differential to employees of the opposite sex in the same establishment based on a factor other than sex.

Equal Pay Enforcement

The Equal Pay Act is enforced by the Equal Employment Opportunity Commission. Its representatives have full investigatory powers to:

1. Enter and inspect place of employment, review records, and interview employees;
2. Advise employers regarding any changes necessary or desirable to comply with the law (If a violation of the law is found, the EEOC will attempt to negotiate a settlement to give the employees back wages due and raise pay levels.);
3. Subpoena witnesses and order production of documents;
4. Supervise back wage payments; and
5. Initiate and conduct litigation.

The names of complaining parties are not to be discussed unless necessary in a court proceeding.

The penalties for Equal Pay violations are covered by the FLSA, and they are discussed in the section, "Penalties and Other Relief Measures," in Chapter 4. Once a prohibited sex-based wage differential has been proved, an employer can come into compliance only by raising the wage rate of the lower paid sex. The Equal Pay Act prohibits an employer from attempting to cure a violation by hiring or transferring employees to perform the previously lower-paid job at the lower rate.

Comparable Worth

The term "comparable worth" describes a theory that every job, by its very nature, has a worth to the employer that can be measured and assigned a precise dollar value. Each employee would then be paid at the same rate as other jobs with the same value. Market factors, such as the availability of qualified workers and the wage rates paid by other employers, would be ignored. Proponents of comparable worth claim that it is needed to eliminate market influences and to close the "earnings gap" between men and women.

U.S. government data confirms that the wide gap between men and women remains little changed since the passage of the Equal Pay Act. Women workers earn about 65% of what men earn. Proponents of pay equity in recent years have introduced legislation in Congress to develop "equitable job evaluation techniques to promote the establishment of wage rates in the federal work force based purely upon the work performed." The rationale is that the Equal Pay Act is insufficient to correct pay discrepancies between the sexes in jobs in which there is a concentration of female workers in a limited number of job classifications. In these jobs, it is argued, the wages are lower than the education, training, skills, experience, effort, responsibility, or working conditions would otherwise warrant.

In 1985, the Equal Employment Opportunity Commission unanimously concluded that Title VII of the Civil Rights Act does not support legal claims based solely on the "controversial concept of comparable worth." That same year the U.S. Civil Rights Commission dismissed comparable worth as "unsound and misplaced." Nevertheless, ten states have adopted written policies on pay equity or comparable worth as they relate to state employees: Hawaii, Iowa, Maine, Michigan, Montana, Minnesota, Ohio, Oregon, Washington, and Wisconsin.

The intensity of the campaign for comparable worth has noticeably subsided since a U.S. Court of Appeals in 1986 reversed what was the most significant, far-reaching court ruling in support of the concept involving Washington state workers. While important legal precedents on this concept are emerging all the time, the fact remains that the concept of comparable worth can "mean all things to all people." Most labor unions, for example, have traditionally opposed job evaluations because they are too subjective a device and, therefore, cannot be relied upon to compare the worth of differing jobs.

"Glass Ceiling" Initiative

This curious term came into prominence in 1990 when the Solicitor of Labor used it in a speech to refer to the invisible, but nonetheless real barriers that may exist, resulting in women and minorities being kept out of higher-level jobs. The Department of Labor initiative is aimed at removing barriers to advancement by women and minorities, through compliance review procedures that focus on managerial positions in the federal contractors' work force.

The Department of Labor's review, which is driven by the demographic realities of the American workplace, is focusing on such issues as practices for selecting employees for executive development programs, succession planning, the structuring of compensation packages, training and rotational assignments, and corporate hiring practices.

While limited now to employers who are federal contractors, the inquiry reminds all employers to use good faith efforts to recruit minorities and women with the requisite skills and to consider them on an even-handed basis for positions at all levels and in all segments of the workforce where they may have been underutilized.

The issue of remedies will be a potential mine field because traditionally the remedy for employment discrimination is to make the victim of discrimination whole through back pay, job placement and/or front pay, if appropriate. Thus, the issue of "bumping" an incumbent employee, who possibly had no role in the act of discrimination, may well arise.

Equal Opportunity and Anti-Bias Laws 7

Legislative Purpose

With the historic passage of the Civil Rights Act of 1964, which contains Title VII — Equal Employment Opportunity, it became the law of the land to bring about equal opportunity for all in the crucial area of employment rights. Congress had found a pattern of restriction, exclusion, discrimination, segregation, and inferior treatment of minorities and women in many employment areas. There was clear evidence that denial of equal rights in employment had led to higher unemployment, lesser occupational status, and the consequent lower income levels of minorities and women. Title VII of the Civil Rights Act provides, therefore, the legal basis for individuals to pursue the work of their own choice and to advance in that work, subject only to consideration of their individual qualifications, talents, and energies.

Congress developed a new national policy defining unlawful employment discrimination to be:

1. To fail or refuse to hire or to discharge any individual, or to discriminate against any individual with respect to compensation, terms, conditions, or privileges of employment because of such individual's race, color, religion, sex, or national origin; or

2. To limit, segregate, or classify employees or applicants for employment in any way which would deprive or tend to deprive any individual of employment opportunities or otherwiseadversely affect his or her status as an employee, because of such individual's race, color, religion, sex, or national origin.

To enforce this anti-discrimination law, the Equal Employment Opportunity Commission was created. The five bipartisan Commissioners are appointed by the President and confirmed by the Senate for a fixed term of five years.

Coverage

Title VII of the Civil Rights Act applies to any employer engaged "in an industry affecting commerce" who has *fifteen* or more employees for each working day in each of twenty or more calendar weeks in the current or preceding year. In 1972, Title VII was amended to include federal, state, and local public employers and educational institutions.

Types of Discrimination Outlawed

The ban on racial discrimination is generally applicable to the protection of persons belonging to minority races; however, the U.S. Supreme Court has held that protection goes to all individuals, including Caucasians, when race is used as a criteria in an employment decision; thus, the recent spate of reverse discrimination suits that have been brought by nonminorities.

Discrimination based on one's color might take place when a choice is made among minority candidates on the basis of the lightest complexion and most apparent Caucasian features.

Where there is a distinction made in employment practices on the basis of sex, male or female, it is illegal unless the job requires specific physical characteristics necessarily possessed by only one sex. In 1978, Congress enacted the Pregnancy Disability Amendment to Title VII which further defines sex discrimination to include disparate treatment of pregnant women for all employment-related purposes. (The Pregnancy Disability Amendment is discussed in greater detail in this chapter).

The prohibition against basing an employment decision on one's religious beliefs or practices is broad in scope. In this instance, neutrality is not enough; there must be an accommodation of the religious needs of employees and job applicants.

The ban on employment discrimination on account of national origin covers all persons residing in the United States, citizens and non-citizens. An employer may deny employment for lack of citizenship, but only to the extent that the refusal does not have the effect of discrimination on the basis of national origin.

Sex Discrimination

The principle of nondiscrimination requires that individuals be considered on the basis of individual capacities and not on the basis of any characteristics generally attributed to the groups, for example, the refusal to hire women on the assumption that the turnover rate among them is higher than men. The key is to avoid stereotyped characterization of the sexes.

The Commission declared that any state laws preferential to one sex over the other are superseded by Title VII and are, therefore, unlawful. Further, it is illegal to have separate lines of progression or a seniority system based on sex. It is an unlawful employment practice for an employer to discriminate between men and women with regard to fringe benefits. In this regard, any benefit payment which is conditioned upon being a "head of the household" or "principal wage earner" will be found to be a *prima facie*

violation of the prohibitions against sex discrimination contained in the Act.

Sexual Harassment

Title VII does not proscribe all conduct of a sexual nature in the workplace. Thus it is crucial to crearly define what sexual harassment is, in the context of the law: only unwelcome sexual conduct that is a term or condition of employment constitutes a violation. The EEOC's Guidelines define two types of sexual harassment: "quid pro quo" and "environmental." The former includes unwelcome sexual conduct when submission to, or rejection of, such conduct by an individual is used as the basis of employment decisions affecting that individual. The latter includes unwelcome sexual conduct that unreasonably interferes with an individual's job performance or creates an "intimidating, hostile, or offensive working environment," even if it leads to no tangible or economic job consequences.

In July 1986, in a landmark case, a unanimous Supreme Court held that Title VII accords employees the right to work in an environment free from discriminatory intimidation, ridicule, and insult. In its first ruling in a sexual harassment case, the Court said, "Without question, when a supervisor sexually harasses a subordinate because of the subordinate's sex, that supervisor 'discriminates' on the basis of sex."

Sexual harassment is "unwelcome . . . verbal or physical conduct of a sexual nature." Because sexual attraction may often play a role in the day-to-day social exchange between employees, "the distinction between invited, uninvited-but-welcome, offensive-but-tolerated, and flatly rejected" sexual advances may well be difficult to discern. But this distinction is essential because sexual conduct becomes unlawful only when it is unwelcome; that is, the challenged conduct must be unwelcome "in the sense that the employee did not solicit or incite it, and in the sense that the employee regarded the conduct as undesirable or offensive." The Supreme Court has said, "The fact that sex-related conduct was 'voluntary,' in the sense that the plaintiff was not forced to

---

EEOC Examples of Sexual Harassment

1. **Consensual Relationships**—Complainant alleges that she lost a promotion for which she was qualified because the co-worker who obtained the promotion was engaged in a sexual relationship with their supervisor. EEOC's investigation discloses that the relationship at issue was consensual and that the supervisor has never subjected complainant's co-worker or any other employees to unwelcome sexual advances. The Commission would find no violation of Title VII in these circumstances, because men and women were equally disadvantaged by the supervisor's conduct for reasons other than their genders. Even if complainant is genuinely offended by the supervisor's conduct, she has no Title VII claim.

2. **Coerced Sexual Favoritism**—Same as above, except the relationship at issue was not consensual. Instead, complainant's supervisor regularly harassed the co-worker in front of other employees, demanded sexual favors as a condition for her promotion, and then audibly boasted about his "conquest." In these circumstances, complainant may be able to establish a violation of Title VII by showing that in order to have obtained the promotion, it would have been necessary to grant sexual favors. In addition, she and other qualified men and women would have standing to challenge the favoritism on the basis that they were injured as a result of the discrimination leveled against their co-worker.

3. **Hostile Environment and Widespread Favoritism**—Same as example *1*, except that complainant's supervisor and other management personnel regularly solicited sexual favors from subordinate employees and offered job opportunities to those who complied. Some of those employees willingly consented to the sexual requests and in turn received promotions and awards. Others consented because they recognized that their opportunities for advancement would otherwise be limited. Complainant, who did not welcome this conduct, was not approached for sexual favors. However, she and other female and male co-workers may be able to establish that the conduct created a hostile work environment. She can also claim that by their conduct, the managers communicated to all female employees that they can obtain job benefits only by acquiescing in sexual conduct.

---

participate against her will, is not a defense to a sexual harassment suit. The core of any sexual harassment claim is that the alleged sexual advances were unwelcome."

The Commission recognizes that sexual conduct may be private and unacknowledged, with no eyewitnesses. Even sexual conduct that occurs openly in the workplace may appear to be consensual. Thus the resolution of a sexual harassment claim often depends on the credibility of the parties. The EEOC investigator will question the charging party and the alleged harasser in detail. The Commission's investigation also will search for corroborative evidence of any nature. Supervisory and managerial employees, as well as co-workers, will be asked about their knowledge of the alleged harassment.

In appropriate cases, the Commission may make a finding of harassment based solely on the credibility of the victim's allegation. As with any other charge of discrimination, a victim's account must be sufficiently detailed and internally consistent so as to be plausible, and a lack of corroborative evidence, where such evidence logically should exist, would undermine the allegation. By the same token, a general denial by the alleged harasser will carry little weight when it is contradicted by other evidence.

The Supreme Court has ruled that for sexual harassment to violate Title VII, it must be "sufficiently severe or pervasive 'to alter the conditions of [the victim's] employment and create an abusive working environment.'" Since "hostile environment" harassment takes a variety of forms, many factors may affect this determination, including: (1) whether the conduct was verbal, physical, or both; (2) how frequently it was repeated; (3) whether the conduct was hostile or patently offensive; (4) whether the alleged harasser was a co-worker or supervisor; (5) whether others joined in perpetrating the harassment; and (6) whether the harassment was directed at more than one individual.

In determining whether unwelcome sexual conduct rises to the level of a "hostile environment" in violation of Title VII, the central inquiry is whether the conduct "unreasonably interferes with an individual's work performance" or creates "an intimidating, hostile, or offensive working environment." Thus, sexual flirtation or innuendo, even vulgar language that is trivial or merely annoying, would probably not establish a hostile environment.

The Supreme Court has agreed with the Commission's position that Congress wanted courts to look to agency principles for guidance in determining an employer's liability for sexual conduct by a supervisor.

As for employer liability, the Court made it clear that employers are not "automatically liable" for the acts of their supervisors. For the same reason, the Court said, "absence of notice to an employer does not necessarily insulate that employer from liability."

The Commission, following the Supreme Court's decision, now requires a careful examination in "hostile environment" cases of whether the harassing supervisor was acting in an "agency capacity." Additionally, whether the employer had an appropriate and effective complaint procedure and whether the victim used it are important factors.

The EEOC's guidelines encourage employers to:

take all steps necessary to prevent sexual harassment from occurring, such as affirmatively raising the subject, expressing strong disapproval, developing appropriate sanc-

tions, informing employees of their right to raise and how to raise the issue of harassment under Title VII, and developing methods to sensitize all concerned.

An effective preventative program should include an explicit policy against sexual harassment that is clearly and regularly communicated to employees and effectively implemented. The employer should affirmatively raise the subject with all supervisory and non-supervisory employees, express strong disapproval, and explain the sanctions for harassment. The employer should also have a procedure for resolving sexual harassment complaints. The procedure should be designed to "encourage victims of harassment to come forward" and should not require a victim to complain first to the offending supervisor. It should ensure confidentiality as much as possible and provide effective remedies, including protection of victims and witnesses against retaliation.

In 1991, a Federal district court in Florida ruled that posting pictures of nude and partly nude women is a form of sexual harassment. This was the first time a court found that pornography was in itself harassment. Prior to this time, courts have found such pictures may have contributed to an atmosphere of sexual harassment. In this case, the court ruled that the pictures created a "visual assault on the sensibilities of female workers" and this sexualized atmosphere had worked to keep women out of the workforce.

What is important to remember is that employers must go beyond the passive policy of posting notices regarding their policy on sexual harassment to ensure that they have adequately communicated their policy. Indeed, in the Florida case the court found that the employer's efforts had little or no effect on what it found to be a sexually hostile work environment. An employer's policy must be clearly and regularly communicated, otherwise an employer is going to be vulnerable when charges of sexual harassment are made.

Pregnancy Discrimination Guidelines

The Pregnancy Discrimination Act of 1978 makes it clear that discrimination on the basis of pregnancy, childbirth, or related medical conditions constitutes unlawful sex discrimination under Title VII.

The basic principle of the Act is that women affected by pregnancy and related conditions must be treated the same as other applicants and employees on the basis of their ability or inability to work.

The Equal Employment Opportunity Commission has issued guidelines, including questions and answers, interpreting the Act. These guidelines provide guidance as to whose employment practices would be considered by the Commission as violating the Act.

Religious Discrimination Guidelines

Denying or limiting equal opportunities to individuals without reasonable effort to accommodate their religious beliefs or practices is a violation of Title VII. Section 701(j) of Title VII established an obligation by employers to reasonably accommodate the religious practices of an employee or prospective employee unless doing so would create an undue hardship upon the employer. In the U.S. Supreme Court's decision in *Trans World Airlines, Inc. v. Hardison* (1977) the Court ruled against a religious observer because the accommodations would have involved the seniority rights of other workers and regular payment of premium wages to the employee who would have had to replace him. Although the Hardison decision left intact the responsibility of business to accommodate, many employers and unions were left uncertain as to the extent of their duty to provide reasonable accommodation for religious practices. Accordingly, the EEOC has published revised *Guidelines on Discrimination Because of Religion*, the major elements of which are summarized below:

Accommodations — The employer is obligated to accommodate an employee's or prospective employee's religious practices once the employer has been notified of the need. The employer must offer the alternative which would least disadvantage the employment opportunities of the religious observant and not cause undue hardship to the employer.

A religious discrimination case involving an interpretation of "reasonable accommodation" became one of the Supreme Court's early decisions in the 1986-1987 term. The High Court ruled that an employer must make a "reasonable" effort to accommodate a worker's religion, but needn't adopt the employee's suggestion on how to go about it. The employer provided for three religious holidays and three days of personal leave, all with pay. The employee, who celebrated six religious holidays a year, argued that he wanted to take three personal days instead of unpaid leave for the remaining three religious holidays. The employer's policy was that personal days could not be used for religious holidays. The High Court ruled that an employer's duty to accommodate the employee's religious belief under Title VII of the 1964 Civil Rights Act does not require the employer to accept the accommodation preferred by the employee. The case is the second in as many years in which the Supreme Court has resolved the competing interests of religious needs of individual employees by ruling in favor of the employer. Earlier, the Court struck down a Connecticut law that required employers to give employees their Sabbath day off. The Court said the law unconstitutionally promoted religious worship.

Alternatives — Examples of alternatives specified by the guidelines include the use of voluntary substitutes and swaps, flexible schedules, lateral transfer, and change of job assignment.

Union Dues — When an employee's religious practices prohibit payment of union dues to a labor organization, the employee must not be made to pay union dues but may be permitted to pay a sum equivalent to the dues to a charitable organization.

Frequently Asked Questions
Relating to Pregnant Employee Rights

Provide Another Job

1. **Q. If, for pregnancy-related reasons, an employee is unable to perform the functions of her job, does the employer have to provide an alternative job?**

   A. An employer is required to treat an employee temporarily unable to perform the functions of the job (because of her pregnancy-related condition) in the same manner as it treats other temporarily disabled employees, whether by providing modified tasks, alternative assignments, disability leaves, leaves without pay, etc. For example, a woman's primary job function may be the operation of a machine, and, incidental to that function, she may carry materials to and from the machine. If other employees temporarily unable to lift are relieved of these functions, pregnant employees also unable to lift must be temporarily relieved of the function.

How To Determine If She Can Work

2. **Q. May an employer place a pregnant employee on leave who claims she is able to work, or deny leave to a pregnant employee who claims she is disabled from work?**

   A. An employer may not single out pregnancy-related conditions for determining an employee's ability to work. However, an employer may use any procedure used to determine the ability of all employees to work. For example, if an employer requires its employees to submit a doctors' statement concerning their inability to work before granting leave or paying sick benefits, the employer may require employees affected by pregnancy-related conditions to submit such statements. Similarly, if an employer allows its employees to obtain doctors' statements from their personal physicians for absences due to other disabilities or return-dates from other disabilities, it must accept doctors' statements from personal physicians for absences and return-dates connected with pregnancy-related disabilities.

Length of Leave

3. **Q. Can an employer have a rule which prohibits an employee from returning to work for a predetermined length of time after childbirth?**

   A. No.

Stay Off Until Delivery?

4. **Q. If an employee has been absent from work as a result of a pregnancy-related condition and recovers, may her employer require her to remain on leave until after her baby is born?**

   A. No. An employee must be permitted to work at all times during pregnancy when she is able to perform her job.

Keep Job Open

5. **Q. Must an employer hold open the job of an employee who is absent on leave because she is temporarily disabled by pregnancy-related conditions?**

   A. Unless the employee on leave has informed the employer that she does not intend to return to work, her job must be held open for her return on the same basis as jobs are held open for employees on sick or disability leave for other reasons.

Status During Leave

6. **Q. May an employer's policy concerning the accrual and crediting of seniority during absences for medical conditions be different for employees affected by pregnancy-related conditions?**

   A. No. An employer's seniority policy must be the same for employees absent for pregnancy-related reasons as for those absent for other medical reasons.

Fringe Benefits

7. **Q. For purposes of calculating such matters as vacations and pay increases, may an employer credit time spent on leave for pregnancy-related reasons differently than time spent on leave for other reasons?**

   A. No. An employer's policy with respect to crediting time for the purpose of calculating such matters as vacation and pay increases cannot treat employees on leave for pregnancy-related reasons less favorably than employees on leave for other reasons. For example, if an employee on leave for medical reasons is credited with the time

Q. & A. Pregnant Employee Rights (continued)

spent on leave when computing entitlement to vacation or pay raises, an employee on leave for pregnancy-related disability is entitled to the same kind of time credit.

Hiring

8. Q. **Must an employer hire a woman who is medically unable, because of a pregnancy-related condition, to perform a necessary function of a job?**

   A. No. An employer can refuse to hire a woman because of her pregnancy-related condition so long as she is unable to perform the major functions necessary to do the job.

Only Marrieds protected?

9. Q. **May an employer limit disability benefits for pregnancy-related conditions to married employees?**

   A. No.

All Female Workforce

10. Q. **If an employer has an all-female workforce or job classification, must benefits be provided for pregnancy-related conditions?**

    A. Yes. If benefits are provided for other conditions, they must be also be provided for pregnancy-related conditions.

Income Maintenance

11. Q. **For what length of time must an employer who provides income maintenance benefits for temporary disabilities provide such benefits for pregnancy-related disabilities?**

    A. Benefits should be provided for as long as the employee is unable to work for medical reasons unless some other limitation is set for all other temporary disabilities, in which case pregnancy-related disabilities should be treated the same as other temporary disabilities.

Long-Term Disability

12. Q. **Must an employer who provides benefits for long-term or permanent disabilities provide such benefits for pregnancy-related conditions?**

    A. Yes. Benefits for long-term or permanent disabilities resulting from pregnancy-related conditions must be provided to the same extent that such benefits are provided for other conditions which result in long-term or permanent disability.

Fringe Benefits

13. Q. **If an employer provides benefits to employees on leave, such as installment purchase disability insurance, payment of premium for health, life, or other insurance, continued payments into pension, savings or profit sharing plans, must the same benefits be provided for those on leave for pregnancy-related conditions?**

    A. Yes, the employer must provide the same benefits for those on leave for pregnancy-related conditions as for those on leave for other reasons.

Vacation

14. Q. **Can an employee who is absent due to a pregnancy-related disability be required to exhaust vacation benefits before receiving sick leave pay or disability benefits?**

    A. No. If employees who are absent because of other disabling cause receive sick leave pay or disability benefits without any requirement that they first exhaust vacation benefits, the employer cannot impose this requirement on an employee for a pregnancy-related cause.

Child-Care Leave

15. Q. **Must an employer grant leave to a female employee for childcare purposes after she is medically able to return to work following leave necessitated by pregnancy, childbirth, or related medical conditions?**

    A. While leave for childcare purposes is not covered by the Pregnancy Discrimination Act, ordinary Title VII principals would require that leave for childcare purposes be granted on the same basis as leave which is granted to employees for other non-medical reasons. For example, if an employer allows its employees to take leave without pay or accrued annual leave for travel or education which is not job-related, the same type of leave must be granted to those who wish to remain on leave for infant care, even though they are medically able to return to work.

Q. & A. Pregnant Employee Rights (continued)

State Laws

16. Q. **If state law requires an employer to provide disability insurance for a specified period before and after child-birth, does compliance with the state law fulfill the employer's obligation under the Pregnancy Discrimination Act?**

    A. No necessarily. It is an employer's obligation to treat employees temporarily disabled by pregnancy in the same manner as employees affected by other temporary disabilities. Therefore, any restrictions imposed by state laws on benefits for pregnancy-related disabilities, but not for other disabilities, do not excuse the employer from treating the individuals in both groups of employees the same. If, for example, a state law requires an employer to pay a maximum of 26 weeks benefits for disabilities other than pregnancy-related ones, but only six weeks for pregnancy-related disabilities, the employer must provide benefits for the additional weeks to an employee disabled by pregnancy-related conditions, up to the maximum provided other disabled employees.

Public Employees

17. Q. **If a state or local government provides its own employees income maintenance benefits for disabilities, may it provide different benefits for disabilities arising from pregnancy-related conditions than for disabilities arising from other conditions?**

    A. No. State and local governments, as employers, are subject to the Pregnancy Discrimination Act in the same way as private employers and must bring their employment practices and programs into compliance with the Act, including disability and health insurance programs.

Spouses of Male Employees

18. Q. **Must an employer provide health insurance coverage for the medical expenses of pregnancy-related conditions of the spouses of male employees? Of the dependents of all employees?**

    A. Where an employer provides no coverage for dependents, the employer is not required to institute such coverage. However, if an employer's insurance program covers the medical expenses of spouses of female employees, then it must equally cover the medical expenses of spouses of male employees, including those arising from pregnancy-related conditions.

    But the insurance does not have to cover the pregnancy-related conditions of non-spouse dependents as long as it excludes the pregnancy-related conditions of such non-spouse dependents of male and female employees equally.

Spouses

19. Q. **Must an employer provide the same level of health insurance coverage for the pregnancy-related medical conditions of the spouses of male employees as it provides for its female employees?**

    A. No. It is not necessary to provide the same level of coverage for the pregnancy-related medical conditions of spouses of male employees.

Dependent Coverage

20. Q. **May an employer offer optional dependent coverage which excludes pregnancy-related medical conditions or offers less coverage for pregnancy-related medical conditions where the total premium for the optional coverage is paid by the employee?**

    A. No. Pregnancy-related medical conditions must be treated the same as other medical conditions under any health or disability insurance or sick leave plan available in connection with employment, regardless of who pays the premiums.

Insurance Protection

21. Q. **Where an employer provides its employees a choice among several health insurance plans, must coverage for pregnancy-related conditions be offered in all of the plans?**

    A. Yes. Each of the plans must cover pregnancy-related conditions. For example, an employee with a single coverage policy cannot be forced to purchase a more expensive family coverage policy in order to receive coverage for her own pregnancy-related condition.

Q. & A. Pregnant Employee Rights (continued)

Medical Expenses

22. Q. On what basis should an employee be reimbursed for medical expenses arising from pregnancy, childbirth, or related conditions?

A. Pregnancy-related expenses should be reimbursed in the same manner as are expenses incurred for other medical conditions. Therefore, whether a plan reimburses the employees on a fixed basis, or on a percentage of a reasonable and customary charge basis, the same basis should be used for reimbursement of expenses incurred for pregnancy-related conditions. Furthermore, if medical costs for pregnancy-related conditions increase, re-evaluation of the reimbursement level should be conducted in the same manner as are cost re-evaluations of increases for other medical conditions. Coverage provided by a health insurance program for other conditions must be provided for pregnancy-related conditions. For example, if a plan provides major medical coverage, pregnancy-related conditions must be so covered. Similarly, if a plan covers the cost of a private room for other conditions, the plan must cover the cost of a private room for pregnancy-related conditions. Finally, where a health insurance plan covers office visits to physicians, pre-natal visits must be included in such coverage.

Insurance Protection

23. Q. May an employer limit payment of costs for pregnancy-related medical conditions to a specified dollar amount set forth in an insurance policy, collective bargaining agreement, or other statement of benefits to which an employee is entitled?

A. The amounts payable for the costs incurred for pregnancy-related conditions can be limited only to the same extent as are costs for other conditions. Maximum recoverable dollar amounts may be specified for pregnancy-related conditions if such amounts are similarly specified for these conditions, and so long as the specific amounts in all instances cover the same proportion of actual costs. If, in addition to the scheduled amount for other procedures, additional costs are paid for, either directly or indirectly, by the employer, such additional payments must also be paid for pregnancy-related procedures.

Deductible

24. Q. May an employer impose a different deductible for payment of costs for pregnancy-related medical conditions than for costs of other medical conditions?

A. No. Neither an additional deductible, an increase in the usual deductible, nor a larger deductible can be imposed for coverage for pregnancy-related medical costs, whether as a condition for inclusion of pregnancy-related costs in the policy, or as payment of the costs when incurred. Thus, if pregnancy-related costs are the first incurred under the policy, the employee is required to pay only the same deductible as would otherwise be required had other medical costs been the first incurred. Once this deductible has been paid, no additional deductible can be required for other medical procedures. If the usual deductible has already been paid for other medical procedures, no additional deductible can be required when pregnancy-related costs are later incurred.

Pre-Existing Condition

25. Q. If a health insurance plan excludes the payment of benefits for any conditions existing at the time the insured's coverage becomes effective (pre-existing condition clause), can benefits be denied for medical costs arising from a pregnancy existing at the time the coverage became effective?

A. Yes. However, such benefits cannot be denied unless the pre-existing condition clause also excludes benefits for other pre-existing conditions in the same way.

Insurance After Termination

26. Q. If an employer's insurance plan provides benefits after the insured's employment has ended (i.e. extended benefits) for costs connected with pregnancy and delivery where conception occurred while the insured was working for the employer, but not for the costs of any other medical conditions which began prior to termination of employment, may an employer (a) continue to pay these extended benefits for pregnancy-related medical conditions but not for other medical conditions, or (b) terminate these benefits for pregnancy-related conditions?

A. Where a health insurance plan currently provides extended benefits for other medical conditions on a less favorable basis than for pregnancy-related medical conditions, extended benefits must be provided for other medical

Q. & A. Pregnant Employee Rights (continued)

conditions on the same basis as for pregnancy-related medical conditions. Therefore, an employer can neither continue to provide less benefits for other medical conditions nor reduce benefits currently paid for pregnancy-related medical conditions.

Extended Benefits Under Different Conditions

27. Q. Where an employer's health insurance plan currently requires total disability as a prerequisite for payment of extended benefits for other medical conditions but not for pregnancy-related costs, may the employer now require total disability for payments of benefits for pregnancy-related medical conditions as well?

A. Since extended benefits cannot be reduced in order to come into compliance with the Act, a more stringent prerequisite for payment of extended benefits for pregnancy-related medical conditions, such as a requirement for total disability, cannot be imposed. Thus, in this instance, in order to comply with the Act, the employer must treat other medical conditions as pregnancy-related conditions are treated.

Self-Insurance

28. Q. Can an employer self-insure benefits for pregnancy-related conditions if it does not self-insure benefits for other medical conditions?

A. Yes, so long as the benefits are the same. In measuring whether benefits are the same, factors other than the dollar coverage paid should be considered. Such factors include the range of choice of physicians and hospitals, and the processing and promptness of payment of claims.

Abortion

29. Q. Can an employer discharge, refuse to hire, or otherwise discriminate against a woman because she has had or is contemplating having an abortion?

A. No. An employer cannot discriminate in its employment practices against a woman who has had or is contemplating having an abortion.

Abortion and Fringe Benefits

30. Q. Is an employer required to provide fringe benefits for abortions if fringe benefits are provided for other medical conditions?

A. All fringe benefits other than health insurance, such as sick leave, which are provided for other medical conditions, must be provided for abortions. Health insurance, however, need be provided for abortions only where the life of the woman would be endangered if the fetus were carried to term or where medical complications arise from an abortion.

Abortion and Complications

31. Q. If complications arise during the course of an abortion, for instance, excessive hemorrhaging, must an employer's health insurance plan cover the additional cost due to the complications of the abortion?

A. Yes. The plan is required to pay those additional costs attributable to the complications of the abortion. However, the employer is not required to pay for the abortion itself, except where the life of the mother would be endangered if the fetus were carried to term.

Abortion and Insurance

32. Q. May an employer elect to provide insurance coverage for abortions?

A. Yes. The Act specifically provides that an employer is not precluded from providing benefits for abortions whether directly or through a collective-bargaining agreement, but if an employer decides to cover the costs of abortion, the employer must do so in the same manner and to the same degree as other medical conditions.

Undue Hardship — Under the guidelines, an employer may assert undue hardship to justify a refusal to accommodate an employee's need to be absent from his or her scheduled duty hours if the employer can demonstrate that the accommodation would require more than a minimal cost. This would be determined by an examination of all the facts and must be in accordance with the *Hardison* decision. Also, undue hardship may be shown where a variance from a *bona fide* seniority system is necessary in order to accommodate an employee's religious practices when it would deny another employee his or her job or shift preference guaranteed by that system.

Selection Practices — The guidelines address selection practices which tend to exclude individuals because of their religious beliefs. Under the guidelines, unlawful practices by employers would include scheduling of examinations and other selection activities during a period which conflicts with an individual's religious practices (or beliefs), and premature inquiries which ascertain an applicant's availability to work during certain time periods.

National Origin Discrimination Guidelines

The Commission broadly defines national origin discrimination as including, but not limited to, the denial of equal employment opportunity because of an individual's place of origin; or because an individual has the physical, cultural, or linguistic characteristics of a national origin group. The Commission will examine, with particular concern, charges alleging that individuals have been denied equal employment opportunity for reasons which are grounded in national origin considerations, such as: (a) marriage to, or association with, persons of a national origin group; (b) membership in or association with an organization identified with or seeking to promote the interests of national origin groups; (c) attendance or participation in schools, churches, temples, or mosques, generally used by persons of a national origin group; and, (d) because an individual's name or spouse's name is associated with a national origin group.

The "Speak-English Only" Rule — The Commission will presume that a rule requiring employees to speak only English at all times in the workplace violated Title VII as a burdensome term and condition of employment. Requiring employees to speak only in English at certain times would not be discriminatory if the employer shows that the rule is justified by business necessity. When the employer believes that the rule is justified by business necessity the employer should clearly inform employees of the circumstance in which they are required to speak only in English and the consequences of violating the rule.

Notice of such a rule is necessary because it is common for individuals whose primary language is not English to inadvertently slip from speaking English to speaking their native tongue. Any adverse employment decision against an individual based on a violation of the rule will be considered as evidence of discrimination if an employer has not given effective notice of the rule.

Accent — In a unanimous decision, the Commission determined an employer must show a legitimate nondiscriminatory reason for the denial of employment opportunity because of an individual's accent or manner of speaking.

Investigations will focus on a claimant's qualifications to do the job and whether the claimant's accent or manner of speaking would have a detrimental effect on job performance.

Requirements that employers or applicants be fluent in English may also violate Title VII if they are adopted for discriminatory reasons or applied in a discriminatory manner, or if they have the effect of excluding individuals of a particular national origin and are not related to successful job performance.

Harassment — The Commission has consistently held that harassment on the basis of national origin is a violation of Title VII. It holds that an employer has an affirmative duty to maintain a working environment free of harassment on the basis of national origin. This rule, which has been adopted by the courts in race and sex cases, clearly applies equally to national origin.

Ethnic slurs and other verbal or physical conduct relating to an individual's national origin constitutes harassment when this conduct (1) has the purpose or effect of creating an intimidating, hostile, or offensive work environment; (2) has the purpose or effect of unreasonably interfering with an individual's work performance; or (3) otherwise adversely affects an individual's employment opportunities.

An employer is responsible for its acts and those of its agents and supervisory employees under Title VII, regardless of whether the acts were specifically authorized or forbidden by the employer and regardless of whether the employer knew or should have known of the acts.

The guidelines distinguish between the employer's responsibility for the acts of its agents or supervisors from the responsibility it has for conduct among fellow employees. Liability for acts of national origin harassment between fellow employees in the workplace exists only when the employer, or its agents or supervisory employees, knows or should have known of the conduct, and the employer cannot demonstrate that it took immediate and appropriate corrective action. In certain circumstances, where an employer may be shown to have the necessary control, it may also be responsible for the acts of non-employees with respect to harassment of employees in the workplace on the basis of national origin.

Hiring Non-Nationals — With its enactment of the Immigration Reform and Control Act of 1986, Congress for the first time made it unlawful for an employer to hire individuals who are not legally authorized for employment in the United States. While adopting these new requirements, Congress was also concerned that some employers might overreact and refuse to hire individuals who appeared or sounded "foreign." Although Congress recognized that the existing prohibitions on national origin discrimination in Title VII of the Civil Rights Act would cover much of the potential discrimination, Congress also included in the Act a new nondiscrimination provision, to

be enforced by the Department of Justice, which prohibits national origin discrimination by small employers not covered by Title VII and discrimination because of citizenship status by all employers with four or more employees.

While the Immigration Act prohibits discrimination on the basis of citizenship in some circumstances, that Act specifically states that it is not a violation *of the Immigration Act* to prefer a citizen over an alien where both are equally qualified. Employers should be aware, however, that such citizenship preferences *may still violate Title VII* if they have the purpose or effect of discriminating on the basis of national origin.

Affirmative Action Guidelines

The EEOC has encouraged voluntary affirmative action to improve opportunities for minorities and women because the legislative purpose of Title VII was first to encourage voluntary action without recourse to legal proceedings. Therefore, in providing guidelines for affirmative action programs, the EEOC helps to define for employers what could become an affirmative good faith defense to any subsequent equal employment discrimination charge. The Commission recommends that such a plan be in writing and be dated so that it could serve as credible evidence of an employer's compliance efforts in case of a subsequent challenge.

In 1986, the Supreme Court strongly endorsed the use of affirmative action, including specific racial goals to remedy past employment discrimination. For the first time, the Court said that federal judges may set goals and timetables requiring employers who have discriminated to hire or promote specific numbers of minorities. It also permitted states and cities even broader discretion to agree to similar racial goals for their work forces without court orders.

In a sweeping extension of a line of decisions on affirmative action, the Supreme Court in 1987 held that employers may sometimes favor women and members of minorities over better qualified men and whites in hiring and promoting to achieve better balance in their work force. The decision upheld a California city's affirmative action plan for women and minority group members.

The ruling was the Court's first involving affirmative action plans giving job preferences to women over men. The Court rejected a civil rights suit by a man who said he had been the victim of illegal sex discrimination when he lost a promotion to a less qualified woman. The decision also marked the first time the High Court had clearly held that in a case where there was no proof of past discrimination against women or minorities by a particular employer, the employer may use racial and sexual preferences in hiring and promoting to bring its work force into line with the make up of the local population or labor market. "In determining whether an imbalance exists that would justify taking sex or race into account, a comparison of the percentage of minorities or women in the employer's work force with a percentage in the area labor market or general population is appropriate in analyzing jobs that require no special expertise."

Supporters of the decision confidently predict that it will increase the percentage of women in jobs historically held by men. Experts contend that the Court's interpretation of Title VII of the Civil Rights Act of 1964 will have a broad impact on strengthening the incentives of private employers around the country to adopt voluntary affirmative action plans.

The most direct impact of the Court's decision will be to bolster the use of affirmative action in relatively unskilled jobs.

In 1989, reflecting a change in the judicial philosophy of the Supreme Court, the justices in a 5-4 ruling allowed previously approved, court-directed affirmative action settlements to be challenged by white workers who had not been parties to consent decrees. The Court affirmed a lower court opinion permitting a suit to go forward on the grounds that the white plaintiffs were entitled to their day in court to challenge a race-based preference for blacks under the decrees. The Court rejected the argument that the reverse bias suit was an "impermissible collateral attack" on the decrees because the white plaintiffs, although not parties to the original suit

filed in 1974, had sufficient notice that their interests might be affected but failed to intervene.

Pre-Employment Inquiries

Employment application forms and pre-employment interviews have traditionally been instruments for eliminating, at an early stage, "unsuited" or "unqualified" persons from consideration for employment and often have been used in such a way as to restrict or deny employment opportunities for women and members of minority groups.

The law, interpreted through court rulings and EEOC decisions, prohibits the use of all pre-employment inquiries and qualifying factors which disproportionately screen out members of minority groups or members of one sex, are not valid predictors of successful job performance, or cannot be justified by "business necessity."

In devising or reviewing application forms or in seeking information from job applicants, employers should ask themselves: (1) Will the answers to this question, if used in making a selection, have a disparate effect in screening out minorities and/or members of one sex (i.e. disqualify a significantly larger percentage of members of a particular group than others) or (2) Is this information really needed to judge an applicant's competence or qualification for the job in question?

The concept of business necessity has been narrowly defined by the courts. When a practice is found to have discriminatory effects, it can be justified only by showing that it is necessary to the safe and efficient operation of the business, that it effectively carries out the purpose it is supposed to serve, and that there are no alternative policies or practices which would better or equally well serve the same purpose with less discriminatory impact.

Title VII specifically excludes from its discrimination ban any employment practices based upon giving and acting upon the "results of any professionally developed ability test, provided that such test, its administration, or action upon the results is not designed, intended, or used to discriminate because of race, color, religion, sex, or national origin." In a technically complex guideline, the EEOC states that the use of any selection procedure which has an adverse impact on the hiring, promotion, or other employment or membership opportunities of members of any race, sex, or ethnic group will be considered to be discriminatory and inconsistent, unless the procedure has been validated. The guidelines also explain validity studies and establish certain minimum technical standards for them.

An employer should be able to demonstrate through statistical evidence that any selection procedure which has a "disparate effect" on groups protected by the law is job related (i.e. validation predicts successful performance in the type of job in question). If this cannot be shown or if the employer cannot or does not wish to perform a technical validation study, the use of that procedure should be discontinued or altered in such a way that there is no longer a discriminatory effect. Even when a procedure having an adverse impact can be validated, it may not be used if there are other procedures which would accomplish the same goal and have less of a discriminatory effect.

Data Required For Legitimate Business Purposes

An employer may justifiably seek and obtain information regarding a job applicant's race, sex, or ethnicity as needed for implementation of affirmative action programs, court-ordered or other government reporting or recordkeeping requirements, and for studies to identify and resolve possible problems in the recruitment and testing of members of minority groups and/or women to insure equal employment for all persons.

Data on such matters as marital status, number and age of children, and similar matters, which could be used in a discriminatory manner in making employment decisions but which are necessary for insurance, reporting requirements, or other business purposes, can and should preferably be obtained after a person has been employed, not by means of an application form or pre-employment interview.

The employer, however, must be able to demonstrate that such data was collected for legitimate business purposes. Such information should be kept separate from the regular permanent employee records to insure that it is not used to discriminate in making personnel decisions. To protect against the improper use of such information by their selected officials, employers should consider collecting the facts by the use of a "tear-off sheet." After completing the application and the tear-off sheet, the latter is separated from the application and used only for purposes unrelated to the selection decision. The tear-off sheet should contain a statement about the purpose for which the information is being collected and that the information will not be made available or used for making employee selections. This should allay the employee's fear that the information might be used to discriminate on a prohibited basis.

It is reasonable to assume that all questions on an application form or in a pre-employment interview are for some purpose and that selection or hiring decisions are made on the basis of the answers given.

To seek information other than that which is essential to evaluate effectively a person's qualification for employment is to increase the exposure to charges of discrimination in legal proceedings.

It is, therefore, in an employer's self-interest to review carefully all procedures used in screening applicants for employment, and any not justified by business necessity should be eliminated or altered.

In 1989, the Supreme Court in *Wards Cove Packing Co. v. Atonia* reversed an 18-year-old precedent that required employers to prove whether a job requirement that is shown statistically to screen out minorities or women is a "business necessity." The court ruled that plaintiff-employees now have the legal burden of proving that the employer had no objective, business-related justification for the challenged practices. In the view of many legal experts, the change tips the scales in favor of employers in this area of civil rights litigation. Indeed, there has already been a significant decrease in the number of lawsuits brought by plaintiffs because of the Supreme Court decision.

Let's examine some specific areas that have been a source of litigation and EEOC comment in the past:

Race, Color, Religion, Sex, or National Origin — Pre-employment inquiries concerning race, color, religion, sex, or national origin are not considered violations of the law in and of themselves. However, inquiries which either directly or indirectly disclose such information, unless otherwise explained, may constitute evidence of discrimination prohibited by Title VII.

Some states' fair employment practice laws expressly prohibit inquiries on employment applications concerning the applicant's race, color, religion, sex, or national origin. In some states it may also be considered illegal to seek related data (former name, past residence, names of relatives, place of birth, citizenship, education, organizational memberships and activities, a photograph, and color of eyes and hair) which could indirectly reveal similar information.

Denial of equal employment opportunity to individuals because of marriage to or association with persons of a specific national, ethnic, or racial origin, or because of attendance at schools or churches, or membership in organizations identified with particular racial or ethnic groups may be considered a violation of Title VII. Charges presented to the EEOC alleging such discrimination will be examined with particular concern to determine if, indeed, the alleged discrimination was based on race or national origin.

Height and Weight — The Equal Employment Opportunity Commission and the courts have ruled that minimum height and weight requirements are illegal if they screen out a disproportionate number of minority-group individuals (e.g. Spanish-surnamed or Asian Americans) or women, and the employer cannot show that these standards are essential to the safe performance of the job in question.

Marital Status, Number of Children, and Provisions for Child Care — Questions about marital status, pregnancy, future child-bearing plans, and number and age of children are frequently used to discriminate against women and may be a violation of Title VII if used to deny or limit employment opportunities for female applicants. Employers are cautioned against use of such non-job-related questions. Information needed for tax, insurance, or Social Security purposes may be obtained after employment.

It is a violation of Title VII for employers to require pre-employment information about child care arrangements from female applicants only. The U.S. Supreme Court has ruled that an employer may not have different hiring policies for men and women with pre-school children.

English Language Skill — When the use of an English language proficiency test has an adverse effect upon a particular minority group and English language skill is not a requirement of the work to be performed, there is a violation of Title VII.

Educational Requirements — The U.S. Supreme Court has found an employer's requirement of a high school education discriminatory where statistics showed such a requirement operated to disqualify blacks at a substantially higher rate than whites, and there was no evidence that the requirement was significantly related to successful job performance. This standard applies to all groups protected under Title VII and is relevant to all questions relating to educational attainment, where no direct job related requirement or business necessity can be proven.

Friends or Relatives Working for the Employer — Information about friends or relatives working for an employer is not relevant to an applicant's competence. Requesting such information may be unlawful if it indicates a preference for friends and relatives of present employees and the composition of the present workforce is such that this preference would reduce or eliminate opportunities for women or minority group members. However, a "nepotism" policy which prohibits or limits employment opportunities of a spouse or other relative also may be illegal if it has an adverse impact on job opportunities for either women or men as a group.

Arrest Records — Because members of some minority groups are arrested substantially more often than whites in proportion to their numbers in the population, making personnel decisions on the basis of arrest records has a disproportionate effect on the employment opportunities of members of these groups. The courts and the commission accordingly have held that without proof of business necessity an employer's use of arrest records to disqualify job applicants is unlawful discrimination. Even if an employer does not consider arrest information, the mere *request* for such information tends to discourage minority applicants and will, therefore, be considered with suspicion by the Commission.

The EEOC recently issued a policy statement on arrest records. The bottom line is refusing to hire any and all applicants based on arrest records will be found to be discrimination under Title VII of the Civil Rights Act. Since it is generally presumed employers ask only questions which are deemed relevant to employment decisions, routinely asking job applicants about arrest records on an employment application or in a job interview may violate Title VII, unless further inquiry is made about the circumstances surrounding an arrest.

An arrest alone is not reliable evidence a person actually committed a crime. Even where the conduct alleged in an arrest record is related to the job at issue, the EEOC states the employer must investigate whether the arrest is proof of a particular conduct. The employer should examine the surrounding circumstances, offer the applicant or employee an opportunity to explain, and, if the person denies engaging in the conduct, make follow-up inquiries to evaluate the person's credibility.

This does not mean information about arrests can never be used to make an employment decision. As with conviction records, arrest records may be considered as evidence of conduct that will render an applicant unsuitable for a particular position, the EEOC explains. But, to use an arrest record to support a refusal to hire, the employer must consider the relationship of the arrest charges to the position applied for, and determine the likelihood the applicant actually committed the conduct alleged in the arrest.

Even asking for conviction records, which do provide reliable proof a person engaged in illegal acts, carries some risks. National law enforcement statistics indicate blacks and Hispanics are convicted in numbers disproportionate to whites. Basing employment decisions on conviction records could thus have an adverse impact on minority groups. The EEOC requires proof the conduct which resulted in a conviction presents a threat to legitimate business goals.

Conviction Records — A conviction for a felony or misdemeanor may not, by itself, lawfully constitute an absolute bar to employment; however, an employer may give fair consideration to the relationship between a conviction and the applicant's fitness for a particular job. Conviction records should be cause for rejection only if their number and nature would cause the applicant to be unsuitable for the position. If such inquiries are made, they should be accompanied by a statement that a conviction record will not necessarily be a bar to employment and that factors such as age and time of the offense, seriousness and nature of the violation, and rehabilitation will be taken into account.

Discharge from Military — Employers should not, as a matter of policy, reject applicants with less than honorable discharges from military service. Minority service members have had a higher proportion of general and undesirable discharges than nonminority members of similar aptitude and education.

Thus, an employer's requirement that to be eligible for employment ex-members of the armed services must have been honorably discharged has a disparate effect upon minorities and may be a violation of Title VII.

One federal district court has held that an employer may inquire about an applicant's military service record if information regarding discharge status is used not in making a hiring decision, but in deciding whether further investigations should be made into the applicant's background and qualifications. If further inquiry reveals nondiscriminatory grounds for denying employment, the employer may then refuse to hire the applicant.

Since a request for this information may discourage minority workers from applying and therefore be grounds for a discriminatory charge, employers should avoid such questions unless "business necessity" can be shown. As in the case of conviction records discussed above, questions regarding military service should be accompanied by a statement that is dishonorable or general discharge is not an absolute bar to employment and that other factors will affect a final decision to hire or not to hire.

Age — The Age Discrimination in Employment Act of 1967, as amended, prohibits discrimination on the basis of age.

A request that an applicant state his age may tend to deter older applicants or may otherwise indicate discrimination based on age. Consequently, employment applicant forms which request such information will be closely scrutinized to assure that the request is for a permissible purpose and not for purposes prohibited by the Age Discrimination in Employment Act.

National Security — It is not unlawful to deny employment to an individual who does not fulfill the national security requirements.

Economic Status — Rejection of applicants because of poor credit ratings might have a disparate impact on minority groups and has been found unlawful by the Commission, unless business necessity can be shown.

Inquiries as to an applicant's financial status, such as bankruptcy, car ownership, rental or ownership of a house, length of residence at an address, or past garnishments of wages, if utilized to make employment decisions, may likewise violate Title VII.

Availability for Work on Weekends or Holidays — Employers and unions have an obligation to accommodate the religious beliefs of employees and/or applicants, unless to do so would cause undue hardship. The EEOC has determined that the use of pre-employment inquiries that determine an applicant's availability has an exclusionary effect on the employment opportunities of persons following certain religious practices. Questions relating to availability for work on Friday evenings, Saturdays, or holidays should not be asked unless the employer can show that the questions have not had an exclusionary effect on its employees or applicants who would need an accommodation for their religious practices, that the questions are otherwise justified by business necessity, and that there are no alternative procedures which would have a lesser exclusionary effect.

The Typical "Charge" Process

Most often, complaints are filed by the aggrieved individual(s), but the EEOC regulations allow complaints to be filed on behalf of the EEOC. Normally the aggrieved party will be interviewed by an Equal Opportunity Specialist (EOS) during the initial intake interview. At that time, the complaining part will be asked to complete a questionnaire which calls for information such as the name, address, and telephone number of the employer, the place where he or she applied for the job, the name of the employee's supervisor (if the individual is actually employed), the date that the alleged discrimination occurred, and the nature of the discrimination.

A complaint must be filed within 180 days of the alleged discriminatory act. If there is a state or local fair employment practice agency in the area, the employee has up to 240 days, and in some cases 300, but if the complaint is not filed on time, the EEOC cannot investigate it.

The EOS will investigate the allegations so that a proper charge may be written. An employee is counseled about the EEOC investigation procedures as well as any rights under the Age Discrimination Act and the Equal Pay Act.

Once the charge is filed, the employer will be notified within 10 days and will be advised as to the date, place, circumstances, and identity of

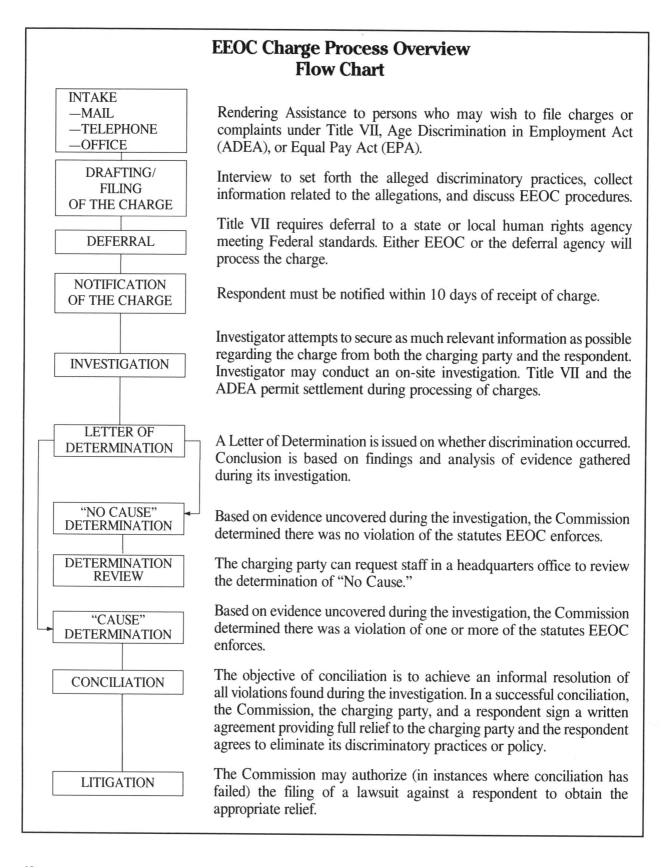

EEOC Charge Process Overview
Flow Chart

INTAKE —MAIL —TELEPHONE —OFFICE	Rendering Assistance to persons who may wish to file charges or complaints under Title VII, Age Discrimination in Employment Act (ADEA), or Equal Pay Act (EPA).
DRAFTING/ FILING OF THE CHARGE	Interview to set forth the alleged discriminatory practices, collect information related to the allegations, and discuss EEOC procedures.
DEFERRAL	Title VII requires deferral to a state or local human rights agency meeting Federal standards. Either EEOC or the deferral agency will process the charge.
NOTIFICATION OF THE CHARGE	Respondent must be notified within 10 days of receipt of charge.
INVESTIGATION	Investigator attempts to secure as much relevant information as possible regarding the charge from both the charging party and the respondent. Investigator may conduct an on-site investigation. Title VII and the ADEA permit settlement during processing of charges.
LETTER OF DETERMINATION	A Letter of Determination is issued on whether discrimination occurred. Conclusion is based on findings and analysis of evidence gathered during its investigation.
"NO CAUSE" DETERMINATION	Based on evidence uncovered during the investigation, the Commission determined there was no violation of the statutes EEOC enforces.
DETERMINATION REVIEW	The charging party can request staff in a headquarters office to review the determination of "No Cause."
"CAUSE" DETERMINATION	Based on evidence uncovered during the investigation, the Commission determined there was a violation of one or more of the statutes EEOC enforces.
CONCILIATION	The objective of conciliation is to achieve an informal resolution of all violations found during the investigation. In a successful conciliation, the Commission, the charging party, and a respondent sign a written agreement providing full relief to the charging party and the respondent agrees to eliminate its discriminatory practices or policy.
LITIGATION	The Commission may authorize (in instances where conciliation has failed) the filing of a lawsuit against a respondent to obtain the appropriate relief.

the person filing the charge. The employer will normally be asked to come to the EEOC office for a fact-finding conference to discuss the allegation in the charge. That conference is conducted by an Equal Opportunity Specialist. Evidence may be presented by both the employee and the employer. The employer may bring along any witnesses who have actual knowledge of the incident. The aggrieved party's witness will have been interviewed prior to the conference. Only those people who have first-hand knowledge of the incident are permitted to speak at the conference. The effort will be to amicably resolve the charge at this fact-finding conference. If it turns out that this is impossible, the charge will be investigated further.

The EEOC has a Continued Investigation and Conciliation Unit which will further investigate the charge, if necessary. If this group has reasonable cause to believe that discrimination has occurred, the EEOC will notify the aggrieved party and the employer. At this point, the EEOC will begin the conciliation efforts required under the statute. Most charges filed with the EEOC, even when the Commission decides to sue, are conciliated or settled before the case actually goes to trial. At all stages of the investigation, the Commission is required by law to attempt to bring the matter to a resolution agreeable to all parties without costly litigation.

If the Commission's investigation shows no reasonable cause to believe that discrimination has occurred, both the aggrieved party and the employer will be notified. The aggrieved party will be issued a "right to sue" letter which permits a private court suit.

If there is reasonable cause to believe discrimination took place and conciliation efforts fail, then the Commission can file a lawsuit in federal district court.

Title VII requires that the Federal government refer charges of discrimination to state or local agencies if the charge meets certain criteria. Depending on the local agreement with the Commission, a charge may be processed either by the EEOC or the state or local agency. (For a further discussion of EEOC complaint handling procedures, read the section, "Age Discrimination 'Charge,'" in Chapter 9.)

Sanctions

A court that finds an employer deliberately engaged in or engaging in an unlawful employment practice may issue an injunction forbidding the employer to continue that practice and requiring such affirmative action as may be appropriate. This may include, but is not limited to, reinstatement or hiring of employees, with or without back pay for a period up to two years prior to the filing date of the charge. The court also may employ other equitable relief as might be appropriate.

Recordkeeping

The EEOC has not adopted any specific recordkeeping requirement for employers. In the case of employers with 100 or more employees, there is an obligation to file Employee Information Report EEOC1 and keep a copy on file at the business location. Every employer is required to post an EEOC Poster (a pull-out copy of which is included at page 171) in a conspicuous place so that employees and applicants for employment will be likely to see it.

Americans with Disabilities Act 8

Legislative Purpose

In 1990, Congress approved the Americans with Disabilities Act (ADA), and immediately it was hailed as landmark legislation that would help to end discrimination against individuals with disabilities and bring these individuals into the economic and social mainstream of American life.

Some 43 million Americans have one or more physical or mental disability. The predominant disabilities are visual, hearing, and mobility-related.

Disability means a physical or mental impairment that substantially limits one or more of the major life functions of an individual.

An infected finger may be an impairment, but it does not impair the performance of a major life activity. The assessment of whether an individual is disabled is made without regard to whether mitigating measures have been taken. For example, hearing aids or medication for diabetes may control the effects of the impairment but the individual is still considered to have a disability.

A record of impairment includes both a past history of having, or being misclassified as having, a mental or physical impairment. Disability also includes an individual who is regarded as having a covered impairment. Basically, this third test covers perceptions, such as the fear of hiring someone because of negative reactions of others, such as co-workers or the consumer. An example is the refusal to hire a severe burn victim because of appearance.

The legislation has four major titles: Employment, Public Services (e.g., public transportation), Telecommunications, and Public Accommodations and Services Operated by Private Entities. This book covers only the Employment title.

Coverage

The law covers employers who have 15 or more full-time employees (e.g., individuals who work more than 20 hours per week) for each working day in each of 20 or more calendar weeks in the current or preceding calendar year. Please note, however, that for an initial two-year period from the effective date for the employment title in the law, the threshold for ADA coverage will be 25 employees (e.g., July 26, 1992 - July 26, 1994).

Discrimination

The ADA provides that no employer shall discriminate against a qualified individual with a disability because of the disability of such individual in regard to job application procedures; the hiring, advancement, or discharge of employees; employee compensation; job training; and other terms, conditions, and privileges of employment.

The term "qualified individual with a disability" means an individual with a disability who, with or without reasonable accommodation, can

71

perform the essential functions of the employment position that such individual holds or desires. For the purposes of the employment title of the ADA, consideration shall be given to the employer's judgment as to what functions of a job are essential, and if an employer has prepared a written description before advertising or interviewing applicants for the job, this description shall be considered evidence of the essential functions of the job.

The ADA describes discrimination to include:

1. limiting, segregating, or classifying a job applicant or employee in a way that adversely affects the opportunities or status of such applicant or employee because of the disability of such applicant or employee;

2. participating in a contractual or other arrangement or relationship that has the effect of subjecting a business's qualified applicant or employee with a disability to the discrimination prohibited by this law (such relationship includes a relationship with an employment or referral agency, labor union, an organization providing fringe benefits to an employee of the covered business, or an organization providing training and apprenticeship programs);

3. utilizing standards, criteria, or methods of administration
   a. that have the effect of discrimination on the basis of disability; or
   b. that perpetuate the discrimination of others who are subject to common administrative control;

4. excluding or otherwise denying equal jobs or benefits to a qualified individual because of the known disability of another individual with whom the qualified individual is known to have a relationship or association;

5. not making reasonable accommodations to the known physical or mental limitations of an otherwise qualified individual who is an applicant or employee, unless the business can demonstrate that the accommodation would impose an undue hardship on the operation of the business; or

6. denying employment opportunities to a job applicant or employee who is an otherwise qualified individual with a disability, if such denial is based on the need of the business to make reasonable accommodation to the physical or mental impairments of the employee or applicant;

7. using qualification standards, employment tests, or other selection criteria that screen out or tend to screen out an individual with a disability or a class of individuals with disabilities unless the test or other selection criteria, as used by the business, is shown to be job-related for the position in question and is consistent with business necessity; and,

8. failing to select and administer tests concerning employment in the most effective manner to ensure that, when such test is administered to a job applicant or employee who has a disability that impairs sensory, manual, or speaking skills, such test results accurately reflect the skills, aptitude, or whatever other factor of such applicant or employee that such test purports to measure, rather than reflecting the impaired sensory, manual, or speaking skills of such employee or applicant (except where such skills are the factors that the test purports to measure).

Reasonable Accommodation

The term "reasonable accommodation" will undoubtedly be the one that is the subject of many lawsuits. After all, it is not a precise formula, but in an effort to give some guidance, there are some helpful comments taken from the legislative history. Congress intended that the reasonable accommodation requirement be utilized as a process in which barriers to a particular individual's equal employment opportunity are removed. The accommodation process focuses on the needs of a particular individual in relation to problems in performance of a particular job because of a physical or mental impairment. A problem-solving approach should be used to identify the particular tasks or aspects of the work environment that limit performance and to identify possible accommodations that will result in a meaningful equal opportunity for the individual with a disability.

To illustrate this provision, consider a job requiring the use of a computer, the essential function of which is the ability to access, input, and retrieve information from the computer. It is not essential that the person be able to use the keyboard or visually read the computer screen, if the provision of adaptive equipment or software would enable the person with the disability—for example, impaired vision or limited hand control—to control the computer and access the information. The relevant question would be whether the acquisition of the adaptive equipment would be a reasonable accommodation, given the factors to be considered in making that determination.

Another example of reasonable accommodation may involve the work schedule or assignments. Part-time or modified work schedules can provide useful accommodation. Some people with disabilities are denied employment opportunities because they cannot work a standard schedule. For example, persons who need medical treatment may benefit from flexible or adjusted work schedules. A person with epilepsy may require constant shifts rather than rotation from day to night shifts. Other persons who may require modified work schedules are persons with mobility impairments who depend on a public transportation system that is not currently fully accessible.

Undue Hardship

An employer is not required to make an accommodation if it imposes an undue hardship. The term "undue hardship" is defined as an action requiring significant difficulty or expense; i.e., an action that is unduly costly, extensive, substantial, or disruptive, or that will fundamentally alter the nature of the program. In determining whether a particular accommodation would impose an undue hardship on the operation of the entity— i.e., require significant difficulty or expense— factors to be considered include: (1) the nature

and cost of the accommodation need under the ADA; (2) the overall financial resources of the facility or facilities involved in the provision of the reasonable accommodation; the number of persons employed at such facility; the effect on expenses and resources, or the impact otherwise of such accommodation upon the operation of the facility; (3) the overall financial resources of the employer; the overall size of the entity with respect to the number of its employees; the number, type, and location of its facilities; and, (4) the type of operation or operations of the covered entity, including the composition, structure, and functions of the work force; the geographic separateness, administrative, or fiscal relationship of the facility or facilities is under the employer's control.

What is apparent is that Congress intended that the weight given to each factor in making the determination as to whether a reasonable accommodation nonetheless constitutes an "undue hardship" will vary depending on the facts of a particular situation and turns on both the nature and cost of the accommodation in relation to the employer's resources and operations. In illustrating this point, the legislative history contains the example of a small day-care center that might not be required to expend more than a nominal sum, such as that necessary to equip a telephone for use by a secretary with impaired hearing, but a large school district might be required to make available a teacher's aide to a blind applicant for a teaching job.

Employment Testing and Job Selection

Under the law, discrimination includes using qualification standards, employment tests, or other selection criteria that screen out or tend to screen out an individual with a disability or a class of individuals with disabilities, *unless* the standard, test, or other selection criteria is shown to be job-related for the position in question, and is consistent with business necessity.

Discrimination includes failing to select and administer tests so as best to ensure that, when the test is administered to an applicant or employee with a disability that impairs sensory, manual, or speaking skills, the test results accurately reflect the individual's job skills, aptitude, or whatever other factor the test purports to measure, rather than reflecting the individual's impaired sensory, manual, or speaking skills (except where those skills are the factors that the test purports to measure).

Medical Examinations

An employer is prohibited from making any inquiries as to the existence or nature of an applicant's disability prior to an offer of employment. The law prohibits pre-offer medical examinations. Employers may ask questions which relate to the applicant's ability to perform job-related functions, but may not ask questions in terms of disability. For example, an employer may ask whether the applicant has a driver's license, if driving is an essential job function, but may not ask whether the applicant has a visual disability.

The only exception to making medical inquiries is narrow. The law allows businesses to require medical examinations after a conditional job offer has been made, so long as they are given to all entering employees in a particular category, the results of the examinations are kept confidential, and the results of such examinations are not used to discriminate against an individual with a disability unless such results make the individual not qualified for the job.

A candidate undergoing a post-offer, pre-employment medical examination may not be excluded, for example, solely on the basis of an abnormality on an x-ray. However, if the examining physician found that there was high probability of substantial harm if the candidate performed the particular functions of the job in question, the employer could reject the candidate, unless the employer could make a reasonable accommodation to the candidate's condition that would avert such harm and such accommodation would not cause an undue hardship.

The law prohibits medical exams of employees unless job-related and consistent with business necessity. Certain jobs require periodic physicals in order to determine fitness for duty. For example, federal safety regulations require bus and truck drivers to have a medical exam at least biennially. In other instances, because a particular job function may have a significant impact on public safety—e.g., flight attendants—an employee's state of health is important in establishing job qualifications, even though a medical certificate may not be required by law.

There are other instances in which medical examinations of employees may be permitted, provided the results of those examinations are not used to limit an employee's eligibility for employer-provided health insurance. For example, several health standards promulgated pursuant to the Occupational Safety and Health Act require that employees exposed to certain toxic and hazardous substances be medically surveyed at specified intervals to determine if the exposures to these substances have had any negative effect on the employees.

Voluntary wellness programs in the workplace often include medical screening for high blood pressure, weight control, cancer detection, and the like. As long as the programs are voluntary and the medical records are maintained in a confidential manner and not used for the purpose of limiting health insurance eligibility or preventing occupational advancement, these activities would fall within the purview of accepted activities.

An employer may invite applicants for employment to indicate voluntarily whether, and to what extent, they have a disability under the following circumstances only:

1. when the employer is taking remedial action to correct the effects of past discrimination,

2. when the employer is taking voluntary action to overcome the effects of conditions that resulted in limited employment opportunities, or

3. when a business is taking affirmative action pursuant to section 503 of the Rehabilitation Act of 1973, provided that:

a. the employer makes clear that the information requested is intended for use solely in conjunction with its remedial action obligations or its voluntary or affirmative action efforts, and

b. the business states clearly that the information is being requested on a voluntary basis, that it will be kept confidential, that refusal to provide it will not subject the applicant to any adverse treatment, and that it will be used only in accordance with the ADA.

Illegal Use of Drugs and Alcohol

A person with a disability who engages in the illegal use of drugs is denied the protection of the ADA. Thus, the law specifically allows employers to discharge or deny employment to persons who illegally use drugs, without fear of being held liable for discrimination.

Rehabilitated individuals and those in treatment who no longer use illegal drugs, and individuals who are erroneously regarded as illegal drug users, however, *are included* within the definition of "individual with a disability." In removing protection from persons who currently use illegal drugs, Congress did not intend to affect coverage for individuals who have a past drug problem or are erroneously perceived as having a current drug problem. Employers are permitted to conduct drug tests or take reasonable actions to ensure that an individual is no longer using illegal drugs. An employer may use other means to ensure that a person is no longer using drugs, as long as those measures are reasonable. An employer:

1. may prohibit the use of alcohol or illegal drugs at the workplace by all employees;
2. may require that employees not be under the influence of alcohol or illegal drugs at the workplace;
3. may require that employees conform their behavior to requirements established pursuant to the Drug-Free Work Place Act of 1988;
4. may hold a drug user or alcoholic to the same qualification standards for employment or job performance and behavior to which it holds other individuals, even if any unsatisfactory performance or behavior is related to the drug use or alcoholism of such individual; and
5. may require employees in sensitive positions, as defined by the Department of Transportation regulations regarding alcohol and drug use, the Department of Defense drug-free work place regulations, and the Nuclear Regulatory Commission regulations regarding alcohol and drug use, to comply with the standards established by such regulations.

It bears repeating that with respect to drug testing, the ADA explicitly states that nothing in the law prohibits or restricts either drug testing or employment decisions taken on the basis of such drug tests. Therefore, an applicant who is tested and not hired because of a positive test result for illegal drugs, or an employee who is tested and is fired because of a positive test result for illegal drugs, does not have a cause action under the ADA.

Defenses

In general, it may be a defense to a charge of discrimination that an alleged application of qualification standards, tests, or selection criteria that screen out or tend to screen out or otherwise deny a job or benefit to an individual with a disability has been shown to be job-related and consistent with business necessity, and such performance cannot be accomplished by reasonable accommodation.

With respect to contagious diseases or infections, the law specifies that the term "qualification standards" may include a requirement that an individual with a currently contagious disease or infection shall not pose a direct threat to the health or safety of other individuals in the workplace. Under this qualification standard, for a person with a currently contagious disease or infection to constitute a direct threat to the health or safety of others, the person must pose a significant risk of transmitting the disease or infection to others in the workplace which cannot be eliminated by reasonable accommodation. Thus, in the case of a food handler who has an infectious or communicable disease that could be transmitted to others, a business may refuse to assign or continue to assign such individual to such a job.

Enforcement

The Equal Employment Opportunity Commission (EEOC) is responsible for enforcement. At present, these remedies include injunctive relief and "make whole" relief, such as back pay. The remedies available are those contained in Title VII of the Civil Rights Act of 1964. An individual may also pursue remedies. Persons with disabilities are to be treated no differently than minorities and women under Title VII, and must follow both the administrative and judicial remedies that are provided in Title VII of the Civil Rights Act of 1964. (For additional information on EEOC procedures, refer to page 67.)

Rehabilitation Act of 1973

Federal contractors have a special obligation toward handicapped persons under Sections 503 and 504 of the Rehabilitation Act of 1973. Section 503 requires most employers doing business with the Federal Government to take affirmative action in employing handicapped persons. About half of all the nation's businesses are covered. Section 504 prohibits discrimination based on handicap by any employer receiving federal funds (e.g., schools, colleges, health care facilities). The Office of Federal Contract Compliance Programs (OFCCP) handles complaints under the Rehabilitation Act.

A "handicap" is a physical or mental characteristic resulting from a disease, injury, congenital condition of birth, or functional disorder. In order to bring a charge of discrimination, a person must show that the condition is unrelated to his or her ability to perform the job in question. Examples include:
— visual impairments
— hearing impairments
— cardiovascular disorders
— orthopedic impairments
— amputations
— nervous system disorders
— respiratory impairments
— sickle cell anemia
— epilepsy
— multiple sclerosis
— cerebral palsy
— muscular dystrophy
— cancer
— learning disorders
— mental retardation
— emotional/mental disorders
— acquired immune deficiency syndrome (AIDS)
Not considered a handicap are conditions which are transitory and insubstantial as well as conditions which are not significantly debilitating or disfiguring.

Employers may request supporting medical documentation from employees who claim to be handicapped in connection with a reasonable accommodation request. An accommodation is a modification to an employer's work process, work site, or work schedule that would enable a handicapped person to perform a specific job. Accommodations that are prohibitively expensive or unduly disruptive are not required.

Age Discrimination 9

Legislative Purpose

In 1967, Congress passed the Age Discrimination in Employment Act (ADEA) to prohibit discrimination in employment because of age in such matters as hiring, job retention, compensation, and other terms, conditions, and privileges of employment. The ADEA establishes as a matter of basic civil rights that people should be treated in employment on the basis of their individual ability to perform a job rather than on the basis of stereotypes about age. Indeed, the ADEA has created a new awareness concerning discrimination against the elderly and has spurred academic research which concludes that chronological age alone is a poor indicator of ability to perform a job. Originally enforced by the Department of Labor, the President, by Executive Order in 1978 with the concurrence of Congress, shifted the enforcement activities to the Equal Employment Opportunity Commission.

Coverage

The ADEA prohibits most employers, employment agencies, and labor organizations from discrimination in employment practices against persons over the age of 40 on the basis of their age. In a highly publicized change in 1978, Congress amended the ADEA, raising the upper age limit on coverage from 65 to 70 and adding a prohibition against the forced retirement based on age of employees below the age of 70.

Then in 1986, Congress unanimously approved another major change to the Age Discrimination in Employment Act by removing the mandatory retirement age of 70 for most of the nation's private sector workers.

By removing the upper age limit, the legislation also requires covered employers to continue the same group health insurance for workers over age 70 as is offered to younger workers. The law applies *to employers having 20 or more employees,* public employers, employment agencies serving such employers, and labor organizations with 24 or more members. The operative language of the statute (incidentally, the ADEA is unusually well written without customary legalese) makes it unlawful for an employer to:

1. Fail or refuse to hire or to discharge any individual or to discriminate against an individual with respect to compensation, terms, conditions, or privileges of employment because of age;

2. Limit, segregate, or classify employees in any way which would deprive or tend to deprive any individual of employment opportunities, or otherwise adversely affect his or her status as an employee because of age; or

3. Reduce the wage rate of any employees in order to comply with the Act.

Some Practical Advice

Two areas that have traditionally been trouble spots for employees are "help wanted" advertisements and job application forms. The EEOC regulations provide some useful guidance:

1. "Help Wanted" Ads — When "help wanted" notices or advertisements contain terms such as "age 25 to 35," "young," "college student," "recent college graduate," "boy," "girl," or other phrases of a similar nature, such a term or phrase deters the employment of older persons and their usage is a violation of the Act, unless one of the exceptions applies. Such phrases as "age 40 to 50," "age over 65," "retired person," or "supplement your pension" discriminate against others within the protected group and, therefore, are prohibited unless one of the exceptions applies. (The "exceptions" are explained in subsequent sections of this chapter).

2. Employment Applications — A request on the part of an employer for information such as "Date of Birth" or "State Age" on an employment application form is not, in itself, a violation of the Act. But because the request that an applicant state his or her age may tend to deter older applicants or otherwise indicate discrimination based on age, employment application forms which request such information will be closely scrutinized to assure that the request is for a permissible purpose. The EEOC recommends that an application form contain language to the following effect:

"The Age Discrimination in Employment Act of 1967 prohibits discrimination on the basis of age with respect to individuals who are over 40 years of age."

The term "employment application," refers to all written inquiries about employment or applications for employment or promotion including resumes or other summaries of the applicant's background.

Exemptions

There are certain situations which are exempt from the ADEA. They are the following:

1. When age is a *bona fide* job qualification reasonably necessary to the normal operation of a particular business, e.g. modeling clothes for teenagers. This exemption is limited in scope and application. The employer asserting this defense must show that the age limit is reasonably necessary.

2. When the differentiation is based on reasonable factors other than age, such as the use of stringent physical requirements necessitated by the nature of the work, ADEA prohibitions do not apply.

3. When differentiations are based on the terms of a *bona fide* seniority system or any *bona fide* employee benefit plan, such as a retirement, pension, or insurance plan. No employee benefit plan, however, can excuse the failure to hire any individual, and no such seniority system or employee benefit plan shall require or permit the involuntary retirement of an individual upon reaching any specific age. By this change, Congress intended "to make it absolutely clear . . . that the exception of a *bona fide* seniority system does not authorize an employer to require or permit mandatory retirement of any employee." The mandatory retirement prohibition applies to all new and existing seniority systems and employer benefit plans. Therefore, any system or plan provision requiring or permitting involuntary retirement is unlawful, regardless of whether the provision was part of an agreement entered into prior to the 1967 Act or the subsequent amendments.

4. Another exception to the prohibition on mandatory retirement at any age, effective January 1, 1986, covers states and localities with mandatory retirement ages for firefighters and law enforcement officers as well as institutions of higher education with a mandatory retirement at age 70 for tenured faculty. A seven-year transition period, beginning October 31, 1986, has been set up for studies to determine what performance-based guidelines may be used in making

employment decisions for firefighters and law enforcement officers and what consequences the elimination of mandatory retirement would have on institutions of higher education.

5. When an individual has for a two-year period prior to retirement been employed in a *bona fide* executive or high policy-making position, and is entitled to an immediate, nonforfeitable, annual retirement benefit from a pension, profit-sharing, savings, or deferred compensation plan which equals at least $44,000, then compulsory retirement at 65 is not prohibited. Therefore, an employee within the exemption can lawfully be forced to retire on account of age at age 65 or above. The "executive" position does not apply to middle-management employees who exercise substantial executive authority over a significant number of employees and a large volume of business. The term "high policy-making position" is likewise expected to have limited application. It is limited to those who are not "executive" but whose position and responsibility are such that they play a significant role in the development of corporate policy and effectively recommend implementing actions.

6. When there is a *bona fide* apprenticeship program, which has been traditionally limited to youths preparing for skilled employment, the ADEA prohibitions again do not apply.

New Benefit Equivalence Provisions

By enacting amendments to the Age Discrimination in Employment Act in 1978 and 1986, Congress now requires that employees 65 and older shall be entitled to coverage under any group health plans offered to employees under age 65 under the same terms and conditions. Similarly, any employee age 65 or older must be offered spousal coverage, if employees under the age of 65 are offered such coverage. Further, each employee in the age group of 65 or older must be offered the opportunity to elect any group health plan offered by the employer. With this group, employers have an additional obligation to explain how Medicare coverage complements the employer's plans.

Older Workers Protection Act

In 1990, Congress passed the Older Workers Benefit Protection Act amending ADEA in two important respects. The law makes clear that discrimination on the basis of age, in virtually all forms of employee benefits, is unlawful. In addition, the law ensures that older workers are not coerced or manipulated into waiving their rights to seek legal relief under the ADEA.

1. Employee Benefits—The new law clarifies and restores one of the original purposes of the ADEA, the eradication of age discrimination in employee benefits. The law overturns both the reasoning and holding of the Supreme Court in a 1989 case, *Public Employees Retirement System of Ohio v. Betts*, in which the Court permitted arbitrary age discrimination in employee benefit plans.

Congress has reaffirmed the "equal benefit or equal cost principle" so as to ensure that productive older workers, an ever-growing segment of the labor force, are not discouraged from remaining actively employed. Employers invoking this defense are required to provide equal benefits to, or to incur equal cost for benefits on behalf of, all employees. For example, if a $100 contribution purchases $50,000 of coverage for an employee age 35 and only $25,000 for an employee age 60, that difference in coverage is lawful. Congress has made clear that employers bear the burden of proving this defense.

The law does set forth several exceptions to this "equal benefit or equal cost" requirement, but these are severely limited. One involves defined benefit pension plans, in which case there is a safe harbor provided for three specified practices. Another exception involves instances in which there is benefit coordination (e.g., retirement health benefits and severance pay). Finally, in the case of early retirement incentive plans, the law will allow them provided they are truly voluntary, are made available for a reasonable period of time, and do not result in arbitrary age discrimination.

Employees eligible for early retirement incentive plans must be given sufficient time to consider their option, particularly in circumstances when no previous retirement counseling has been provided. Eligible employees must be provided complete and accurate information regarding the benefits available under the plan. If subsequent layoffs or terminations are contemplated or discussed, employees should be advised of the criteria by which those decisions will be made. The critical question involving allegation of involuntary retirement is whether, under the circumstances, a reasonable person would have concluded that there was no choice but to accept the offer.

2. Waiver of Rights—For the first time, the law now provides that waivers of rights under the ADEA not supervised by the EEOC may be valid and enforceable if they meet certain threshold requirements and are otherwise shown to be knowing and voluntary. The law also distinguishes between individually tailored separation agreements and employer programs targeted at groups of employees.

For waivers executed as part of individually tailored separation agreements, the legislation provides certain threshold requirements that must first be met. The waiver must be part of a written settlement agreement which specifically identifies that rights and claims under the ADEA are being waived. The agreement may not waive any rights or claims that may arise after the date the agreement is executed. The ADEA rights and claims may be waived only in exchange for consideration that exceeds what the individual already was entitled to by contract or law. The employee must also be advised in writing to consult an attorney prior to executing the agreement. In the case of an individual separation agreement, the employee must be given at least 21 days within which to consider the agreement. Thus, Congress rationalized, "An employee who is terminated needs time to recover from the shock of losing a job, especially when that job was held

for a long period. The employee needs time to learn about the conditions of termination, including any benefits being offered by the employer." Following the execution of the document, an individual has a period of seven days within which to revoke. The agreement becomes binding and enforceable, assuming it meets all the requirements of the law and is knowing and voluntary, only after the expiration of the revocation period.

Group termination programs raise additional issues, and the law requires additional protection for individuals from whom a waiver is sought. Thus, in these case employees are given at least 45 days to consider these agreements. The employer must provide at the outset detailed information regarding the class of individuals covered by the program, the program's eligibility requirements, and any applicable time limitations. The employer also must include a listing of the job titles and ages of all those individuals eligible for the program, and similar information for individuals who are not eligible. Finally, employers must notify eligible employees of any adverse action (such as a layoff) the employer knows or should know may occur, if the individual declines to participate in the program, along with the approximate date on which such adverse action would occur.

The new law covers waivers executed after October 16, 1990, the enactment date of the Older Workers Protection Act.

Age Discrimination "Charge"

Typically, information is submitted in person, by telephone, or by mail to the EEOC offices. When the information involves a violation, then a charge is drawn up with EEOC assistance, if desired, which generally contains the following information:

1. The full name, address, and telephone number of the person making the charge;
2. The full name and address of the employer; and
3. A clear and concise statement of the facts, including pertinent dates constituting the alleged unlawful employment practices.

The identity of a complainant, a confidential witness, or the aggrieved party on whose behalf a charge is filed will ordinarily not be disclosed without prior written consent.

Parties making a charge may not file a civil suit until 60 days after a charge has been filed. Further, the charge must be submitted to the EEOC within 180 days of the alleged discriminatory action to be timely. In the case where the alleged discriminatory action occurs in a state which has its own age discrimination law, it must be filed within 300 days of the discrimination, or 30 days after receipt of notice of the limitation of state proceedings, whichever date is earlier.

In November 1990, the Age Discrimination Claims Assistance Amendments of 1990 were enacted. This law provides a limited group of individuals a 15-month extension in the normal statute of limitations for bringing charges under the ADEA. Those individuals in this limited group include:

1. Individuals who filed timely age discrimination charges after April 6, 1985, but did not have a civil court action lodged on their claims.
2. Individuals who filed claims, but neither EEOC conciliation took place nor did the EEOC advise of disposition of claims and their right to sue.
3. Individuals whose claims have expired or will have expired after April 6, 1988, but before May 3, 1991.

This legislation followed the discovery that the EEOC, having been weighed down with an enormous backlog of cases, failed to act on hundreds of cases which had been filed in a timely manner. The Commission is required to give notice to those individuals covered by the amendments and to advise them of their restored rights.

EEOC Enforcement

Upon receipt of a charge, the EEOC will promptly notify the employer. Thereafter, the agency will immediately pursue informal methods of conciliation to resolve the controversy. If this conciliation process in which the Equal Opportunity Specialist will try to persuade the employer to resolve the problem fails, the charging party is notified and permitted to file a private lawsuit without waiting 60 days.

Once the investigative process begins, the charging party may request a withdrawal of a charge. Note, however, the EEOC has independent investigative authority; therefore, it may continue an investigation notwithstanding a request to withdraw.

Equal Opportunity Specialists have investigative powers. They may enter and inspect establishments and records, as well as interview employees. They may advise changes to assure proper compliance, and, if necessary, they have full subpoena powers. Finally, if a violation is found, they may supervise the payment of wages owed and other appropriate relief.

The conciliation agreement, if any, is always in written form signed by the employer, charging party, and EEOC representative.

The EEOC will honor a request for an opinion letter. Such request should be sent to the Chairman, EEOC, 1801 L Street, N.W., Washington, D.C. 20507, and contain the following.

1. A concise statement of the issues;
2. A full statement on the relevant facts and law; and
3. The name(s) and address(es) of the person(s) making the request.

Good faith reliance upon an opinion letter, written administrative regulations, order, ruling, approval, or interpretation is an affirmative defense to the imposition of any liability under the ADEA.

Recordkeeping

There is no precise order or form for the required records for ADEA compliance. The following information is required to be kept for three years:

1. Employee's Name
2. Address
3. Date of Birth
4. Occupation

5. Rate of Pay
6. Compensation Earned Each Week

The following information must be kept for one year from the date of the personnel action to which any records relate:

1. Job applications, resumes, or any other form of employment inquiry that was submitted to the employer in response to an advertisement or other notice of existing or anticipated job openings, including records pertaining to the failure or refusal to hire any individual;
2. Promotion, demotion, transfer, selection for training, layoff, recall, or discharge of any employee;
3. Job orders submitted by the employer to an employment agency or labor organization for recruitment of personnel for job openings;
4. Test papers completed by applicants or candidates for any position which disclose the results of any employer-administered aptitude or other employment test considered by the employer in connection with any personnel action;
5. The results of any physical examination where such examination is considered by the employer in connection with any personnel action; and
6. Any advertisements or notices to the public or to employees relating to job openings, promotions, training programs, or opportunities for overtime work.

Finally, there are two further special requirements concerning benefit plans and application forms:

1. Every employer must keep on file any employee benefit plan such as pension and insurance plans, as well as copies of any seniority systems and merit systems which are in writing, for the full period the plan or system is in effect, and for at least one year after its termination. If the plan or system is not in writing, a memorandum fully outlining the terms of such plan or system and the manner in which it has been communicated to the affected employees, together with notations relating to any changes or revisions, must be kept on file for a like period.

2. Application forms and other pre-employment records of applicants for positions which are, and are known by applicants to be, of a temporary nature, must be kept for a period of 90 days from the date of the personnel action to which the record relates.

Every employer has an obligation to keep the EEOC notice which contains a section on age discrimination in a prominent and accessible place at all times so that it can be viewed by employees.

Relief Measures

The ADEA penalty provisions include the right to seek legal or equitable relief. The latter may include, without limitation, the right to employment, reinstatement, promotion, and the payment of wages lost and an additional equal amount as liquidated damages when the violations are willful.

These actions may be brought in a federal or state court, and no party may be made a plaintiff unless written consent is given. Any judgment awarded may allow for reasonable attorneys' fees and court costs to be paid by the employer. Once the EEOC has filed suit, no further private action is permitted.

National Labor Relations Act 10 and Union Organizing

Coverage

The National Labor Relations Board (NLRB) is charged with administering the National Labor Relations Act (NLRA), the country's basic labor relations law. The NLRB conducts representation elections to determine whether or not the employees in an appropriate bargaining unit wish to be represented as a union. The NLRB headquarters are in Washington, D.C., but it has a number of regional offices located throughout the country, each headed by a Regional Director.

Bargaining Unit

The group of employees that a union represents is known as a bargaining unit. To obtain representation over a group of employees, the unit sought must be deemed "appropriate" for the purposes of bargaining. The NLRB is primarily responsible for determining the appropriateness of a bargaining unit. The underlying concept the NLRB has historically used in determining appropriateness of a unit is "community interest" (i.e. those employees who share similar terms and conditions of employment). Some of the criteria considered in making unit determinations are similar wages and benefits, working conditions, employee transfers and interchange, supervisors, integration of work product, and geographical location. It should also be noted that a unit may be deemed "appropriate" even if it is not the most appropriate unit.

The National Labor Relations Act provides that a representative chosen by "the majority of employees in a unit appropriate for such purposes" is to be the "exclusive" representative for all employees of such a unit. The structure and operation of a particular employer's operation will be critical in ascertaining the appropriateness of a bargaining unit. The NLRB focus will be directed toward the nature of the management and administration. To the extent that the components of an employer's business are administratively and functionally integrated, there is greater likelihood that the NLRB will examine not only the particular facility but also the history of bargaining by other employers in the industry.

A brief listing of some common types of bargaining units follows:

1. Production and Maintenance Units. This is the kind of unit usually found in manufacturing facilities and is favored by the NLRB in industrial and similar establishments. Plant clerical employees who work with production are ordinarily included in production and maintenance units.

2. Craft Units. Craft units are composed of a distinct and homogeneous group of skilled craftsmen, working as such, together with their apprentices and/or helpers.

3. Technical Units. These are composed of employees whose work is of a technical nature. These employees are involved with the use of specialized training, ordinarily obtained either in colleges or in technical schools.

4. Department Units. The NLRA sanctions a subdivision of a plant unit. Although these employees lack the skills of craftsmen, they are treated as separate units.

5. Office Clerical Units. The NLRB has consistently held that the interests of office clerical employees are different from those of other employees.

6. Guards. The NLRA prohibits including in a unit any individual employed as a guard.

7. Single vs. Multi-Plant Units. The NLRB relies upon the presumption that one plant of a multi-plant operation may be an appropriate unit.

Basic Union Organizing Techniques

Authorization Cards — The union's major aim through the initial steps of an organizing campaign is to obtain authorization cards. There are two basic kinds of authorization cards: pure and dual purpose. "Pure" cards designate the union as the signer's exclusive bargaining representative. The "dual purpose" card carries both the exclusive bargaining representative designation and a request for an election.

Certification — Although a union may become the designated bargaining agent for a company's employees, through the employer's voluntary recognition, unions generally try to obtain certification from the NLRB. Certification provides the union with several advantages. For example, unless there are unusual circumstances, an employer is required to bargain with a certified union for at least one year. Furthermore, any petition for an election, whether filed by the employees, the employer, or another union, will be barred from certification for one year.

Filing Petitions

A representation case is initiated by filing a petition for an election at one of the NLRB's regional offices.

A union will file an "RC-Certification of Representation" petition. The petition must be accompanied by documentary proof (usually authorization cards) showing that at least 30% of the employees in the proposed bargaining unit support the petition. The proof submitted by the petitioning union is held in strict confidence by the NLRB. The Board is solely responsible for evaluating the sufficiency and validity of a union's showing of interest. An employee may question the validity of a showing of interest by alleging, for example, that the authorization cards were obtained by fraud. The Regional Director will investigate the charges and administratively determine, without a hearing, whether the employee's allegations are true.

An employer may also file a petition with the NLRB, referred to as an "RM-Representation" (Employer Petition). An RM petition may be filed only after a union has made a demand upon the employer to be recognized as the employees' bargaining representative. When the employer files the election petition, no showing of interest is required.

After a petition is filed, an NLRB representative will investigate the matter to determine if a question concerning representation exists which warrants holding an election. The investigation will center around such issues as whether the union is a *bona fide* labor organization, whether the NLRB has jurisdiction over the employer, whether a contract exists which would bar an election, and whether the designated bargaining unit is an appropriate one.

Initial Correspondence

Initial NLRB correspondence with the employer will include a request that the employer post a "Notice to Employees" concerning union and employer conduct while the representation question is being resolved. This posting is purely voluntary and is not required under the Board's rules. Employers are also requested at that time to submit to the NLRB:

1. A payroll list covering the employees in the proposed bargaining unit, as of the date of the petition. This list is used to check the union's showing of interest and should not be confused with the *Excelsior* list described later in this chapter;

2. Data indicating the nature of the employer's business and the volume of the operations for jurisdictional purposes (discussed below); and

3. A position statement on the appropriateness of the unit and whether the employer is willing to consent to an election.

Included in the initial correspondence are several other NLRB forms which inform the Board if the employer will be represented by counsel, a designation of a representative for the purposes of serving documents, and a brief statement of representation procedures.

Hearings

At the time the petition is filed, the NLRB will usually schedule a formal hearing for the purpose of resolving any election issues that cannot be resolved informally. Generally, the parties' informal discussions will deal with such questions as the appropriateness of the unit, which employees are eligible to vote, voting hours, and the place and date of the election. Although in most cases the parties will be able to resolve a good number of these issues, if they cannot, a fact-finding hearing will be held.

If a hearing is necessary, the Regional Director will serve a notice of hearing on all interested parties. Technically, representation hearings are nonadversarial, investigatory proceedings. The NLRB agent assigned to the case will most likely preside as hearing officer, and evidence will be presented by the parties of the issues in dispute. The hearing is open to the public. A verbatim transcript of the hearing is made by an official reporter of the NLRB. Any party has the right to appear in person, by counsel, or by other

representative. After the hearing is closed, the parties may submit briefs to the Regional Director on any or all of the questions raised. The hearing officer also submits a report to the Regional Director. It consists of an analysis of the issues presented at the hearing and a summary of the evidence. The Regional Director will then issue a decision; in rare instances he may transfer a particulary complex or novel case to the Board in Washington, D.C. The Regional Director's decision will set forth findings of fact and conclusions of law, and include either a direction for an election or an order dismissing the petition. Review of the Regional Director's decision by the NLRB in Washington, D.C., is procedurally available, but it is not a matter of right and most requests for review are denied.

Consent Agreements

A hearing will not be necessary, of course, if the parties are able to resolve their differences. In such an event, they will enter into a formal consent agreement which provides for holding a representation election. There are two different kinds of such agreements: one is called an "Agreement for Consent Election" (Consent), and the other is called a "Stipulation for Certification upon Consent Election" (Stipulation). Both agreements provide for the wording on the ballot, a payroll period eligibility date, hours and place of the election, and identity of the appropriate bargaining unit. The Consent, however, vests final authority on the Regional Director (with limited review by the Board in Washington, D.C.) to investigate and rule upon challenged ballots and objections to the conduct of the election. The Stipulation, by contrast, provides that the Board in Washington, D.C., shall determine all election questions, including challenges and objections to the conduct of the election. Even where there is a Stipulation, however, the Regional Director will investigate a dispute for the Board and may issue a report and recommendations with respect to the disposition of the issues in question. In either case, the election will be supervised by the NLRB's regional office.

Excelsior List

Within seven days after the direction of an election or the execution of an election agreement, the employer must furnish the NLRB with an alphabetical list of the employees eligible to vote and their home addresses. This list, known as the *Excelsior* list, is then made available to the union for use during its election campaign. An election may not be held sooner than 10 days after the *Excelsior* list is received, and failure to furnish the list is grounds for setting aside an election.

Notice of Election

Unlike the original "Notice to Employees," the official "Notice of Election" must be posted before the election. This notice includes details of the upcoming election and a facsimile of the official ballot. It is intended to inform all eligible voters about the details of the election. Failure to post these notices properly may be sufficient grounds for setting aside an election.

Misleading Campaign Propaganda

The NLRB's position on regulating campaign propaganda has fluctuated over the years. Therefore, any employer statement or action during an election campaign should be carefully examined to determine if it meets the Board's standards.

Under current NLRB rules, the Board will not probe into the veracity of campaign statements, but will intervene if a party has used forged documents, thereby preventing the voters from recognizing the material as propaganda.

The Board rule on campaign statements is limited to misrepresentations. It will, however, continue to enforce its rules against threats of reprisal, promises of benefits, and other prohibited practices.

Threats of Reprisal, Promises of Benefits, and Other Prohibited Practices

Section 8(c) of the National Labor Relations Act expressly prohibits an employer from making any statement that threatens employees or promises them benefits. Threats by an employer are considered an illegal inducement to vote against union representation.

Although direct threats are clearly impermissible, the employer is confronted with a dilemma when he wishes to emphasize some of the detrimental economic consequences of union representation. On the one hand, this is the kind of information an employee who is about to make an important decision should have. On the other hand, it may be regarded as a threat of reprisal for a pro-union vote. Several years ago, the Supreme Court tried to establish some guidelines for evaluating employer statements concerning the possible adverse consequence of unionization. The employer must be prepared to demonstrate that the stated consequences of any such prediction (1) are probable and (2) are based on economic considerations alone. The employee must be left with the impression that anti-union feeling has nothing to do with the employer's comment. This framework necessitates that an employer use care in formulating any statement about the economic consequences of unionization.

Just as threats of reprisals cannot be made, neither are promises or grants of benefits allowed. A promise or grant may be unconditional, that is, not tied to a vote against the union, but may still be regarded as improper if there appears to be no valid business reason for it. Therefore, when an employer can establish a *bona fide* business reason for increasing benefits, such as past practice, the grant or announcement will be permissible.

Visits to Employees' Homes — Although union representatives may visit employees' homes and speak to them about the election, an employer may not do so.

Appeals to Racial Prejudice — The standard used by the Board in evaluating racially oriented statements in the context of an election campaign is whether the party making the statement truthfully sets forth the other party's position on racial matters. Any inflammatory or irrelevant statements are clearly prohibited.

Duplication of NLRB Ballot and Other Official Documents — One of the strictest Board election campaign policies is that parties are not permitted to reproduce copies of the official ballot. Any tampering with a facsimile ballot is regarded as grounds for setting an election aside, regardless of the motive or effect of the action. This rule is not limited to ballots only. It applies to all official NLRB election documents.

Discrimination — Discrimination against union supporters is prohibited by the National Labor Relations Act. Employers must be careful, therefore, in dealing with union adherents. Any action taken against them which could be construed as discriminatory could lead to an unfair labor practice charge. Before an employer takes any action against a known union supporter, the nondiscriminatory basis for such action should be firmly established. Even where there are obvious nondiscriminatory reasons for the employer's actions, the NLRB will find that the company has engaged in unlawful discrimination if any part of the decision was motivated by anti-union sentiment.

Surveillance — Surveillance of employees engaged in union activity is forbidden by the NLRB. It is immaterial whether the surveillance is conducted by the employer, supervisors, employees, or outsiders. Furthermore, there may be a violation even if the surveillance is apparent rather than actual.

Peerless Plywood Rule — Under the Board's holding in the *Peerless Plywood* case, an employer is forbidden from delivering a captive audience address within the 24 hours immediately preceding the beginning of an election. Other forms of campaigning within the 24-hour period are permissible, if employee attendance is voluntary.

Campaigning Within the Voting Area — An election can be set aside if a party engages in electioneering near a polling place. This rule applies to employers and unions equally. The Board agent will indicate an area within which no campaigning may occur. The rule is so strictly enforced that conversations with voters in the restricted area, by either employer or union representatives, are sufficient to set aside an election.

The foregoing is only a summary of some of the conduct that may invalidate an election. The admonition to the employer is that he must be cautious regarding conduct during a campaign since even harmless and unintentional actions may have serious legal consequences.

The Election

The election itself is conducted by an NLRB agent. Election observers will be designated by the parties involved to represent the company and the union during the election. Under Board policy, in most cases the observers must be nonsupervisory employees.

The NLRB agent will instruct the observers about their duties: identifying voters, checking names against the *Excelsior* list, challenging individuals if necessary, and assisting in counting the ballots. If an employee is ineligible to vote, he or she must be challenged when asking for a ballot. The NLRB agent will then permit the challenged employee to vote, but the ballot will be placed in an envelope and sealed, its status to be determined later, if necessary. If a prospective voter is not on the eligibility list, the NLRB agent should automatically challenge that individual.

Tally of Ballots and Certification on Conduct of Election

As soon as the polls close, the NLRB agent will count the ballots. To win representation rights, the union must receive a majority of the votes cast.

The NLRB agent, after counting the ballots, will prepare two documents. One is a "Tally of Ballots" showing the results of the count and a statement that the tabulation was accurate. The Tally will be signed and a copy will be served to both parties. He or she will also prepare a "Certification on Conduct of Election" to be signed by the parties' observers. The Certification states that the election was conducted fairly and the secrecy of the ballot was preserved. If there is any question about the way in which the election was conducted, the Certification should not be signed. However, signing the Certification does not preclude a party from thereafter filing objections.

Finally, if the number of challenged ballots is sufficient to affect the results of the election, then the eligibility of the challenged voters will have to be resolved before the outcome can be determined.

Objections

Within seven days after the "Tally of the Ballots" has been prepared, any objections to the election must be filed with the Regional Director, with copies served to the other parties. Objections may be based on the manner in which the election was held, or based on conduct which affected the results of the election. If the objections are sustained, the election will be set aside, and a new one will be conducted.

The Regional Director has the authority to conduct an investigation into the objections. If substantial factual issues exist, he may order a hearing. After completion of the investigation, the Regional Director's actions are determined by whether the election was a directed election, a Stipulation, or a Consent. Essentially, the Board or the Regional Director will resolve the objections and/or challenges. In either case, a decision will be rendered overruling the objections and certifying the results, or sustaining the objections, in whole or part, and setting the election aside.

If the union wins the election, the NLRB will certify it as the bargaining representative for the employees in the designated appropriate bargaining unit. There is no direct court review of the NLRB's representation determination. The employer may, however, refuse to bargain with the union, thereby committing an unfair labor practice which can then be reviewed by a United States Circuit Court. If, on the other hand, the union loses the election, the NLRB will issue a "Certification of Results," legally precluding another election in that bargaining unit for a one-year period.

Occupational Safety and Health 11

Legislative Purpose

In 1970, Congress passed landmark legislation establishing the Occupational Safety and Health Administration (OSHA) within the Department of Labor. The first decade of its existence was especially stormy. Employers resisted what was thought to be excessive regulation of the workplace, and the agency's operations often were cited as a political issue. In 1981, President Ronald Reagan dispelled any notion that he would seek OSHA's abolition when he stated, "there is a compelling need for an effective program to improve safety and health in the workplace." Indeed, his statement echoed the sentiment of Congress when it passed the legislation. The legislative history reveals the Act's purpose:

1. Encourage employers and employees to reduce workplace hazards and implement new or improved existing safety and health programs;
2. Provide for research in occupational safety and health and develop innovative ways of dealing with occupational safety and health problems;
3. Establish "separate but dependent responsibilities and rights" for employers and employees for the achievement of better safety and health conditions;
4. Maintain a reporting and recordkeeping system to monitor job-related injuries and illnesses;

5. Develop mandatory job safety and health standards; and
6. Provide for the development, analysis, evaluation, and approval of the state occupational safety and health programs.

In 1990, Congress approved legislation that significantly increased OSHA civil penalties for both willful and nonwillful violations of the law.

Coverage

In general, compliance with OSHA workplace standards and regulations extends to every employer of the 50 states and the District of Columbia, and all territories (Puerto Rico) under federal jurisdiction. The Act defines an "employer" as "any person engaged in a business affecting commerce who has employees." This broad definition encompasses virtually all business enterprises. There are several exceptions, however, which are not covered by the Act (e.g. self-employed individuals, farms on which only immediate family members of the owner are employed, and workplaces already protected by other federal agencies or laws, such as mines).

Workplace Standards

The Occupational Safety and Health Act requires that all employers "shall furnish a place of employment which is free from recognized hazards that are causing or are likely to cause death or serious physical harm to his employees." To carry out this statutory requirement, OSHA is authorized to issue legally enforceable workplace safety standards, such as limitation on worker exposure to hazardous chemicals and maximum workplace noise levels.

OSHA can begin the standards-setting procedure on its own initiative or upon petition from other parties, such as employers or labor organizations, the federal National Institute for Occupational Safety and Health, or even interested individuals. Once OSHA determines that there is a need to propose, amend, or delete a workplace standard, the agency will publish its intentions in the Federal Register. This notice will include the rationale for the regulation and provide an opportunity (usually 60 days) for affected organizations and individuals to comment on the proposal. Often, public hearings are held to solicit additional information. Following the close of the comment period, OSHA evaluates all information and makes a determination whether to issue a final standard. OSHA also has the option of deciding that no standard or amendment is required. In certain limited circumstances, OSHA may set emergency safety standards which can take effect immediately, but the agency must first conclude that workers are in "grave danger."

OSHA workplace standards fall into four major categories: general industry, construction, agriculture, and maritime. All employers are responsible for complying with the OSHA regulations affecting their particular businesses.

The Workplace Inspection

OSHA's considerable authority to regulate working conditions is enhanced by the agency's power to conduct workplace inspections and impose citations and penalties for workplace conditions which violate OSHA regulations.

Obviously, not all of the estimated five million businesses covered by the Occupational Safety and Health Act can be inspected on a regular basis. (OSHA currently employs about 1,200 workplace inspectors). OSHA, therefore, has established a system of priorities which targets a business for inspection.

"Imminent danger situations" are given top priority. An imminent danger situation is defined as "any condition where there is reasonable certainty that a danger exists that can be expected to cause harm to employees."

Second priority is given to investigation of "fatalities and catastrophes" resulting in hospitalization of five or more employees. These situations must be reported to OSHA by the employer, and inspections are made to determine if OSHA standards were violated and to avoid recurrence of similar accidents.

Self-Inspection Checklist

An OSHA Self-Inspection Checklist recommended by the agency is reproduced below:

	OK	ACTION NEEDED
1. Is the required OSHA workplace poster displayed in your place of business as required where all employees are likely to see it?	☐	☐
2. Are you aware of the requirement to report all workplace fatalities and any serious accidents (where 5 or more are hospitalized) to a federal or state OSHA office within 48 hours?	☐	☐
3. Are workplace injury and illness records being kept as required by OSHA?	☐	☐
4. Are you aware that the OSHA annual summary of workplace injuries and illnesses must be posted by February 1 and must remain posted until March 1?	☐	☐
5. Are you aware that employers with 10 or fewer employees are exempt from the OSHA recordkeeping requirements, unless they are part of an official Bureau of Labor Standards or state survey and have received specific instructions to keep records?	☐	☐
6. Do all employees know what to do in emergencies?	☐	☐
7. Are emergency telephone numbers posted?	☐	☐
8. Are all electrical cords strung so they do not hang on pipes, nails, hooks, etc.?	☐	☐

Self-Inspection Checklist
(continued)

	OK	ACTION NEEDED		OK	ACTION NEEDED
9. Is there no evidence of fraying on any electrical cords?	☐	☐	21. Are stairways in good condition with standard railing provided for every flight having four or more risers?	☐	☐
10. Are metallic cable and conduit systems properly grounded?	☐	☐			
11. Are portable electrical tools and appliances grounded or double insulated?	☐	☐	22. Are portable wood ladders and metal ladders adequate for their purpose, in good condition, and provided with secure footing?	☐	☐
12. Are switches mounted in clean, tightly closed boxes?	☐	☐	23. Are all machines or operations that expose operators or other employees to rotating parts, pinch points, flying chips, particles, or sparks adequately guarded?	☐	☐
13. Are all exits visible and unobstructed?	☐	☐			
14. Are all exits marked with a readily visible sign that is properly illuminated?	☐	☐	24. Are mechanical power transmission belts and pinch points guarded?	☐	☐
15. Are there sufficient exits to ensure prompt escape in case of emergency?	☐	☐	25. Are hand tools and other equipment regularly inspected for safe condition?	☐	☐
16. Are portable fire extinguishers provided in adequate number and type?	☐	☐	26. Are approved safety cans or other acceptable containers used for handling and dispensing flammable liquids?	☐	☐
17. Are fire extinguishers recharged regularly and properly noted on the inspection tag?	☐	☐	27. Are your first-aid supplies adequate for the type of potential injuries in your workplace?	☐	☐
18. Are fire extinguishers mounted in readily accessible locations?	☐	☐	28. Are hard hats provided and worn where any danger of falling objects exists?	☐	☐
19. Are NO SMOKING signs prominently posted in areas containing combustibles and flammables?	☐	☐	29. Are protective goggles or glasses provided and worn where there is any danger of flying particles or splashing of corrosive materials?	☐	☐
20. Are waste receptacles provided and are they emptied regularly?	☐	☐			

General Inspections

OSHA answers complaints based on the most immediate risk of injury or illness. An inspection will be conducted if reasonable grounds are established to conclude that physical harm or imminent danger is a possibility. If OSHA decides an inspection isn't needed, it will still notify the employer of the possible violation and needed corrective action. The employer who receives such a letter and fails to respond or take corrective action may be subject to an on-site inspection.

OSHA will inspect only in cases of "imminent danger." However, OSHA will send a letter to the employer outlining the nature of the complaint and requesting that any potentially hazardous situation be corrected. OSHA may contact the complainant to ensure that corrective measures have been taken.

Inspection Exemptions

Workplaces with 10 or fewer employees will be exempted from general schedule safety inspections if they are in an industry that has a lost workday occupation injury rate lower than 3.6 cases per 100 workers, the national average injury rate for the private sector for 1984. This is the most recent period for which such data has been reported by the Bureau of Labor Statistics.

To compute your "Lost Workday Injury Rate":

1. From the OSHA Form 200, "Log and Summary of Occupational Injuries and Illnesses," count the number of injuries involving lost workdays (column 2).

2. Determine the number of hours all employees actually worked during the year; use payroll or other time records. All employees include salaried and sales forces. The "hours worked" figure should not include any non-worked time even though paid, such as vacation, sick leave, holiday, etc. The lost workday rate may be computed from the following formula:

$$\frac{\text{Number of Lost Workday Injuries} \times 200,000}{\substack{\text{Total Hours Worked By All Employees} \\ \text{During Period Covered}}}$$
$$= \text{Lost Workday Rate}$$

What the OSHA Inspector Will Do

Normally, the OSHA health inspector meets with an employer representative and an employee representative in an **"opening conference"** to discuss procedures for the inspection.

When it is not practical to hold a joint conference, separate conferences will be held. OSHA will, on request, provide written summaries of each conference.

If the inspector feels that it is necessary to observe workplace conditions without delay, the opening conference can be kept brief and, if appropriate, can be continued later.

In most cases, the inspector reviews the employer's records on health problems, noise or ventilation monitoring, and use of hazardous materials before beginning the inspection. This helps the inspector identify probable health hazards.

Next, the inspector makes a **"walkaround" inspection,** looking for signs of health hazards. Danger signals include:
- eye irritation
- strong odors
- visible dust or fumes in the air
- excessive noise
- spilled or leaking chemicals
- use of substances which are known to be dangerous even when handled properly.

After identifying possible hazards, the OSHA inspector takes measurements and samples, using a number of instruments to determine the levels of noise, dust, chemical vapors, and other hazards.

It may be necessary to attach some of these instruments to the workers in order to make proper measurements. Some sampling must be done over an entire shift, while other samples can be taken in a few minutes.

Some other things the inspector will look for include the following:

- Has the employer made use of engineering controls (changes in the physical work environment) or administrative controls (changes in work procedures) to reduce health hazards?
- If personal protective devices (such as respirators) are being used, are they effective in controlling the hazard involved? Are they properly fitted to the workers and properly maintained? Have workers been trained in their use?
- Are areas for eating, washing, and resting being kept isolated from work areas where there are hazardous substances?

The inspector gathers information about the employer's efforts to provide a healthful workplace, including the following:

- **Monitoring of health hazards.** Does the employer have qualified personnel and the right equipment to keep track of the levels of hazardous substances?
- **Medical program.** Does the employer provide regular medical examinations, if required, as a way of identifying health problems?
- **Education and training.** Does the employer conduct a training program on hazards and their control, and on emergency procedures? Are workers participating in the program?

At the end of the inspection, the inspector meets with the employer and employee representatives in a **"closing conference"** to discuss hazards which have been found.

If it is not practical to hold a joint conference, separate conferences will be held, and OSHA will provide written summaries, on request.

It may be necessary to send the test samples for laboratory analysis, which may take several weeks. When the results are available, second conferences will be held.

Sampling results will be provided to a workers' representative.

During the closing conference, an employee representative can describe what hazards exist, what should be done to correct them and how long it should take. The employee representative also can provide facts about the history of health and safety conditions at the workplace.

Any citation issued must be posted by the employer at or near the place where each violation occurred. Employees then have the right to:

- help check to be sure the employer corrects hazards within the deadlines OSHA sets,
- appeal those hazard correction deadlines,
- give the employee's side of the story if the employer appeals OSHA actions.

Recordkeeping and Reporting

With certain exceptions (listed below), employers of 10 or more workers must maintain records of occupational injuries and illnesses as they occur.

Records must be maintained for each business establishment, defined as "a single physical location where business is conducted or where services are performed." Recordkeeping forms are kept on a calendar year basis. *These forms are not sent to OSHA or any other agency.* Rather, they must be kept for a minimum of five years and be available for inspection by representatives of OSHA, the Department of Health and Human Services, the Bureau of Labor Statistics, and certain designated state agencies. Two forms are necessary to fulfill the recordkeeping requirements. Employers must post a notice (a pull-out copy of which is at page 171) in a conspicuous place, and in states operating under an OSHA-approved plan the equivalent state poster. For your reference, there is provided in the Appendix at page 159 a sample company policy statement covering safety and health in the workplace. If used, it is recommended that it be placed adjacent to the OSHA poster where all employees can see it.

OSHA No. 200. Log and Summary of Occupational Injuries and Illnesses. Each recordable occupational injury and illness must be logged on this form within six working days from the time the employer learns of it. If the log is prepared at a central location by automatic data processing equipment, a copy current to within 45 calendar days must be present at all times in the establishment. A substitute for the OSHA No. 200 is acceptable if it is as detailed, easily readable and understandable as the OSHA No. 200.

The OSHA No. 200 must be completed for the calendar year and then conspicuously posted for the entire month of February of the following year.

OSHA No. 101. Supplemental Record of Occupational Injuries and Illnesses. The form OSHA No. 101 contains much more detail about each injury or illness. It also must be completed within six working days from the time the employer learns of the work-related injury or illness. A substitute for the OSHA No. 101 (such as insurance or workers' compensation) may be used if it contains all required information.

In addition, many specific OSHA workplace standards have additional recordkeeping and reporting obligations.

An occupational injury is an injury such as a cut, fracture, sprain, or amputation which results from a work-related accident or from exposure involving a single incident in the work environment. An occupational illness is any abnormal condition or disorder, other than one resulting from an occupational injury, caused by exposure to environmental factors associated with employment. Included are acute and chronic illnesses which may be caused by inhalation, absorption, injestion, or direct contact with toxic substances or harmful agents.

Occupational injuries must be recorded if they result in: one or more lost workdays; restriction of work or motion; loss of consciousness; medical treatment (other than first aid); transfer to another job; or death.

If an on-the-job accident occurs which results in the death of an employee or in the hospitalization of five or more workers, all employers, regardless of the number of employees, are required to report the accident in detail to the nearest OSHA Regional Office.

In 1982, OSHA exempted certain types of businesses from maintaining the annual record of occupational injuries and illnesses because of their low incidence of workplace mishaps. Types of businesses exempted from the recordkeeping requirements are:

1. Retail trade, *except* for general merchandise,

food, building materials, and garden supply retailers;
2. Real estate, insurance, and finance establishments; and
3. Service, *except* for hotels and other lodging places, repair facilities, amusement and recreational services, and health services.

OSHA Standards Most Frequently Cited for Violations in 1990

Subject	% of Total Violations
Hazard Communication/ Construction Industry	11.4
Hazard Communication/ General Industry	10.6
Recordkeeping	3.1
Mechanical Power Transmission Equipment	3.0
Scaffolding	2.7
OSHA Notice	2.5
Guardrails	2.5
Wiring Design	2.5
Machine Guarding	2.4
Wiring Methods/General Industry	2.4
Respiratory Protection	2.4
Employee Exposure/ Medical Records Access	2.2
Abrasive Wheel Guarding	2.0
General Environmental Controls/ Standards Sources	1.8
Flammable and Combustible Liquids	1.6
Noise	1.6
General Electrical Rules	1.6
Wiring Methods/Construction	1.5
Spray Finishing	1.5
Woodworking Machinery	1.4
General Duty Clause	1.4

OSHA Hazard Communication Standard

More and more substances in today's workplace are being viewed as hazardous — not necessarily life threatening, although many can be. In fact, OSHA estimates there are some 575,000 existing chemical products in the workplace. OSHA also estimates 32 million workers are potentially exposed to one or more chemical hazards.

As a result, *all* employers covered by OSHA must comply with OSHA's Hazard Communication Standard. While some states also require employers to disclose to employees the use of hazardous chemicals, the Hazard Communication Standard is broader in scope and pre-empts state law where applicable. Given the broad scope of the rule, and the fact that it requires employers to undertake certain affirmative action to educate and train workers, it is important that every employer become familiar with the basic rule.

Purpose — To ensure that the hazards of all chemicals produced or imported by chemical manufacturers or importers are evaluated and that information concerning their hazards is transmitted to affected employers and employees. This transmittal of information is to be accomplished by means of comprehensive hazard communication progams, which are to include container labeling and other forms of warning, material safety data sheets and employee training.

Scope and Application — Requires all chemical manufacturers or importers to assess the hazards of chemicals which they produce or import. Employers are then responsible for informing their employees about the hazardous materials to which they are exposed:

A chemical is considered hazardous if it:

1. is on the OSHA Z list;
2. is listed in the "Threshold Limit Values for Chemical Substances and Physical Agents in the Work Environment," American Conference of Governmental Industrial Hygienists;
3. is a carcinogen;
4. is a physical hazard because it is a combustible liquid; compressed gas; explosive; flammable; organic peroxide; oxidizer; pyrophoric; unstable (reactive); or water reactive; or
5. is a health hazard because of the existence of statistically significant and scientifically valid evidence that exposure to the chemical can cause acute or chronic adverse health effects.

Written Hazard Communication Program — Employers must develop and put into practice a written hazard communication program for their workplaces which describes their procedures for using material safety data sheets, labels and other forms of warning, and employee information and training. The written program should also contain a list of the hazardous chemicals known to be present, the methods of safety training for non-routine tasks where chemicals are involved, and the methods for insuring that independent contractors are properly trained.

Labels and Other Forms of Warning — The chemical manufacturer, importer or distributor must ensure that each container of hazardous chemicals is labeled, tagged or marked with: the identity of the hazardous chemical(s) (this identity should correspond with the name on the material safety data sheet); an appropriate hazard warning (including the target organ); and, the name and address of the chemical manufacturer, importer, or other responsible party. The employer must ensure that labels or other forms of warning are legible, in English, and prominently displayed on the container, or readily available in the work area throughout each work shift.

Material Safety Data Sheets (MSDSs) — Chemical manufacturers and importers must develop or obtain an MSDS for each hazardous chemical which they use, and must ensure that copies of the required MSDSs are readily accessible during each work shift to employees when they are in their work area(s), and make them available, upon request, to designated representatives of the employees and to OSHA officials.

Employee Information and Training — Each employee who routinely works with any hazardous chemical must be trained regarding:

■ the physical and health hazards of the chemicals in the work area;

■ methods and observations that may be used to detect the presence or release of a hazardous chemical in the work area;

■ the protective measures available, including specific safety procedures, appropriate work practices, emergency procedures, and personal protective equipment to be used; and

■ the details of the employer's hazard communication program, including an explanation of the labeling and MSDSs.

Work Environment Issues

Physical working conditions are becoming increasingly important to employees. Since the enactment of the Occupational Safety and Health Act (OSHA), workplace safety has been widely publicized. Therefore, employee opinions on what they regard as hazardous working conditions should be solicited and acted upon. Safety on the job should be encouraged and rewarded.

Apart from safety, employers must consider other physical aspects of the working environment to make it as conducive to productivity and employee morale as possible. Facilities such as cafeterias, lunch rooms, vending machines, break areas, and lounges should be made available if practical. In addition, keeping these areas clean and properly maintained demonstrates appropriate consideration and respect for the employees' general well-being.

Restricting Smoking in the Workplace — Increasingly, workers are requesting a workplace free of tobacco smoke, and some employers have taken it even further by not hiring smokers. One tobacco-producing state, Virginia, has passed a law prohibiting employment discrimination against smokers, but six other states have considered similar legislation.

A non-smoking policy that is limited to the workplace should withstand a legal challenge based upon discrimination. Management can rationalize the benefits of a smoke-free workforce by pointing to increased productivity and decreased health care claims.

Recent data reveal that smokers have an absenteeism rate 33 to 45 percent greater than that of nonsmokers and use medical systems 25 percent more than nonsmokers, and are significantly more likely to experience disability and premature death. The smoking habits of employees reportedly cost industry some $12.8 billion annually.

The Environmental Protection Agency and the U.S. Surgeon General have concluded environmental tobacco smoke is a major contributor of particulate indoor air pollution. Thus, the Federal government is recommending that "employers and employees should ensure that the act of smoking does not expose nonsmokers to environmental tobacco smoke, by restricting smoking to separately ventilated areas or banning smoking from buildings."

Video Display Terminals — There has been considerable media attention given to VDT health and safety issues. Employers, therefore, can anticipate some questions from employees on such subjects as physical discomfort, eye fatigue, radiation, etc. If an employee asks questions about such issues, you should advise that VDTs present no known health or safety risks to users, when they are ergonomically well designed and used in suitable work environments.

A highly publicized municipal ordinance regulating video display terminals was passed in San Francisco in 1990. In that city, employers with more than 15 employees who work on VDTs for more than four hours a day will have to install flexible work stations and ergonomic equipment to reduce the potential for eye and wrist strain. In addition, an employer must provide adjustable chairs, glare shields, tables and special lamps, and glare screens. A fifteen-minute break after every two hours from continuous VDT work is required. The legislation does allow employers a fair amount of time, four years, to bring their work environment into compliance.

Congress has so far declined to regulate the use of video display terminals in the workplace, rationalizing that legislative standards would "inhibit the flexibility of employers and employees in getting the best use of VDTs."

Employee Insurance and Pension Laws **12**

The Crisis in Health Care Costs

Health care costs for employees and their dependents are a major concern for most employers. The soaring costs of health care have made it one of the central public policy issues of our time. As a result, bold initiatives that were once summarily dismissed are now receiving another look.

Employee insistence on an adequate health care program, the ever-rising cost of such benefits, and government's gradual shifting of these costs onto the employer sector of the economy, have forced employers to rethink the traditional group insurance package. ERISA, COBRA, and other mandated benefit laws increase employer awareness of the direct relationship between employee wellness and "the bottom line" — all have brought attention to what just a few years ago was a largely ignored area of the employer-employee relationship.

Historically, employees were insulated from the costs of their health care buying decision. The Health Research Institute has found, however, that unless the employee is paying at least 25% of the bill, there's no attention paid to the cost. Therefore, employers have focused on plans which encourage prudent buying decisions, and which change buying habits for health care.

Most employee health care plans now include some form of deductible. Other incentives for cost-control include: pre-admission testing (tests which can be performed before entering the hospital); outpatient surgery (many procedures once routinely performed in the hospital can now be

---

Health Care Cost Savings Checklist

☐ Identify doctors and hospitals that are more proficient and cost-effective.

☐ Provide incentives that encourage employees to make use of these medical services.

☐ Monitor, continually, medical services' quality and cost (e.g. one major company pays a greater percent of the medical bill if the employee uses doctors and hospitals in the company's network).

☐ Design handbooks to inform employees how to use the health care system and how to encourage wiser decisions by employees.

☐ To emphasize who is covering the cost, place the company's own name, in addition to the name of its insurance claims handler, on the checks with which it pays medical bills.

☐ Break out the amounts spent on health care costs in the annual benefits summary.

☐ Train "health service advisors" to advise in cases of severe illness.

done on an outpatient basis); audit programs (approximately 70-90% of all hospital bills have errors); generic drugs; birthing centers; free-standing emergency medical centers; hospice care; and second-opinion surgery. Some forms of disincentive or "punishment for imprudent spending" include reducing benefits by 50% if there is no second opinion and not paying for weekend hospital pre-admission.

As Congress wrestles with the problem of health care costs, some employers have tried some noteworthy options other than shifting health care costs to employees.

Employee Wellness Programs

Employers have seen that certain chronic disease problems among their employees are a result of poor lifestyle habits. Studies have shown that roughly 50% of large case costs could be mitigated substantially by improvement in four areas of wellness — smoking cessation, proper diet, regular exercise, and moderate consumption of alcohol. To foster these improvements, the employer can offer employees wellness-oriented programs. These include on-site screening for major diseases and employer education programs aimed at informing employees about lifestyle choices which lead to optimum health. Employers who invest in these programs feel that the long-term payoff will be a workforce with improved lifestyle habits, which will, in turn, lower health care costs.

An example of a wellness program used by one employer is based on simple flexibility stretching, for business and home. This program aims at the reported source of 50 percent of workers' compensation claims and 25 percent of health claims — sprains and strains of the torso, with specific emphasis on the lower back. The cost of the program depends on the number of participants, but the company contends that it breaks down to approximately two percent of the monthly employee health care premium, or $24 annually per employee. In this case, preventing just one back injury (average cost is more than $10,000) would pay for this wellness program

for as many as 300 employees for an entire year.

Employee Assistance Programs

A wide range of problems, not indirectly associated with a person's job function, can have an effect on that individual's job performance. Significant changes in any of the following areas can indicate that an employer is troubled:

- Low productivity
- Poor work quality
- Interpersonal conflicts with co-workers or customers/clients (e.g. inappropriately hostile, angry, withdrawn, or exhibition of inappropriate attitudes or behaviors)
- Excessive waste
- Excessive accidents/mistakes
- Excessive absenteeism (especially on Mondays)
- Poor judgment
- Reduced efficiency
- Disappearance from work
- Extending or not returning from lunch or other breaks
- Consistently missing deadlines
- Minimal contact with co-workers, especially supervisors

Typical problems employees can be expected to have include:

- Alcohol and/or drug dependency
- Family (which includes marital, children, extended families, parents, etc.)
- Financial
- Legal
- Work related

In most instances employees overcome such personal problems independently and the effect on job performance is negligible. In other instances, normal supervisory assistance either serves as motivation or guidance by which such problems can be resolved, thereby returning job performance back to an acceptable level. In some cases, however, neither the efforts of the employee or the supervisor have the desired effect and unsatisfactory job performance persists.

Many employers, recognizing that almost any human problem can be successfully treated if it is identified in its early stages, and if referral is made to an appropriate professional care facility, are now offering an Employee Assistance Program (EAP). Such EAPs are designed to help employees resolve personal problems which may adversely affect their jobs or lives.

EAP services are normally available to employees on a voluntary, self-referral basis through an outside agency or by supervisory referral to the EAP agency. Resources through the EAP agency include professional counseling, doctors, and information resources to which employees may not have access or about which they may not be aware. Employers with EAPs make it clear to employees that neither a request for treatment nor program participation will jeopardize the employee's job security or advancement opportunities.

COBRA — Legislative Purpose

A major provision of the Consolidated Omnibus Budget Reconciliation Act of 1986 (COBRA) allows for the extension of group insurance coverage to employees and/or their dependents on a self-pay basis, who would otherwise lose their coverage.

Group health care plans providing "medical" benefits as defined in Internal Revenue Code Section 213, such as medical, dental, vision, and prescription drug plans (but not life insurance and disability benefit plans) are covered. Thus, not only group insurance plans, but self-insured plans, HMOs, and PPOs are included under the scope of COBRA.

Eligible employees and/or dependents are entitled to continue their group health benefits for varying periods of time (maximum of three years) by paying up to 102% of the current premium (including both employee and employer payments) or of the reasonable estimate of the self-insured plan cost.

In 1989, the COBRA law was amended to require employers to cover former employees whose medical condition keep them from immediately getting coverage under a new employer's plan. Thus, an individual may continue to pay for COBRA coverage even after becoming

covered by another group plan if that plan excludes or limits the coverage of a preexisting condition.

By the terms of a recent amendment, the continuation coverage is extended to 29 months, from 18 months, in the event a worker is disabled at the time of termination or reduction of hours.

Coverage and Eligibility

Virtually every employer, private and public, with a group health plan as described above is included, except the Federal government, District of Columbia, churches and synagogues, and employers with fewer than 20 employees.

Employees losing coverage on or after the effective date due either to termination of employment for any reason except discharge for gross misconduct, or a reduction in hours of work, must be extended the continuation privilege. In 1990, the Internal Revenue Service ruled that COBRA coverage must be offered military reservists and their families, unless an employer "voluntarily" maintains full coverage under a group health plan for these individuals and their families. Spouses and dependent children of covered employees are also eligible if they lose coverage on or after the effective date due to the employee's death, termination (other than for gross misconduct), reduced work hours, or becoming eligible for Medicare; divorce or legal separation from the employee; or ceasing to satisfy the plan's coverage requirements for dependent children. Employees over 69 and their over-69 spouses are entitled to continue coverage for as long as they are actively working.

Benefits and Duration

The individual has the right to continue the same coverages he or she had the day before the qualifying event as an ongoing participant or dependent in the plan, and no evidence of insurability can be required. Coverage on this self-pay basis can continue from the date coverage would have stopped for varying periods of time from 18 to 36 months. Coverage may be stopped if the employer terminates the plan, if the individual fails to pay the premium, if the individual becomes covered under another health care plan (regardless of the benefits included), or if the individual becomes eligible for Medicare. The employee must notify the plan administrator within 60 days of divorce, legal separation, or loss of dependent child status.

Employees have to accept or reject continued coverage within a minimum of 60 days after notice, and pay the premium within 45 days after election of continued coverage.

Notification Requirements

The employer must give written notice to employees and spouses when the employer's plan year begins and compliance with COBRA becomes required. (See a "model" COBRA statement for employers' use in the Appendix). An explanation of how COBRA applies must also be included in the employer's Summary Plan Description. Within 30 days of an employee's death or change in employment status, the employer must notify the plan administrator. Employees or "qualified beneficiaries" must notify the plan administrator when there is a divorce or legal separation or when the dependent has reached the contractual age limit.

The plan administrator has 14 days to notify the beneficiary of continuation rights (ensuring that the ex-spouse or dependent is aware of their options). The individual has 60 days to elect coverage, and 45 more days to start paying the premium.

Penalties for Noncompliance

A private sector employer's failure to comply could result in the following:
1. Loss of a federal income tax deduction for the plan costs;
2. The cost of coverage for highly compensated employees would become taxable income to them;
3. The plan administrator and the plan fiduciary are liable for $100 per day personal damages for failure to give notice if

requested to; and
4. Attorneys' fees and costs can be awarded for breach of fiduciary responsibility.

A public sector employer's penalty for noncompliance is injunctive relief.

Suggestions for "Coping With COBRA"

1. All notices — initial and ongoing — should be sent Registered/Return Receipt Requested to verify notice in case of subsequent charges of notification not being made.
2. Enrollment forms for continuation coverage should identify eligibility and conditions of coverage.
3. Clearly state your policy for premium payment and cancellation provisions for nonpayment of premiums.
4. Tickler files should be maintained for:
   a. 180-day pre-continuation trigger notice for conversion application
   b. Notification to beneficiaries and/or administrator/insurer of end of continuation period for an individual.
5. Procedure for updating of beneficiary addresses — needed for premium overdue notices, plan revision information, etc.
6. Offer continuation of benefits on all-or-nothing basis (e.g., must continue dental and health, not dental only). This limits some effects of anti-selection which would add to your benefit costs.
7. Require declination forms for those individuals indicating no wish to continue.
8. Notify claims personnel to screen for other sources of payment on providers' bills which should then be followed up for potential ineligibility of the individual to continue on your plan.
9. Implementation of mandatory managed care plans to preclude inappropriate or excessive utilization patterns — studies suggest that nonworking persons have higher utilization trends.

10. Create a system to log in and out all administrative notices and receipts.
11. Establish "premium" amounts (even if self-insured) prospectively; update annually. Use "worst-case scenario" in developing "premium" even if you must, as a consequence, adjust the employer contribution level to maintain current payroll deductions.
12. If you terminate or lose employees shortly after hiring, determine the average time they are with your firm. Use this time period to set your plan eligibility date. This will cut down on typical benefit paperwork and also preclude a short-term employee from gaining significant coverage.

Workers' Compensation— Purpose

The basic tenet of workers' compensation laws is that employers are to provide compensation in the form of wage replacement and the cost of all reasonable and necessary hospital, surgical, and medical expenses, for all accidental injuries or illnesses and death arising out of and in the course of employment.

Each of the 50 states has its own workers' compensation law. In addition, there are federal laws, including the District of Columbia Workers' Compensation Act, the Federal Employee's Compensation Act, and the Longshoremen's and Harbor Workers' Compensation Act (covering both private and public employees in nationwide maritime work).

There are six basic objectives underlying workers' compensation laws:

1. Provide sure, prompt, and reasonable income and medical benefits to work accident victims, or income benefits to their dependents, regardless of fault;
2. Provide a single remedy and reduce court delays, costs, and workloads arising out of personal-injury litigation;
3. Relieve public and private charities of financial drains — incident to uncompen-

sated industrial accidents;
4. Eliminate payment of fees to lawyers and witnesses as well as time-consuming trials and appeals;
5. Encourage maximum employer interest in safety and rehabilitation through an appropriate experience-rating mechanism; and
6. Promote frank study of causes of accidents (rather than concealment of fault), thereby reducing preventable accidents and human suffering.

As with other runaway insurance costs issues, workers' compensation is being threatened by out-of-control costs, unnecessary litigation, and underfunded, understaffed state-administered agencies. For example, the country's largest workers' compensation insurer recently stopped writing insurance altogether in Maine because its premium income did not cover losses and expenses. In fact, in recent years, workers' compensation medical costs outpace both health care increases and inflation.

Coverage

Virtually every employer in the public and private sectors is covered. Employers are required to obtain insurance or prove financial ability to carry their own risk (self-insurance). Six states require employers to participate in a monopolistic state fund. Thirteen states offer, as an alternative to private insurance companies, a competitive state fund. Twenty-eight states and the Longshoremen's Act authorize group self-insurance for smaller employers with similar risk characteristics who pool their risks and liabilities. Forty-seven states permit self-insurance for individual employers. Coverage is elective in only three states: South Carolina, New Jersey, and Texas.

Occupational Diseases

All states now recognize responsibility for occupational diseases. Coverage extends to all diseases arising out of, and in the course of, employment. Most states do not provide compensation for a disease that is an "ordinary disease of life" or which is not "peculiar to or characteristic of" the employee's occupation.

Benefits

Since workers' compensation is viewed as a beneficial system, it is liberally interpreted in favor of the intended beneficiary.

Medical benefits are usually provided without dollar or time limits, although many programs base maximum medical costs on a "reasonable and customary" test. Income replacement for lost work time is most often based on two-thirds of the employee's average earnings with some dollar maximum, such as the state's average weekly wage. Cash benefits may also be paid for specific physical impairments (permanent partial disability). The great majority of workers' compensation dollars are paid out for temporary total disability income replacement and permanent partial disabilities. Rehabilitation, both medical and vocational, is provided for those cases involving severe disabilities.

Loss Control and Prevention

In a report on loss control and prevention, the National Council on Compensation Insurance recently stated:

"Insurers are no longer content to share the risk; they are committed to decreasing risks as well. The insurance specialties of loss control, risk control, and loss prevention are dedicated to the dual goals of reducing the chances that a loss will occur and minimizing the financial impact of losses which cannot be prevented.

"In the areas of workers' compensation, this means the establishment of a safe workplace. For greater safety in the workplace, it is necessary to increase the awareness of employers and employees that loss prevention and loss reduction prior to an accident are the most effective methods of minimizing injury and compensation costs. Safety awareness should not be limited to the workplace. A societal focus on safety as a 'cradle to grave' goal is highly recommended. Good safety habits should be universal, and not confined to

the workplace. Further, employer involvement in safety issues must be sustained. An employer motivational campaign is essential to achieving a long-term commitment to safety.

"The initial minimization or prevention of injury should remain the primary focus of loss control. However, it also is essential to establish, through analysis of job hazards and incidents, procedures to reduce and eliminate the effects of incidents that do occur, to prevent recurrence and to establish return-to-work programs."

Cost Control Suggestions

In every instance of an alleged work-related accident, injury, or illness, the employer should take the following steps to control costs:

1. Conduct a prompt, thorough, and accurate investigation;

2. Set up a file for all of the information;

3. Critically evaluate all of the information gathered to be sure it supports the decision to pay, or not to pay;

4. Update and review the file regularly, keeping in mind that to act reasonably doesn't necessarily mean the decision will be upheld;

5. When in doubt, particularly as to questions of law or government agency procedure, the employer should confer with an attorney, insurance carrier, or service organization representative, and get their written opinions for the file.

   Note: Many employers rely on their insurance carrier to handle the entire claim. It takes a partnership, however, to really keep on top of every claim. The insurance carrier needs any and all information you can supply so the proper steps continue to be taken.

6. Provide safety training programs to prevent accidents. Approximately 85% of all work-related accidents are attributable to unsafe employee acts caused by a lack of worker knowledge or skill. Research has shown

that employers pay an additional 5-10% on top of workers' compensation in hidden and indirect costs. The major hidden cost is lost productivity, including the lost production time of the injured worker and co-workers. Training and administrative costs are added when a replacement must be hired. Moreover, upon return to work, the injured worker may not be as productive as before the accident. There are also costs attached to an accident investigation.

7. Ensure appropriate rehabilitation so the injured worker can return to work quickly.

8. Demand sensible medical fee schedules. Eliminate "doctor shopping" and unnecessary testing. Consider cost containment programs.

9. Encourage simpler procedures and better communication of rights and benefits, plus teamwork between doctors, employers, and state regulatory agencies.

10. Support alternative methods for resolving legitimate disputes short of going to court.

11. Provide suitable alternative employment in the event a worker can't return to his or her original job.

Unemployment Insurance— Purpose

Unemployment insurance is a national social insurance program, whose major objective is to provide unemployed workers the means of getting through a temporary period of involuntary unemployment without having to face a needs test.

Administration

Unlike workers' compensation, there is a Federal Unemployment Tax Act (part of the U.S. Internal Revenue Code) which oversees the individual unemployment insurance laws of the 50 states and U.S. possessions by: 1) providing a continuing incentive for the states to adopt and maintain their own unemployment compensation laws; 2) controlling the taxes collected under both the state and federal unemployment compensation laws; 3) providing sound administration through the monies given each state for "proper and efficient" administration as determined by the U.S. Department of Labor; and 4) establishing minimum program standards regarding eligibility, benefit amount, and duration of benefits.

The states, in turn, establish their own criteria for eligibility, benefit amounts, and duration.

Coverage and Eligibility

Virtually all employers, with the exception of small farms and some minor categories of services, are covered. The program is financed almost entirely from employer taxes. Two states, Alaska and New Jersey, tax employees as well; and two states, Pennsylvania and West Virginia, require employee contributions under limited conditions. The employer pays both a state unemployment compensation tax and a federal tax (FUTA). Public employers are exempted from the FUTA tax.

The Federal tax is 6.2% of the first $7,000 in wages paid to each employee. Employers receive credit for up to 5.4% of this tax for taxes they pay under state unemployment compensation laws. The difference is used to finance state and federal administrative costs, 35% of extended benefits during periods of unusually high unemployment, and loans to states which have exhausted their own unemployment compensation funds. Each state unemployment compensation tax goes entirely for unemployment compensation benefits. The state assigns a rate to each employer based on his experience with unemployment in relation to other employers.

All claimants, in order to qualify for benefits, must be able to work and be available for suitable work. All states disqualify persons who voluntarily quit without good cause, are discharged for misconduct, or refuse an offer of suitable work.

Most states provide for denial of benefits for the duration of the disqualified individual's unemployment, or until one has obtained another job, worked on that job for a minimum period, and is separated from that job for nondisqualifying reasons.

As the result of more stringent administration of the unemployment insurance system, there are fewer workers eligible for benefits with each passing year. Another reason for the decline is the shift in the economy away from manufacturing jobs to service industry employees, who tend to earn less and change jobs more frequently. Many are part-timers who have not worked enough hours or earned sufficient pay to qualify under the tougher rules.

Benefits

The generally accepted objective is to provide a wage replacement in the form of a weekly unemployment compensation benefit which is high enough to cover the individual's nondeferrable expenses while not serving as a disincentive to return to work. The weekly benefit is usually 35% of the individual's average weekly wage, with a maximum benefit amount based on the state's average weekly wage.

All states provide at least a potential duration of 26 weekly benefits, with a few providing for more. The federal law provides for additional benefits during periods of high unemployment to individuals who have exhausted their entitlement to regular benefits.

The benefits and the duration of payments for workers vary enormously among the states. Longtime employees can generally get 26 weeks of benefits. In 1989, the average weekly payment was $152. Most states tie benefits to the amount of wages last earned and the length of time worked for the last employer.

Cost Control Suggestions

Suggestions for effective unemployment insurance cost control include the following steps:
1. Keep a numerical Social Security number listing of all current and former employees (former within past three years). State and federal agencies identify every applicant by Social Security number on all forms, whereas names are often abbreviated or misspelled beyond recognition;
2. Determine which unemployment compensation claims you should protest, and be ready to do so within the time limits if notified of such a claim;
3. Have one person responsible for all unemployment compensation claims, records, protests, and tax reports;
4. Audit every monthly or quarterly statement from the state agency. Be ready to properly protest within the time limits if any mistakes are noted. Consider these statements as bills, because they determine the unemployment compensation tax or charge which will be assessed the employer; and
5. Audit the annual state and federal (FUTA) tax notices and be ready to protest in the proper manner within the specified time.

The Scope and Coverage of ERISA

The private pension system covers over 40 million active and retired workers who have been promised that they will receive or will continue to receive benefits during their retirement years. The Employee Retirement Income Security Act (ERISA) does not require that such promises be made, but once they are, it does provide safeguards to ensure that they be kept.

When Congress passed the ERISA legislation in 1974, it wanted to establish four basic concepts:
1. Workers must become eligible for benefits after a reasonable length of service;
2. Adequate funds must be set aside to provide promised benefits;
3. Those managing the plan and its funds must meet certain standards of conduct; and
4. Sufficient information must be made available to determine if the law's requirements are being met.

ERISA regulations cover any employer engaged in business or in any industry or activity affecting commerce.

Pension Plans

There are two general types of pension plans: *Defined benefit plans* promise employees specific monthly benefits at retirement. They may state the exact dollar amount (e.g., $150 a month) or they may provide a formula to calculate the benefits (e.g., $15 per month for every year of service with the employer).

Defined contribution plans provide benefits based on employer contributions and investment earnings of the pension trust. An individual account is established for each employee. The employer may promise to contribute a specific amount of money (e.g. five percent of the employee's annual earnings), as in a money purchase plan, or contributions may vary with the company's profits, as in a profit-sharing plan. However, no exact benefit is promised at retirement.

Defined contribution plans include target benefit plans, thrift and savings plans, 401(k) arrangements, and employee stock ownership plans (ESOPs).

In recent years, many employers have begun supplementing existing defined benefit plans.

Plan Requirements

To protect the rights of plan participants, ERISA imposes certain requirements for pension plans. (Author's note: The following text is taken from the Employer's Pension Guide, a publication of the Department of Labor, the Internal Revenue Service, and the Pension Benefit Guaranty Corporation. It is a very useful reference.)

Plan Purpose

A pension plan must be operated solely in the interest of participants and beneficiaries. Pension funds must be held in a trust fund separate from an employer's assets or be used to purchase insurance policies that are held as plan assets. Trust fund assets or insurance policies must be used exclusively to provide benefits for plan participants and, with very few exceptions, may not be returned to the employer while the plan is in operation.

Virtually any transaction involving an employer and the assets of any pension plan maintained by the employer is prohibited. For example, an employer is not allowed to borrow money from its pension fund, even if it is willing to pay a higher interest rate than the plan could obtain in the open market. However, a plan may hold a limited amount of the employer's stock as part of the plan's assets.

If a company is sold or merged, the assets of the pension plan do not become the property of the new company, but must remain in the trust fund for the benefit of the plan participants.

Participation

Generally, employees must be allowed to participate in a plan if they are at least age 21 and have completed one year of service with the employer. However, two years of service may be required if a plan provides for full and immediate vesting. An employee may not be excluded from a pension plan because of age, even if he or she is hired within a few years of retirement age.

Vesting

Being "vested" means an employee has completed the years of service required under the plan to attain a permanent legal right to receive his or her pension, whether or not the employee continues to work for the same employer. Despite the years of service requirement, an employee is entitled to 100 percent of his or her accrued benefit upon attaining the normal retirement age under the plan. For this purpose, the plan cannot define a normal retirement age that is later than age 65 or the time a person has five years of participation. In addition, an employee must always be fully vested in his or her own contributions to the plan. This means that if the employee leaves the company, he or she is entitled to the money he or she contributed, plus interest.

Single-employer pension plans must provide

vesting for employees *at least as rapidly* as either of the following two methods:

Cliff Vesting — employees are fully vested after five years of service.

Graded Vesting — employees are at least 20 percent vested after three years of service and receive at least an additional 20 percent vesting for each of the next four years, with full vesting coming after no more than seven years.

If the plan's vesting schedule is changed, individuals with three or more years of service must be able to remain under the prior schedule if they wish to do so.

Years of Service — Ordinarily, for vesting purposes, a year of service is defined in the plan as a 12-month period during which an employee performs at least 1,000 hours of service, which generally are defined as:

■ hours for which an employee is paid or entitled to be paid (including pay for vacation and sick leave); and

■ hours for which an employee is awarded back pay.

Pension plans also are permitted to use an "elapsed time" method of counting service. Under this system, the total period of time from the date of employment to the date of severance is computed, regardless of actual hours worked.

Exclusions — Service that may be excluded when determining employee vesting includes: years of service before age 18; periods during which an employee declined to contribute to a plan for which employee contributions were required; periods when the employer did not maintain the plan or a predecessor plan; years during which an employee has a break in service; and certain periods preceding breaks in service.

Break in Service — A plan may regard a year in which an employee does not complete more than 500 hours of service as a "break in service," and this may result in an employee receiving credit for less service for vesting purposes.

However, if an employee takes leave because of pregnancy, birth, or adoption of a child, or for purposes of caring for the child immediately following birth, or adoption, up to 501 hours of

that leave must be counted as hours of service to the extent that such hours prevent the occurrence of a break in service.

Absence due to certain military service also cannot be counted as a break in service.

Disclosure Requirements

There are certain disclosure requirements to which plan sponsors and plan administrators must comply under ERISA. The plan administrator must automatically provide employees with the following information:

Summary Plan Description — A booklet or similar document written in easily understandable language that includes such information as: how the plan operates; when employees are eligible to receive their pensions; how they can calculate the amount of their benefits; and how to file claims. This information must be provided free of charge within 90 days after an employee becomes a participant in the plan. All updated versions of the Summary Plan Description that reflect changes in the plan also must automatically be provided to the plan participants.

Summary of the Annual Report — A summary of the annual report—information on the financial activities of the plan—must be provided to participants annually. (The full annual report also must be provided to any participants who request it in writing.)

Survivor Coverage Data — Information on the plan's survivor coverage, and how it affects employees and their spouses, must be provided to participants.

Benefit Statement — In general, the plan administrator must furnish to any participant or beneficiary who so requests *in writing*—but not more frequently than once a year—a statement of the participant's total accrued benefit and the earliest date on which he or she will become vested.

Additionally, administrators of all pension plans covered by ERISA must file an annual report with the IRS using the Form 5500 series. The IRS transmits the report to the Department of Labor and specific information from the report to the Pension Benefit Guaranty Corporation.

Drug and Alcohol Abuse in the 13 Workplace

The "War" on Drugs

America is waging a "war" on drugs. Illegal drugs — and the illegal use of legally manufactured drugs — pose a growing threat to American society. Drugs are stronger, cheaper, more available, and, in some circles, more accepted than ever before.

The price tag is immense — in excess of $110 billion annually. Drug dependency and fatality rates are at record high levels.

The nexus of drug abuse to major crime and urban blight is well known. However, the relevance of drug abuse to the workplace is just now being fully recognized. The National Institute on Drug Abuse estimates that if every employee aged 18 to 40 were tested for drug use on any given day, anywhere from 14 percent to 25 percent would test positive.

Every community is affected by drug abuse. So is virtually every employer.

Employers Can Help

Police officials alone cannot win the war on drugs. A concerted effort by the various segments of society is necessary — especially by schools and businesses.

Is there an employer role in preventing drug abuse? Yes. An effective employer program to prevent drug abuse is in the interests of both the community and the individual business. Such a program is not only humane, but cost-effective as well.

Furthermore, many people believe employers are best equipped to deter drug abuse because of the "power of the paycheck." If employees and job applicants know that their jobs are contingent on their being "drug free," they have a compelling incentive to get off, or stay off, drugs.

More and more businesses are recognizing and responding to the problems created by drug abuse in the United States. They recognize the enormity of our country's drug abuse problem, its costs economically and in human suffering and lives, and employers' responsibility to act firmly but fairly to combat drug abuse. The ultimate employer goals should be deterrence and rehabilitation. Ultimately, effective drug abuse prevention programs can save lives — and businesses.

How Drug Abuse Hurts Business

Perhaps drug abusers themselves tell the story most clearly. A recent study of drug abusers in rehabilitation resulted in admissions that:

- 75 percent had used drugs on the job
- 64 percent had experienced adverse job performance as a result of drug use
- 44 percent had sold drugs to co-workers
- 18 percent had stolen on the job to support their habits

The negative effects of drug abuse on the workplace include:

■ lost productivity
■ increased absenteeism
■ increased on-the-job accidents
■ increased medical costs
■ increased employee theft

An employee with drugs in his or her system is one-third less productive. That employee also is: 2.5 times more likely to have absences of eight days or more, 3.6 times more likely to injure himself or another person on the job, and 5 times more likely to file a workers' compensation claim. Drug-abusing workers also incur 300 percent higher medical costs and benefits.

Employers also face other "hidden" costs of drug abuse, costs which are difficult to calculate but easy to recognize:

■ Lower employee morale
■ Compromised product integrity
■ Decreased quality of customer service
■ Increased absenteeism for the family members of drug users
■ Increased insurance costs
■ Increased destruction of company property
■ Impaired judgment regarding day-to-day decisions affecting the company
■ The introduction and influence of the criminal element in the workplace

The Elements of a Drug Abuse Prevention Program

Drug testing is *not* an answer unto itself. Drug testing, performed as fairly and accurately as is reasonably possible, may be part of the solution for many employers, but it is only one element of an overall drug abuse prevention program.

Employer programs for drug abuse prevention have three major goals:

1. To keep drug abusers out of the workforce by screening job applicants,
2. To deter employees from developing a drug abuse problem, and
3. To rehabilitate employees who have a drug abuse problem.

Employers should keep in mind that this last goal — rehabilitation — is the ultimate and most humane purpose of a drug abuse prevention program. Employers also should recognize that no testing at all is highly preferable to inaccurate testing.

An employer program for drug abuse prevention should include:

1. Commitment — It is essential that top management on a corporate-wide basis understand how comprehensive a drug abuse prevention program must be and commit to that level of involvement.

2. Analysis and Development — Thoroughness is necessary. Analyze personnel, productivity, absenteeism, compensation claims, and safety and health records. Find out if your company has a drug problem significant enough to warrant a corporate response. Develop a formal, written company policy which includes whether and when drug testing will be performed, and what disciplinary actions are anticipated. Coordinate your company's policy — before implementation — with personnel, benefits, legal, medical, security, safety and health, and labor relations staff persons or outside counselors, and, if present, union representatives.

3. Education and Training — "Sell" your drug abuse prevention program to your employees. Communications regarding the company policy, the company's commitment, the dangers of drug abuse, and the availability of rehabilitation services or referral will encourage cooperation, give the program credibility, and prevent undue resentment or morale problems. Education may deter drug abuse as effectively as testing or disciplinary action. Training of supervisors also is critical, particularly regarding how to react to a workplace drug incident.

4. Drug Testing — Everyone is hurt by inaccuracies, misidentifications, or unconfirmed tests. Commit the resources necessary to have a professional drug testing program. Strive to assure the integrity, accuracy, and fairness of the testing program in order to: (1) produce the most conclusive and useful test results, (2) minimize the intrusion on and discomfort of the individual, and (3) decrease legal vulnerability. Split the specimen taken for urinalysis into two samples, so that a second confirming test can be performed using the same specimen if the first half of the specimen tests "positive" for the presence of drugs. These second tests, called confirmation assays, should be performed using a different chemical process.

No disciplinary or job action should be taken unless both tests prove "positive." Take reasonable steps to preserve the confidentiality of employees' test results.

5. Disciplinary Action — Consistency is the key. Do not selectively enforce your company's drug abuse prevention program. Be prepared to take the same response for all employees, irrespective of their seniority and their value to the company. Document as fully as possible a relationship between drug use and declining performance. Dismiss chronic drug abuse cases who: (1) are unable or unwilling to rehabilitate, (2) present a significant safety or security risk, (3) are unable to perform their job responsibilities because of their illegal drug use, or (4) are engaged in criminal activities such as selling drugs.

6. Rehabilitation — Employee assistance programs (EAPs) best serve the ultimate goal of rehabilitation. Usually structured as an adjunct to company health care programs, EAPs generally include counseling, medical monitoring, treatment, retesting, and family support and reinforcement. EAPs can be effective, cost-effective, and good for employee morale. In the absence of company-provided programs, referrals to local counseling and treatment centers is an alternative. Suspension, rather than dismissal, for first-time cases and continuation of pay are humane policies which should be considered. However, a high level of accountability — with the requirement of strict adherence to the rehabilitation program and retesting — is entirely appropriate for employees in rehabilitation.

Guidelines to Prevent Liability for Drug Testing

Drug testing programs are not appropriate for all employers. They may not be appropriate for most employers. But they can be an effective and integral part of an employer's drug abuse prevention program, and all employers should at least adopt an anti-drug abuse policy. Drug testing should be performed as accurately and fairly as is reasonably possible — or it should not be performed at all.

Employers are well-advised to stay current and in compliance with continuing legal and legislative developments in the field of drug abuse in the workplace.

No federal legislation has received extensive consideration by Congress, thus far, regarding a private employer's ability to perform employee drug testing.

The Supreme Court, however, has given its approval to drug testing programs in two federal programs involving railroad industry workers and Customs Service drug-enforcement positions. The rulings are seen as the first of a series which will define the limit of testing under the Fourth Amendment's ban against "unreasonble searches." It should be noted that private-sector employees have no constitutional protection against testing; therefore, the court's decisions are not expected to materially affect testing in private industry. In 1990, the U.S. Court of Appeals ruled the federal government's efforts to test federal employees suspected of using narcotics while off duty illegal. In a related finding, the court found unconstitutional regulations that allowed for intrusive monitoring of federal employees who provided urine samples for testing. "The Government may investigate and punish wrongdoing within the walls of its offices. What the Government may not do in the case of ordinary employees is justify drug testing procedures that intrude upon constitutionally protected privacy interests with speculation about possible future job impairment or rules violations." It should be noted, however, that courts have determined that testing

Six Reasons Not to Test

Why should an employer *not* implement a drug testing program in the workplace?

1. To avoid morale problems — Drug testing can upset even those employees most opposed to illegal drug use. It is, despite precautions, somewhat intrusive and somewhat of an invasion of privacy. Unless handled fairly and with full explanations, drug testing can create resentment in the workforce.

2. To avoid union grievances or union organizing — Most unions actively oppose drug testing in the workplace. To attempt to implement drug testing may cause grievances and defeat or detract from other collective bargaining goals. In non-union workplaces, implementation of drug testing, particularly if handled inequitably, can provide the union organizer with a major weapon against the employer.

3. To avoid an "overreaction" — Employers may conclude that the best response is no response, or a prevention program without testing. A company may evaluate its situation and find that a drug abuse prevention program is unnecessary because: (1) it does not have a significant enough drug abuse problem in its workforce to warrant a program, or (2) it is not the type of business that has safety, health, or security concerns which warrant efforts to assure a completely "drug free" workforce.

4. To avoid additional expenses — Given the level of commitment necessary to maintain an effective drug abuse prevention program, employers also face a question of cost. Even if a business recognizes that it does have a drug abuse problem, it may not be able to afford a comprehensive program to address it. Development and implementation of a program is expensive. Drug testing, if done right, is expensive. Rehabilitation services are expensive. (Nonetheless, given the costs to employers of drug abuse, the more appropriate question may not be "can you afford a program?", but rather "can you afford not to have a program?")

5. To avoid legal claims — In our increasingly litigious society, employers face a plethora of legal claims, especially in the employee rights area. Even when an employer is legally "right" on the merits, the cost of litigation can be substantial. Some employers may see the implementation of a drug testing program as an invitation to legal challenges, and may avoid testing to avoid litigation.

6. To observe privacy interests of employees — An employer may feel that the legitimate individual rights and privacy interests of employees outweigh a company or societal interest in preventing drug abuse. However, most employers believe that while these interests are both valid and compelling, a balance must be struck.

Six Reasons to Test

Why should an employer implement a drug testing program in the workplace?

1. To help the community — By addressing the drug abuse problem effectively, employers "do their part" in addressing the needs of the community. All segments of society — government, schools, law enforcement, and businesses — must fight the war on drugs.

2. To maintain productivity — At this time of heightened national concern about the competitiveness of American business, can employers afford to carry significant numbers of employees who are one-third less productive because they have drugs in their systems?

3. To protect employees and customers — Safety and health are major employer concerns because of their moral and legal obligations to provide a workplace free of recognized hazards. In many occupations, workers on drugs present a clear and present danger to themselves, co-workers, and members of the public. Employers cannot and should not allow the safety and health of others to be jeopardized by drug abusers in the workplace.

4. To contain health care costs — American business, like American society in general, faces a crisis in health care costs. Drug users are not only more likely to injure others on the job, they also incur four times the medical expenses of the average employee. In order to contain medical costs and preserve an employer's ability to continue to provide comprehensive and affordable benefits for all employees, employers should limit the drug user's access to the workforce.

5. To deter drug abuse — Contingency of employment is a powerful disincentive to illegal drug use. If drug users know a company makes "being drug free" a condition of employment, they are more likely to refrain from illegal drug use or to apply for employment elsewhere.

6. To rehabilitate employees — The first step to rehabilitation is recognition of the problem. To the extent that drug testing uncovers drug dependency problems and forces people to face up to them, it can be constructive, humane, and even life-saving.

in jobs related to public safety and national security must be unfettered.

There is a great deal of activity at the state and local level. Ten states — Connecticut, Rhode Island, Vermont, Minnesota, Iowa, Montana, Maine, Oregon, North Carolina, and Utah — have enacted laws regarding drug abuse and employment. Some of these states restrict, in some cases severely, who and how an employer can test for the presence of drugs. Only the Utah law is considered pro-employer on the drug testing issue because it shields employers from legal liabilities if certain procedures are followed.

The city of San Francisco has enacted an ordinance prohibiting random drug testing in both the public and private sectors. More state and local laws are sure to follow.

Employers can minimize the legal risks of drug testing by taking appropriate steps:

1. Contract with a reliable, professional drug testing service — Businesses should contract with a service or use an in-house testing program which is staffed by well-trained and certified personnel who will follow acceptable professional procedures. Check out the service with medical professionals and other businesses. Ask for references. Make sure it has qualified professionals available to serve as expert witnesses if necessary.

2. Assure that chain-of-custody is maintained for specimens — Human error is the most common reason for inaccuracies in testing today. Maintaining chain-of-custody is vital in preventing tampering, substitution, misidentification, or misplacement.

3. Confirm "positive" tests before taking any job action — Initial specimens should be split into two samples so that a second test can be performed using the initial specimen if the first half of that specimen tests "positive" for the presence of illegal drugs. The confirmatory assay should be conducted using a different chemical process. The most common initial screens use immunoassay techniques and are relatively simple and inexpensive. The most common confirmatory assays — gas chromatography/mass spectrometry, gas chromatography, or high performance

liquid chromatography — are more complex and expensive, but highly advisable from a legal standpoint. Employers should not take disciplinary action against employees — except in extraordinary circumstances — based on the results of a single laboratory test.

4. Enforce the company policy consistently — Critical to employee acceptance of a company's drug abuse prevention program is even-handed enforcement. Perhaps even more important than *what* response an employer takes, is that the *same* response be taken for each similar offense of company policy. Be prepared to take the same action when a "positive" test is confirmed for a long-term, highly placed employee as you do when it involves a newly hired employee whose performance is marginal.

5. Maintain thorough, secure, and confidential records — For both drug test results and reports on drug-related accidents or incidents, a secure and comprehensive documentation record should be established and maintained. The best legal defense to disciplinary action based on drug abuse — and an important safeguard for innocent employees — is documentation. Equally important, employers should make every reasonable effort to observe employee expectations of privacy and confidentiality (1) as a sound employee relations policy, and (2) as a precaution against such tort actions as defamation and intentional infliction of emotional distress. Employers also should retain "positive" test samples as evidence for a reasonable period of time.

6. Make sure reliable witnesses are present — When confronting an employee suspected of being under the influence of drugs or involved in any other drug-related incidents, make sure supervisors know how to act and what to say. It is especially important that supervisors do not act alone and that reliable witnesses be present.

7. Document declining performance — The safest legal policy for employers regarding disciplinary action is to document as fully as possible a relationship between an employee's declining performance and the employee's drug use.

8. Request job applicant waivers of legal claims — Employers, as a legal safeguard, may consider requesting — not requiring — a job applicant, at the time that the drug test is administered, to sign a waiver of legal rights of action against the employer. Such releases of employer liability permit both the test and the employer's right to act on the test's results, but must be signed knowingly and willingly.

Of course, a critical first step for employers is the development of a formal written company policy and the effective and repeated communcation of that policy to all employees. Common forms of communication which should be used include company bulletin boards, paycheck envelope inserts, and company newsletters.

When to Test: Seven Options

When an employer decides to include drug testing in its drug abuse prevention program, it must decide under what conditions to test. The options of when and who to test include:

1. Job applicant testing — The drug screening of job applicants prior to employment is the most common employer drug testing practice, has the greatest deterrent effect, and is the most cost-effective — by keeping drug users out of the work force, it helps avoid costly problems involving safety, productivity, and absenteeism.

2. Testing of employees in safety-conscious jobs — Jobs involving the safety, health, and security of the employee, his or her co-workers, and the public represent a compelling public interest and may warrant special employer precautions to assure that its work force is "drug free." Transportation, construction, and utility industries are common examples.

3. Incident-driven drug testing — Specific incidents may trigger employer suspicions of drug abuse and warrant drug testing. A medical emergency which appears to be drug-related, the observance of drugs or drug paraphernalia at an employee's desk or work station, or other evidence that an employee's behavior is influenced by drugs may prompt an incident-driven drug test.

4. Post-accident investigation drug testing — On-the-job accidents which may have involved human error often trigger drug testing of those employees involved. This is common, for example, in investigations of train or mass transit accidents.

5. Retesting of employees during and after rehabilitation — Employees who are, or have participated in, drug rehabilitation programs are commonly and appropriately retested for the presence of drugs in their systems. Continued employment is often predicated on an employee being successfully rehabilitated. Without retesting, successful rehabilitation may be difficult to assure.

6. Periodic drug testing with advance notice — Scheduled in advance, usually as part of an annual employee physical, and uniformly administered, periodic testing is common for jobs involving stress, requiring physical endurance, or involving senior-level decision making.

7. Random, unannounced drug tests — Random testing without pre-notification is most likely to identify drug users. However, it also is most likely to create morale problems and trigger union grievances or employee legal claims. Employers should proceed with caution before selecting this option.

Job Applicants Versus Employees

There are several reasons why the testing of job applicants is much more common than the testing of incumbent employees:

1. Testing of job applicants is more legally defensible than the testing of employees for various reasons:
   a. There is no employer-employee relationship.
   b. There are no issues of job performance.
   c. Employers generally do have a right to make being "drug free" a condition of employment prior to hiring.
   d. Job applicant testing is less likely to be of concern to union representatives than

employee testing, and less likely to result in union-filed grievances.

2. Job denial for applicants, unlike employee dismissals, are not complicated by benefits, severance pay, or pension issues.

3. Job applicant testing is less likely to hurt employee morale than employee drug testing.

4. Job applicant testing, by keeping drug users out of the workforce, is cost-effective because it has a preventive impact on drug-related workplace problems. It also frees up limited employer resources so employers can provide more comprehensive rehabilitation programs for those employees who do develop drug abuse problems (since, presumably, there will be fewer problems due to application drug screening).

5. Job applicant testing is likely to have the greatest deterrent effect since it is disproportionately geared toward young people entering the workforce — the age group for whom drug use is most common — and communicates a forceful and consistent anti-drug abuse policy at the outset of their careers.

Drug Testing and Collective Bargaining

The National Labor Relations Act (NLRA) requires employers whose employees are represented by a union to bargain not only on wages and benefits, but also on terms and conditions of employment. Clearly, drug testing and a requirement that workers be "drug free" are terms and conditions of employment.

Therefore, it is clear that unionized employers cannot act unilaterally to implement drug testing programs. Unionized employers must notify their unions of their intentions and, upon request, bargain in good faith prior to the implementation of drug testing.

Drug testing can only be implemented after: (1) management and labor representatives reach an agreement, or (2) negotiations deadlock in a good faith impasse. While employers are required under the NLRA to bargain in good faith, they are not required to reach an agreement, take a particular position, or make a particular concession.

Special Concerns for Federal Contractors

Companies that receive $2,500 or more in federal contracts, or that receive federal financial assistance such as research grants or Small Business Administration loans, are subject to the Vocational Rehabilitation Act of 1973. The Rehabilitation Act prohibits employers who receive federal funds from discriminating against handicapped persons.

"Handicap" is defined to include: (1) prior drug abuse or alcoholism, and (2) current drug and alcohol abuse, unless this substance abuse detrimentally affects job performance or endangers the employee or others.

As a result, covered employers cannot refuse to hire a job applicant because he or she has a drug abuse history, or ask a job applicant if he or she has ever abused drugs or been treated for drug abuse.

Drug Testing and the Americans with Disabilities Act

With respect to drug testing, the ADA explicitly states that nothing in the law prohibits or restricts either drug testing or employment decisions taken on the basis of such drug tests. Therefore, an applicant who is tested and not hired because of a positive test result for illegal drugs, or an employee who is tested and is terminated because of a positive test result for illegal drugs, does not have a cause of action under the ADA. If an employer performed a test which actually measured the current use of illegal drugs and the test was positive for the use of illegal drugs, the applicant or employee has no protection under the ADA. It is not a question of the employer having a defense in an action by the applicant or employee. The employer needs no such defense because the applicant or the employee has no cause of action. Thus, employers will not face litigation under the ADA on the part of current users of illegal drugs and alcohol either for testing or for taking disciplinary action against such individuals based on such testing.

During the legislative debate on the ADA, an important principle was highlighted. The law recognizes the need to protect employers, workers, and the public from persons whose current illegal drug use impairs their ability to perform a job and whose employment could result in serious harm to the lives or property of others. At the same time, the law recognizes that treatment for those in the grips of substance abuse is not only the compassionate thing to do but an essential component of a comprehensive attack on drugs. Treatment can save the lives of individual abusers, and it can also return them to productive roles in society. By providing protections against discrimination for recovered substance abusers and those in treatment or recovery who are no longer engaged in illegal drug use, the law provides an incentive for treatment. Under the law, no one who seeks treatment and overcomes a drug abuse problem need fear discrimination because of past drug use.

Drivers and Drug Testing

The safe operation of commercial vehicles (includes any truck over 10,001 pounds operating in a business affecting interstate commerce) has become a major area of concern for the American public. As a result, Congress and the Department of Transportation (DOT) have added to, or renewed their emphasis on, motor carrier safety regulations. These DOT regulations provide that no driver shall be on duty if the driver uses any controlled substances. No driver is to be on duty if that individual tests positive for the use of controlled substances. A person who refuses to be tested is not to be permitted to operate a commercial motor vehicle. Additionally, an employer shall require a driver to be tested, upon reasonable cause, for the use of controlled substances. Furthermore, any applicant for a

driving position must be tested for the use of controlled substances.

For further information, interested employers should refer to the applicable DOT regulations.

Drug-Free Workplace Act

The Drug-Free Workplace Act of 1988 provides that federal contractors receiving awards of $25,000 or more must maintain a drug-free workplace. A contractor who fails to comply is subject to suspension of contract payments, and to contract termination, and could be barred from future federal contracts for up to five years. All federal procurement contracts exceeding $25,000 must now contain a clause in which the contractor undertakes to do the following:

- Publish a policy statement notifying employees that the unlawful manufacture, distribution, dispensation, possession, or use of a controlled substance is prohibited in the workplace, and specifying what actions will be taken against employees for violations of such prohibitions;
- Establish a program to inform employees of, among other things, the dangers of drug abuse in the workplace and the availability of drug counseling, rehabilitation, and employee assistance programs;
- Provide all employees working under the contract with a copy of the policy statement;
- Notify the employee in the policy statement that, as a condition of continued employment under the contract, the employee will abide by the statement and notify the employer if he or she is convicted of a criminal drug offense occurring in the workplace within five days after the conviction;
- Notify the contracting officer of an employee conviction within 10 days after the contractor learns of the conviction;
- Within 30 days after receiving notice of a conviction, impose a sanction on the convicted employee, up to and including termination, or require the employee to satisfactorily complete a drug rehabilitation program; and,
- Make a good faith effort to continue to maintain a drug-free workplace by meeting the requirements of the federal legislation.

Questions-and-Answers on the Drug-Free Workplace Act

Q. What is a minimum set of components for an employer program to meet the requirements of the Drug-Free Workplace Act?

A. Each employer must meet the specific requirements of the Act with a good faith effort, including having a policy statement and a drug awareness program. Neither the law nor the final rules require employers to establish an Employee Assistance Program (EAP), to conduct any drug testing, or to incorporate any particular component in an employer's program.

Q. What are examples of other possible components of an employer drug-free workplace program for contractors and grantees?

A. Here is a partial list of other possible components of an employer program. The list is provided for information only; there is no intention for the Federal Government to require any particular component.

Employee Education

Conduct education/outreach of employees/families via:
- Discussion groups on drug abuse/company policy
- Videotapes/pamphlets on drugs in workplace
- Brown bag lunch discussions
- Communication of available employee assistance
- Communication of available health benefits for drug/alcohol treatment

Employee Assistance
- Establish an EAP
- Identify treatment resources
- Assemble resource file on providers of assistance
- Provide problem assessments
- Provide confidential counseling
- Provide referral to counseling and/or treatment
- Provide crisis intervention
- Establish hot-line
- Provide family support services
- Conduct followup during and after treatment
- Conduct evaluation of job performance pre- and post-program contact

- Review insurance coverage (to include outpatient as well as inpatient treatment)
- Institute mechanism to review employee complaints

Supervisory Training

Conduct management/supervisory/union training on:
- Drug Abuse education
- Signs and symptoms of drug use
- Company policy on drug use
- Employee assistance resources
- How to deal with an employee suspected of drug use
- How and when to take disciplinary action

Drug Detection

Institute a program of drug testing of:
- All employees — testing of applicants or pre-employment; testing of employees based on reasonable suspicion, post-accident, during and after counseling and/or rehabilitation
- Employees in health and safety or national security sensitive positions — random unannounced testing

Increase security

Alcoholism and Employers

Alcohol abuse remains the most widespread and debilitating form of drug abuse in America and for American businesses.

Twelve million Americans are alcoholics, and another 90 million are "social drinkers" who have alcohol at least once a month.

While alcohol does not pose a danger to most people who drink it, it does remain a common and costly problem which adversely affects the workplace with:

■ Increased absenteeism

■ Reduced productivity

■ Increased accident rates

■ Increased health care costs

Between seven and nine percent of all workers abuse alcohol — four times the abuse rate for marijuana.

Employers are unwise if they implement prevention and rehabilitation programs for drug abuse, but ignore alcohol abuse. The annual cost of alcohol abuse to business is nearly equivalent to that for drug abuse.

Employers need to address both problems — alcohol and drug abuse — in parallel programs which are humane and effective.

Under the Americans with Disabilities Act, an employer may hold an employee who is an alcoholic to the same qualification standards for employment or job performance and behavior that the employer holds other employees, even if an unsatisfactory performance or behavior is related to the alcoholism of the employee. Thus, an employer under the reasonable accommodation provisions of the ADA does not have to provide a rehabilitation program or an opportunity for rehabilitation for any job applicant who is an alcoholic or for any current employee who is an alcoholic.

Alcohol Control Program Checklist

☐ Provide policy statement affirming the belief that alcoholism is an illness that can be treated successfully in most cases. The employer must show a readiness to help those with drinking problems.

☐ Both employer and employees should jointly develop and administer the program.

☐ Make available information and education about the nature of alcohol so as to dispell myths. The problem requires an intelligent response based upon facts.

☐ Middle management or, in larger companies, the first level supervisor, are the key individuals to insure implementation of an effective control program. These individuals are in daily contact with the largest part of the workforce and can most easily detect the signs of a person who needs help. They must be trained to recognize the signs of declining performance and how to approach the problem with an employee.

☐ Professional staff services must be chosen once a troubled employee is identified. There must be someone to whom the employee can be referred for diagnoses and assistance. The referral is usually to a doctor, but the function can also be performed by a nurse, psychologist, counselor, personnel worker, or other staff specialist. While these latter persons may be able to provide a counseling function, treatment should be left to private physicians or hospitals.

☐ Early identification of the problem should be emphasized. An alcoholic will be masterful at developing rationales to deny the existence of a problem.

☐ There should be controls in place to be sure that ongoing efforts are not abandoned once an employee has been referred for assistance. Information should be gathered to review the progress made by employees who have been referred for aid.

☐ The records of people who voluntarily seek assistance should be maintained. If employees know this will occur, they will be more likely to make effective use of the treatment program.

Setting Up an Alcohol Assistance Program

Alcohol abuse is one of the major reasons for lost productivity in the workforce and is a major element contributing to growing healthcare costs. Employers who want to reduce costs from ineffective performance by impaired workers, accidents, lost time from work, and disability, should consider the possible advantages of establishing an alcohol counseling program.

Any alcohol counseling program must be aggressive in its efforts to discover and control the problem. Early detection is the key, as the employee must be persuaded to admit the problem exists, or the employer must take more coercive action by requiring the employee to straighten up work performance or face discharge. The initial step, then, is getting the employee some sort of professional help either through in-house referral or through staff employed by the firm.

AIDS in the Workplace **14**

What AIDS Is and Is Not

Acquired Immune Deficiency Syndrome (AIDS) is a major — and growing — health problem for American society. Its impact on workplace relationships is significant, and will become even greater in the future.

AIDS is a relatively new and highly misunderstood health problem. Understanding what AIDS is — and is not — is a critical first step to addressing and preventing the disease and the fears that accompany it. Education regarding AIDS is also critical to minimizing afflicted employees' suffering, workplace disruption, and legal challenges against employers.

1. What AIDS Is — AIDS is a condition that destroys a person's natural ability to fight disease. AIDS leaves a person vulnerable to diseases that would not otherwise be life-threatening. AIDS is caused by a virus which enters the blood system and kills T-cells, the type of white blood cells necessary to prevent the disease by sustaining the body's immune system. The virus, human T-cell lymphotrophic virus type-III, is commonly referred to as HIV virus or HTLV-III. Not everyone infected with the HIV virus will develop AIDS. The body does not attempt to counterattack the virus by producing antibodies, referred to as AIDS antibodies.

At the present time, how the virus works and how it evolves into the AIDS condition is not totally known. While AIDS has become the short-hand description for this health care problem, it is only the tip of the iceberg. At this time, AIDS is incurable and, in its advanced stages, is most often — if not always — fatal. Currently, there is no vaccine to prevent AIDS.

2. How AIDS Is Transmitted — The HIV virus is an infectious disease contagious in the way that sexually transmitted diseases such as syphilis and gonorrhea are. It is not contagious in the way of a common cold, or the measles.

AIDS can be prevented by refraining from high risk behavior. In the overwhelming majority of cases (more than 90 percent), the HIV virus is transmitted by either sexual contact — usually involving homosexual or bisexual men — or shared use of intravenous needles and syringes.

However, heterosexual transmission is expected to account for an increasing proportion of those infected with the HIV virus in the future. Furthermore, persons with hemophilia and other blood coagulation disorders, and infants born to HIV-infected mothers, also account for a relatively small but growing number of AIDS cases (1 percent of the total each).

AIDS is not spread by common everyday behavior. You cannot be infected with the HIV virus from such casual social contact as shaking hands, hugging, social kissing, crying, coughing, or sneezing. Futhermore, AIDS is not transmitted from eating in cafeterias or restaurants, even if a food service worker is infected, and is not contracted from using public restrooms, water fountains, shower facilities, telephones, office machinery, furniture, towels, dishes, or door knobs.

3. Identified High Risk Groups — Homosexual and bisexual men are, by far, the highest risk group for AIDS. Nearly three out of every four AIDS victims have been homosexual or bisexual males. Intravenous drug users also are a high risk population. One study of intravenous drug users in New York City found that nearly nine out of ten had been exposed to the HIV virus.

Hemophiliacs, because they receive frequent blood transfusions, are also at high risk. Although they only account for one percent of all AIDS victims, studies have shown that as many as 72 percent of all hemophiliacs may have been exposed to the virus.

4. AIDS Symptoms — The majority of persons infected with the HIV virus show no symptoms. Some develop symptoms after a latency period (time from infection to illness) of as long as nine years. Symptoms include persistent tiredness, fever, weight loss, diarrhea, night sweats, and swollen glands.

5. The Stages of AIDS — There are three stages of HIV-infected conditions: seropositive, AIDS-related complex (ARC), and AIDS.

The first stage is exposure to the HIV virus, an exposure which produces an AIDS antibody. The presence of this antibody in the blood system is called seropositive. The U.S. Public Health Service estimates that 1.5 million Americans are seropositive. All are capable of transmitting the virus through homosexual and heterosexual contact or through use of shared needles or syringes. Most will not suffer impaired immune systems or any of the clinical symptoms associated with ARC or AIDS. However, medical experts predict that between 20 and 30 percent of these 1.5 million seropositive Americans will advance to more severe and life-threatening stages of AIDS within five years.

The second stage, AIDS-related complex (ARC), is characterized by the existence of one or more of the symptoms of AIDS for at least three months. Although the immune system is not as severely impaired as it is for those with AIDS, ARC itself can be fatal and is almost certain to lead to AIDS.

The third, and almost certainly fatal stage is AIDS, a natural progression of infection by the HIV virus. With the destruction of the body's immune system, otherwise controllable infections invade the body and cause additional diseases. The final stage after HIV virus infection — the AIDS condition — usually is fatal within two years.

6. Treatment — While neither a cure for AIDS nor a preventive vaccine exists, medical research and testing is being pursued vigorously. There has been some success in developing drugs which inhibit the HIV virus on a short-term basis, thereby extending the lives of AIDS victims. However, these drugs do not restore the immune capabilities, and AIDS, to date, remains incurable.

7. Prevention — On a personal level, restraint is the key to the prevention of AIDS. The risk of AIDS increases dramatically for certain active — not passive — personal behavior. The safest course of action is to refrain from "casual" sexual contact, particularly with homosexual and bisexual males or the female partners of bisexual males. Multiple sexual partners or sexual contact with a partner whose sexual background and experience is unknown obviously increases the risk of infection. A wide range of health and medical professionals have recommended the use of condoms as an AIDS-preventive precaution during sexual contact.

Similarly, personal restraint regarding intravenous drug use — advisable for many reasons — is critical to AIDS prevention. Risk of HIV virus infection exists when needles and syringes are shared.

On an employment level, dissemination of information on the causes of AIDS is critical to help prevent its spread.

Education is of paramount importance in the health care industry because a small number of workers in this industry actually are at a higher risk than normal of contracting an HIV virus infection.

Care and instruction must be maintained in the collection, storage, handling, and testing of blood and other body fluids, and in the administration of transfusions and other intravenous injections.

Extent of the AIDS Problem

The number of persons with the HIV virus infection and the AIDS condition is growing exponentially. There have been more AIDS cases identified in the last year than in the entire period prior to last year and dating back to the first identified American case in 1981. U.S. Public Health Service data indicate that AIDS already is at epidemic proportions.

Furthermore, the public at large is increasingly at risk. While more than two-thirds of the current AIDS victims are homosexual or bisexual men, that percentage is decreasing and is likely to decrease further as heterosexual transmission increases.

1. The Human Costs of AIDS — Since 1981, when the Center on Disease Control began to compile statistics on the AIDS epidemic, 112,241 cases have been reported in the U.S. Of those individuals, 66,493 have died. These figures, however, reflect only the reported cases. Health officials believe that between 800,000 and 1.5 million people are infected with the HIV virus, but do not have AIDS symptoms.

2. The Economic Costs of AIDS — In 1987, the average lifetime hospital cost of AIDS patients was $147,000 per patient. This estimate was based on surveys finding an average hospital stay of 168 days, an average survival time of 392 days (approximately 13 months), and an average hospital charge of $878 per day per AIDS patient.

Within the next two years, the estimated direct cost of medical care for people with AIDS is expected to range between $2.5 and $15.1 billion.

For the individual, the question is how can an AIDS victim and his or her family afford even the minimal direct medical costs associated with the condition? For the company, the questions involve higher health insurance and other benefit costs at a time when health care costs already have skyrocketed.

These problems are exacerbated by the expected six-fold increase in the number of AIDS patients in the next few years. The strain on the health care industry, insurance carriers, insurance policy holders, and company benefit plans will be enormous. These costs and effects need to be addressed promptly and effectively.

Furthermore, while medical research to date has produced several drugs for AIDS treatment, only one has been approved and is commercially available, at a very high cost. Other drugs which may be available soon also are expected to be very expensive and to offer only short-term relief. While some of these drugs appear temporarily to arrest the health deterioration of AIDS victims, they currently offer no hope of recovery. While they prolong survival time, they also can prolong suffering and require continued and substantial expense. In this regard, these drugs and continued medical developments could produce mixed results — a "good news/bad news" practical effect on AIDS victims. They also could have profound ramifications on the costs incurred by an employer for an AIDS-afflicted employee.

Of course, health care costs are only one element of the economic costs of AIDS. The indirect costs (lost productivity and lost income) are estimated to be nearly three-and-a-half times the direct medical costs. Furthermore, *Business Week* reported that lost productivity due to illness and premature deaths caused by AIDS could cost American businesses more than $55 billion in 1991 alone.

The business community, like society as a whole, has an immense stake in the AIDS crisis.

Guidelines for Employers

The U.S. Public Health Service, through the Centers for Disease Control (CDC), has issued guidelines for preventing transmission of the HIV virus in the workplace.

1. General Guidelines — The CDC guidelines for employers include two critical points:

AIDS Testing

Don't do it.

This is not only good advice for individuals regarding high risk behavior, it also is good advice for most employers regarding testing of employees for the presence of the AIDS antibody.

1. Testing for AIDS — There is no test for AIDS, only testing which may detect the presence of the AIDS antibody in the blood system, a presence that indicates past exposure to the HIV virus. No test currently exists which can determine if a person has or will get AIDS.

2. Testing for the AIDS Antibody — Normally, exposure to viral infections produces antibodies in the blood that help the immune system resist the spread of the infection. However, while exposure to the HIV virus does create antibodies, these antibodies do not assist the immune system in preventing development of the AIDS condition.

There are several tests available which can determine if a person is seropositive, the first stage of AIDS. These tests detect the AIDS antibody in the blood system, a presence that only can be produced following exposure to the HIV virus.

These tests do not indicate whether a person will develop or transmit AIDS, nor do they indicate whether a person is still infected. A positive test does indicate however, that the individual should take extra precautions to avoid transmission of the HIV virus.

3. Testing of Employees — This test is of little practical value to employers because it is:

   a. Inconclusive as to whether the tested person will ever get the AIDS condition, be incapacitated for work, or require extensive benefits,
   b. Prohibited or severely restricted in a significant number of states and cities and with more prohibitions and restrictions pending and likely to be enacted in the near future,
   c. Inconclusive in that a negative test result still can mean that a person is seropositive because there is a time lag between exposure and the development of antibodies, and
   d. Likely to create a potential plaintiff cause of action against an employer by an employee or a job applicant, even if no job action is taken based upon the results of the test.

This last point — the possibility that the employer will face litigation which is expensive and difficult to defend against — is sufficient reason alone not to require tests for the AIDS antibody. The difficulty of defending against such litigation is based on the current medical consensus that there is *no risk* of transmission of the HIV virus to co-workers or customers in the overwhelming majority of employment situations.

Furthermore, the U.S. Public Health Service states that compulsory testing of individuals for the AIDS antibody is "not necessary," and that the procedures could be "unmanageable and cost prohibitive."

a. "No known risk of transmission to co-workers, clients, or consumers exists."

b. "Workers known to be infected (with the HIV virus) should not be restricted based on this finding."

2. Health Care Workers — Generally, our nation's 6.8 million health care workers are at no greater risk of exposure to the HIV virus than the population in general. However, there is potential for exposure if precautions are not taken, particularly as the number of AIDS patients increases. Obviously, careful handling of needles and syringes by health care workers is vital.

The CDC recommendations for the health care industry (hospitals, laboratories, nursing homes, clinics, and doctors' and dentists' offices) include:

■ "Extraordinary care" in the use of needles, syringes, scalpels, and other sharp items to prevent accidental injuries (including the prompt disposal of contaminated needles and syringes in puncture-proof containers)

■ The use of gloves and, as necessary, gowns, masks, and eye-coverings when dealing with blood and other body fluids

■ The use of mouth pieces, resuscitation bags, or other ventilation devices to minimize the risks of transmission during mouth-to-mouth resuscitation

■ Proper sterilization and disinfection procedures

■ Proper disposal of infected body wastes

■ The need for health care workers to consider all patients as potentially infected with the HIV virus

■ The need for health care workers with skin lesions or dermatitis to refrain from direct patient care and equipment handling until such conditions clear up

■ The necessity of employer-provided education and training programs for all health care workers

■ The necessity of employer monitoring of workplace practices to assure adherence to these recommended precautions

The CDC notes, significantly, that at this time the hepatitis B virus poses a much greater risk than the HIV virus to health care workers.

Regarding hepatitis B, the HIV virus, or any other infectious disease, the keys for health care workers are good personal hygiene and safe practices appropriate and necessary to any normal hospital setting.

The CDC recommendations are common sense and would be appropriate even without the risk of HIV virus infection. The possibility of HIV virus infection merely makes the consequences of carelessness or an accident much greater.

It is important that these guidelines be known and observed not just by employers and employees in the health care industry, but also by those individuals in any company responsible for medical treatment and first aid. Failure to assure compliance with these guidelines by the company nurse, for example, could unnecessarily subject more employees to AIDS and could subject the company to tort claims of negligence.

3. Personal Service Workers — Another area of heightened public and worker concern about AIDS exposure is personal services — jobs involving close personal contact with clients, such as hairdressers, barbers, cosmetologists, manicurists, and massage therapists.

There have been no reported cases of transmission of the HIV virus between personal service workers and their clients. Worker, client, and public fears appear to be unjustified.

Nonetheless, precautions should be taken so that:

a. Open lesions do not come in contact with the blood or other body fluids of an HIV virus carrier

b. Instruments contaminated with blood are sterilized and disinfected

4. Food Service Workers — Like personal service workers, food service workers and the people they come in contact with on the job are at virtually no additional risk of HIV virus infection. There is no recorded case of AIDS being transmitted through the preparation or serving of foods or beverages.

Nonetheless, food service workers — including cooks, caterers, waiters, dishwashers, bartenders, and flight attendants — should take precautions. These include:

a. Following established standards for good personal hygiene
b. Refraining from preparing or serving foods if they have open lesions
c. Taking care to avoid hand injuries such as cuts during food preparation
d. Disposing of food contaminated with blood

Food service workers who are infected with the HIV virus need not be restricted from their jobs unless they have other medical conditions which would justify removal or reassignment for any other worker. For an employer to take such a job action would invite litigation.

Under the provisions of the Americans with Disabilities Act, an individual who has an infectious or communicable disease that is transmitted through the handling of food may be reassigned to a job not involving food handling. The underlying requirement of the ADA is simply that a reasonable accommodation must be made if such accommodation will eliminate the risk of the disease being transmitted in the particular job. For example, if an individual has an infectious disease that can be eliminated by taking medication for a specified period of time, the employer must offer the employee the reasonable accommodation of allowing the individual time off to take such medication. Unless the Secretary of Health and Human Services puts HIV on a list of infectious and communicable diseases that are transmitted through handling the food supply, it will be a violation of the ADA to take any adverse action involving such an individual carrying the HIV virus. This list will be updated annually, and is intended to reassure the public that the Secretary will review the relevant scientific and medical evidence regarding the transmissibility of diseases through food handling.

AIDS and the Vocational Rehabilitation Act

The Vocational Rehabilitation Act of 1973 applies to: (1) federal contractors or subcontractors receiving $2,500 or more in federal funds, and

(2) all employers who receive federal funds or federal financial assistance through grants or loans. This Act prohibits discrimination against "qualified handicapped individuals."

It appears extremely likely that the Rehabilitation Act would apply in the AIDS context. Although technically unresolved by law, there is sufficient related case law to suggest that AIDS is a "handicap" and that the Rehabilitation Act therefore prohibits discrimination against individuals with AIDS who appear to be "otherwise qualified" for employment.

In a 1987 case, the Supreme Court pointed out that a person should not be denied access to employment simply because of ignorance and the "irrational fears" of others — a decision with obvious implications for the AIDS issue. The Court held that the Rehabilitation Act applies to both those individuals who are actually impaired *and* those who are regarded or perceived to be impaired by others. A 1988 Justice Department opinion, based on the Supreme Court decision, concluded that a person with AIDS or the HIV virus should be protected by the Act.

The Rehabilitation Act therefore is likely to prohibit covered businesses from discriminating against job applicants or employees with AIDS unless their medical condition: (1) so detrimentally affects job performance that they cannot perform the duties of their jobs, or (2) continued employment poses a significant risk of communicating the disease to others in the workplace.

Futhermore, application of the Rehabilitation Act to job applicants and employees with AIDS also imposes on employers a duty of "reasonable accommodation." Businesses must provide an available job to an AIDS victim as a handicapped individual as long as he or she is "otherwise qualified" and able to perform the job, or can do so by being reasonably accommodated. "Reasonable accommodation" typically may involve: (1) the transfer of a handicapped individual no longer capable of performing his or her job to another job which is reasonably available under the employer's current policies, (2) the modification of workplace facilities and equipment to make them more accessible, or (3) the tailoring of work schedules to increase flexibility.

"Reasonable accommodation" does *not* require creation of a job, nor does it require an employer to incur undue financial or administrative burdens, or fundamentally alter the nature of the business being performed.

The AIDS Issue's Impact on Employment Laws

AIDS in the workplace presents numerous personnel and legal issues for employers. Those issues often have crossover effects on other labor and employment laws:

1. The OSHA "General Duty Clause" — The Occupational Safety and Health Act's general duty clause requires employers to provide employment and a workplace "free from recognized hazards that are causing or likely to cause death or serious harm." Based on current medical evidence, virtually no employer or employee could prove that the mere presence of, or working relationship with, a co-worker with AIDS creates a "recognized hazard." Futhermore, various federal and state "right-to-know" laws cannot be reasonably interpreted to require employers to disclose to co-workers the presence of an HIV virus carrier or AIDS victim in the workforce.

2. NLRA — Under the National Labor Relations Act, the decision by a unionized employer to implement AIDS testing in the workplace for current employees is clearly a mandatory subject of collective bargaining. Furthermore, based on the NLRB General Counsel's September 1987 memorandum on drug testing (a similar legal issue), it appears likely that AIDS testing for job applicants also would be considered a mandatory subject of bargaining (at least by the General Counsel's side of the NLRB).

3. ERISA — The Employee Retirement Income Security Act has a handicap anti-discrimination provision which may apply to employees with AIDS. Furthermore, ERISA prohibits employers from discharging or otherwise discriminating against employees "for the purpose of interfering with the attainment of any right" to which the employee is entitled under an ERISA-covered benefit plan. Although there is no case on point to date, ERISA *may* prohibit an employer from dismissing an employee in order to avoid anticipated expenses under medical, long-term disability, or other benefit plans.

4. Workers' Compensation — An employee who proved that he or she contracted the HIV virus on the job from an infected co-worker during the normal performance of his or her duties would be entitled to workers' compensation payments. However, to date, establishing such eligibility would be extremely difficult. It also is possible that employees could claim workers' compensation coverage because of psychiatric conditions which have disabled them based on a good faith fear of contracting the HIV virus from a co-worker. However, such a scenario is theoretical and could be rebutted by evidence of an employer-provided educational program on AIDS.

5. Unemployment Compensation — Unemployment compensation may be available to AIDS victims and co-workers. If a worker is dismissed because he or she is suspected of having AIDS, he or she would be entitled to unemployment compensation, absent a demonstration by the employer that the employee currently was unable to perform his or her job responsibilities. A co-worker of an employee with AIDS who voluntarily resigns from work due to a reasonable, good faith fear of harm to his or her health from contact with the co-worker, also could be entitled to unemployment compensation benefits. However, as discussed in the case of workers' compensation, demonstration that the employer provided factual information about AIDS could rebut this claim.

State and Local Laws Prohibiting AIDS Testing

While there is no federal law that has been enacted that specifically addresses AIDS and employment issues, the number of state and local laws that have been enacted is growing.

125

These laws generally protect AIDS victims against workplace discrimination by prohibiting employers from either requiring tests for the AIDS antibody or acting upon the results of those tests.

At least 20 states now have laws either defining AIDS as a protected handicap or expressly prohibiting discrimination against persons with AIDS or those who have tested positive for the HIV virus. Only two states—Georgia and Kentucky—have gone against the trend by enacting statutes that specifically exclude communicable diseases, such as AIDS, from their states' statutory definition of handicap. Many local jurisdictions have also enacted ordinances banning discrimination against persons with AIDS.

The scope of these statutes varies greatly. In California, state law specifically bans the use of test results for determining suitability for employment. In Maine, insurers, nonprofit hospitals, medical service organizations, or nonprofit health care plans are prohibited from requiring persons to reveal whether they have been tested for AIDS prior to applying for insurance. In a number of states, employers are prohibited from requiring AIDS tests as a condition of employment, and many states require the consent of the individual prior to testing for the HIV virus.

Clearly, the law in this area is still evolving, particularly at the state and local levels. Employers are advised to keep abreast of the laws regarding AIDS and the workplace — laws that, like the AIDS cases themselves, are multiplying in number and complexity.

Ten Employer Concerns About AIDS

Employers certainly are concerned for their workers who are AIDS victims. However, they also are concerned about AIDS victims' co-workers and their willingness and ability to work side-by-side with victims of this deadly disease. They also have to be concerned about medical and benefit costs, and the impact the AIDS epidemic will have on their ability to afford and deliver coverage for all workers.

Employer concerns about AIDS should include:

1. Absenteeism
2. Inability to perform job assignments
3. Safety and health
4. Futility of involving victims in long-range employment and training programs
5. Co-worker morale, productivity, and refusals to work
6. Legal liability to co-workers and the public
7. Health insurance costs
8. Liability insurance costs
9. Workers' compensation costs
10. Unknown health risks

These concerns may be valid in the eyes of an employer, but most would not be valid defenses in the eyes of the law.

The best available and only truly workable legal defenses to AIDS handicap claims are absenteeism (#1 on the above list) and inability to perform job assignments (#2). These involve more than a "reasonable accommodation," and would, if proven, successfully defend against claims based on any handicap, not just AIDS.

Two other employer concerns have some merit from a legal perspective, but in most instances are unlikely to prevail against allegations of AIDS discrimination. Safety and health (3) has not been shown to be a realistic enough threat to co-workers or the public in virtually any workplace environment to justify exclusion of HIV virus carriers or AIDS victims. Failure of the employer to enroll HIV virus carriers or AIDS victims in long-term employment and training programs (4), because the disease is fatal and the individual would not be employable for a sufficient enough period of time to justify training time and expense, has some marginal merit as a defense, but only regarding those employees at advanced stages of the illness.

Co-worker morale and control of the workforce (5) is never a valid basis for discrimination, and although it certainly may be a valid employer concern, it is not a valid legal defense to claims of handicap discrimination.

Similarly, employer concerns about potential liability (6) or health care, liability insurance, and workers' compensation costs (7, 8, and 9) may be valid concerns, but are irrelevant to the legal process.

Finally, unknown health risks (10) do present a variable to the equation. Recognizing that medical and scientific research regarding AIDS is still in the embryonic stage, and that a great deal remains unknown or uncertain — even about the causes and transmission of AIDS and the HIV virus — employers, like all members of American society, remain somewhat in a "holding pattern" regarding the ultimate resolution of AIDS issues.

Co-Workers and AIDS

The fear and misunderstanding regarding AIDS and its victims is pervasive in the workplace. Co-workers can be confused, afraid, and bitter towards those employees who are afflicted. A potentially disruptive, costly, and even cruel workplace situation can arise — however irrational or unfounded it may be.

Employers must act to defuse such explosive situations. Step one is education — informing the workforce about AIDS and how it is and is not transmitted. Explaining to workers that there is no known danger of transmission occupationally in virtually any business setting can help alleviate unfounded fears. Nonetheless, unreasonable and reasonable fears exist and will continue to exist, and that is why a comprehensive and fair employer program, as outlined in this chapter, can be both necessary and appropriate.

Two potential legal claims by the co-workers of HIV virus carriers or AIDS victims currently exist: (1) concerted refusal to work, and (2) negligent exposure.

Employees' refusal to work with a co-worker who is an HIV virus carrier or AIDS victim, even though the fear is unfounded, may still be a "protected concerted activity" under the National Labor Relations Act. All that is required is a "good faith, reasonable belief" in the danger, not a well-founded or justifiable fear.

If the refusal to work is "protected," an employer cannot take disciplinary action or discharge employees for refusing to work. However, an employer can hire replacements.

Furthermore, if the collective bargaining agreement includes a "no strike" clause, an employer may be able to discipline employees for violation of this provision.

Employees also could sue based on a claim of negligent exposure to an HIV virus carrier in the workplace. However, the current medical consensus recognizing only non-occupational AIDS transmission, and the Rehabilitation Act's very probable prohibition of employer discrimination against those with the "handicap" of AIDS who are "otherwise qualified," certainly provide adequate defenses.

Potential Tort Claims for AIDS Testing

Employers also may face legal claims in tort law for either (1) testing employees for the presence of the AIDS antibody or (2) unnecessarily revealing to personnel the medical condition of an HIV virus carrier or AIDS victim. These causes of action in tort law include:

1. Invasion of Privacy — An employee has a reasonable expectation of privacy, especially regarding medical conditions. This right is balanced by the courts with the employer's need to know. The actual taking of a blood sample, because it is an invasive procedure, also may be claimed by an employee/plaintiff to be an invasion of privacy.

2. Defamation — Employees may bring an action in tort law because information was revealed about the employee to persons in the workforce without a need to know. Disclosure of information regarding an employee's medical condition or status as a carrier of the HIV virus, or statements or information-sharing by an employer that created or contributed to the co-worker's or the public's inference or perception that an employee is homosexual, bisexual, or an intravenous drug user, all can serve as the basis of legal actions.

3. Intentional Infliction of Emotional Distress — A cause of action also may arise if an employee is subjected to an AIDS test under threat of termination, feels there are attempts to "drive"

Checklist to Minimize Liability on AIDS

AIDS is a major health problem in the United States — a health problem for society and for businesses. In the workplace, AIDS presents numerous personnel, benefits, and legal issues to employers.

The *wrong* employer response can: (1) exacerbate the suffering of AIDS victims, (2) perpetuate unfounded fears in the workforce (thereby causing unnecessary disruption and loss of productivity), and (3) subject employers to lengthy and costly litigation. The *right* employer response to AIDS is not only fair and humane, it is cost-effective.

Legal risks regarding AIDS can be minimized for employers if they follow these recommendations:

☐ Issue a formal, written company policy on AIDS and communicate that policy to all workers.

☐ Include in the company policy a provision that a refusal to work by a co-worker of an HIV virus-afflicted employee is subject to discipline.

☐ Educate employees about AIDS, its causes, prevention, and relevance to the workplace. Emphasize the virtually unanimous medical consensus that there is no risk of contracting AIDS in a normal working environment.

☐ Make every reasonable and appropriate effort to preserve the confidentiality and right of privacy of HIV virus-infected and AIDS-afflicted employees, limiting dissemination of medical reports and other information only to those persons with a need to know.

☐ Treat AIDS victims who, as a result of their illness, are no longer able to perform their job responsibilities, the same way the company treats any other worker with a life-threatening or debilitating illness.

☐ Coordinate the efforts of benefits, legal, medical, and personnel staff members or advisors to assure that your company's policies: (1) are consistent with current legal and legislative developments in this evolving area of employment law, (2) assure not only fairness, but also consistency of response to employees, and (3) are revised to reflect up-to-date medical and scientific evaluations of the AIDS problem.

☐ Provide gloves, eye-covers, masks, and other protective items as necessary and on request for those employees exposed to human blood or other body fluids on the job.

☐ Implement a comprehensive drug abuse prevention program to deter drug abuse and rehabilitate drug abusers, with a particular emphasis on prevention of intravenous drug use.

☐ Monitor adherence to company rules and guidelines for work practices designed to eliminate or minimize employee exposure to the HIV virus.

☐ Train company medical staff, nurses, safety and health specialists, and those responsible for first aid about the dangers of certain exposures to open wounds or lesions, and the advisability, if feasible, of using protective inserts when administering mouth-to-mouth resuscitation.

☐ Do not implement mandatory testing of employees for the AIDS antibody or other screening procedures to detect job applicants infected by the HIV virus (due to testing's limited utility and reliability, and the high probability of legal challenges to such screenings).

☐ Assume that every employee infected with the HIV virus, no matter at what stage of AIDS — seropositive, ARC, or AIDS — is covered by handicap discrimination laws and, accordingly: (1) take steps to reasonably accommodate, and (2) do not take adverse employment action (dismissal, unwanted transfer, or job or promotion denial) against employees based solely on their medical condition absent other substantial legal justification (such as extensive absenteeism or inability to perform job responsibilities).

☐ Allow HIV virus-afflicted workers to continue to work as long as they are able and willing to, provided that their remaining on the job does not pose a safety or health threat to others or a heightened safety or health threat to themselves.

What Employers Should Know About AIDS

Employers need to know the facts about AIDS for several reasons. The well being of employees is a major concern, and employers want to protect them from discrimination related to illness. Employers also need to protect their business from legal challenges stemming from the treatment of workers with AIDS.

Everything an employer needs to know about AIDS in the workplace is based on conclusive scientific evidence. Employers already know enough to prevent the spread of AIDS and to calm fears among employees and managers.

Generally, employers should treat people with AIDS the same as they would treat people with a serious illness such as cancer. Employers should respect their need for confidentiality and be compassionate. Employers need to use good judgment and know about the laws that apply to employees with AIDS.

Important Facts about AIDS:

1. Acquired immune deficiency syndrome (AIDS) is caused by a virus known as the Human Immunodeficiency Virus (HIV). Over one million Americans are infected with HIV. Most, if not all of them, will experience a variety of illnesses, symptoms, and disabling conditions over several years and will eventually die of related conditions.

2. Many new cases of AIDS will be among heterosexuals and will appear outside of the major cities already affected — in people 20 to 40 years old. The number of "AIDS cases" we read about so often is only the tip of the iceberg: Many more people have AIDS-related conditions caused by HIV. The HIV infection is treatable, but not curable. There is no vaccine to prevent infection, but infection can be prevented through education and by changing certain behaviors.

3. A company-wide AIDS policy should be developed before it is needed (a sample draft of one is included in the Appendix). This will benefit your employees and protect your company by ensuring that you are aware of the legal protections afforded people with AIDS. If an employee tells you he or she has AIDS, you may violate employee confidentiality by calling a meeting to ask for compassion from co-workers. At that point, issuing a policy may not work. It is better to act *before* an employee gets AIDS. Surveys show that many businesses already have employees with AIDS.

4. AIDS cannot be transmitted in typical workplace activities among employees or between customers and employees. AIDS is *not* transmitted though sweat, tears, or saliva. The virus does *not* survive on telephones, paper, or even food.

5. Prudent managers do not discriminate. The Rehabilitation Act of 1973 and the Americans with Disabilities Act of 1990 prohibit discrimination against the handicapped. Almost every state and many local governments have similar laws. Courts and regulatory agencies have ruled that AIDS is a handicap and should be treated like other handicapping conditions, and damages have been awarded to employees who experienced discrimination.

   Consult your own legal counsel to inquire about the legal precedents that exist in your state and locale. Meanwhile, prudent managers will treat an employee with AIDS like other employees, because it is best for the business and best for the employee.

6. Confidentiality of employee health information must be strictly protected to avoid lawsuits and to protect your employees' rights. Again, your lawyer can cite applicable laws in your state; meanwhile, follow the spirit of the laws and guard health information carefully.

7. Company health plans can benefit employees with AIDS — and keep health costs down at the same time. Expanding health benefits to include home health care *now* will probably reduce unnecessary hospitalization costs later.

What Employers Should Know About AIDS (continued)

The Presidential Commission on the HIV epidemic notes that only about 1.4 percent of the nation's overall health care costs will be attributed to the AIDS virus by 1991. Just as home health care is the best medical strategy for people with AIDS, it is also the best strategy for employers who need to control health benefits costs.

8. Employment should continue for persons who develop AIDS. People who test positive now for evidence of the HIV virus may work for years before they have any symptoms of the disease. Even with symptoms, they will *not* be contagious at the workplace, and good managers will make accommodations so they can continue to work as called for in relevant laws. Indeed, the availability of continued employment for individuals with an illness can be therapeutic.

9. Everyone should know how the HIV virus is transmitted and how to prevent the spread of the virus. Lives can be saved through education.

10. Education of all employees, including top management, is needed *before* the first case of an employee with AIDS arises and causes concerns. Although we know that AIDS cannot be transmitted by casual contact in the workplace, employees who do not know this may have some fears about the illness. These fears may lead to disruption of work flow or unnecessary complaints to supervisors or regulatory agencies. Education about AIDS can help reduce these problems.

Your local chapter of the American Red Cross can send a trained group leader to your business to explain how AIDS is transmitted and how to prevent the spread of AIDS. Brochures, videotapes, and other educational materials are available.

---

him or her out of the workforce which are encouraged or condoned by the employer, or is ridiculed, humiliated, or otherwise treated in a careless or undignified manner regarding his or her medical condition.

4. Assault and Battery — The administration of a blood test in order to test for the presence of the AIDS antibody involves physical contact of an invasive nature which could be considered offensive, harmful, or threatening to an individual — especially if their consent to the test was uninformed, reluctant, or otherwise tainted — and could lead to additional legal claims of assault and battery.

How to Discharge **15**
Employees and Avoid Liability

An Overview

The termination of an employee can be traumatic for the employee, and at the same time it is one of the most onerous and sensitive tasks that an employer has to perform. Because of these circumstances, there is probably no chapter in this book that will be turned to for guidance as often as this one will be. Today, every employer's decision to dismiss an employee represents a potential lawsuit.

At the heart of the issue is the conflict between two legal concepts, one favoring employers and the other, employees.

Employment-at-will is a pro-employer doctrine that states, in the absence of an agreement that specifically fixes the term of employment, that an employee is free to resign and an employer is free to dismiss its employees at any time and for any reason. Thus, resignation by, or dismissal of, employees can be for good cause, inappropriate cause, or no cause at all.

On the other hand, wrongful discharge is a more recent legal development and is pro-employee. This concept states that employees have a right to their jobs and can only be dismissed for "just cause." As plaintiffs, dismissed workers claiming wrongful discharge can seek such court-ordered remedies as back pay, punitive damages, and reinstatement.

Before discussing these two legal concepts in greater depth, it is proper to deal with the termination itself.

Termination: A Planned Event

The decision to discharge an employee should be carefully planned. It is not something to be left to spontaneity. Obviously, the degree of planning is much less necessary in those circumstances where the employee has committed crimes (i.e. theft, assault, etc.) or serious infractions of an employer's work rules or policies.

In the vast majority of dismissals there should be a "paper trail" documenting the circumstances leading to the decision to terminate an individual. If it is insubordination, then the employee's personnel file should have a record of incidences. Signed periodic reviews should reflect earlier dissatisfaction.

If it is a matter of economics, then there should be a straightforward recitation of those facts (i.e. the loss of a major customer or a general business slowdown). What is important in these circumstances is to reveal the true basis for dismissal. There are many wrongful discharge suits that are brought to find the "real reasons" for termination, and some of these could have been avoided by forthrightly explaining the dismissal.

I have often advised employers who were anguishing over a decision to terminate an individual that there is no guaranteed right to a position. The decision to hire or dismiss an employee is ultimately the employer's, but should be based on principles of fairness and respectful of the dignity of employees. If these two guideposts are followed, then there is greater certainty that a disgruntled former employee will not prevail in a wrongful discharge lawsuit.

How to Handle a Termination

The catalyst for a wrongful discharge claim often can be an inappropriately handled notice of termination — a notice that is poorly timed, poorly stated, and/or too publicly handled. A discharged employee who feels that he or she has been humiliated, lied to, or provoked, is much more likely to sue.

In some instances, the decision to dismiss may not be as critically important as how that decision is carried out.

Employers therefore should keep in mind the following recommendations regarding the elements of a termination:

Dismissal — Review all proposed dismissals at a centralized higher management level before they are implemented. Seek clearance from legal counsel. Standardize the methods used for termination. Do not vary in the application of company policies. Give the reasons for the discharge. Be honest, straightforward, and complete. Recognize that timing, tone, and confidentiality are important.

Severance Pay — Be humane. Recognize the hardship and trauma which accompanies worker dislocations. When possible and appropriate, consider providing: (1) a reasonable amount of notice prior to dismissal, (2) a generous severance "package," (3) continuation of benefits for a reasonable time, and (4) outplacement counseling. Such practices help ease the transition for dismissed employees, help maintain the morale of employees continuing in the workforce, lessen the likelihood of legal challenges being filed, and help build a compelling case that the employer has acted fairly.

Releases from Liability — Releases and convenants not to sue should be considered standard procedures in finalizing severance agreements. By signing such agreements, employees forego specified legal remedies and waive their right to sue the employer over the dismissal — generally in return for enhanced severance pay or other benefits. Severance pay should not be disbursed without receipt by the employer of a signed and valid release agreement and covenant not to sue. However, it is important that employees be given a reasonable time to review and confer on the agreements, and that their decision be knowing, willing, and voluntary.

Termination Checklist

☐ Know precisely why the employee is being dismissed; the grounds should be based, obviously, upon nondiscriminatory reasons.

☐ Once the decision is made, set a private appointment in your office to ensure control and privacy. Under no circumstances should the dismissal be done on the telephone or in a social setting.

☐ There is never a "good" time to dismiss, but an early Monday or Tuesday is preferred to a 5:00 p.m. on Friday. Emphasize that after a complete review of all relevant factors, the decision is final and irrevocable.

☐ Keep the meeting brief. Get the bad news across at the outset. Avoid platitudes.

☐ Let the dismissed employee have an opportunity to get his "side" across, without interruption. Yet, keep control of the meeting, and in no way waver in your determination that the decision is final.

☐ Do not discuss the situation with any other employee.

☐ Have any final payroll checks, benefits, or vacation payments prepared in advance.

☐ Regardless of the reason for termination, be sure the employee understands his/her rights regarding employee benefits (e.g. group insurance continuation, pension plan electives, unemployment insurance).

☐ While most employees respond to a dismissal with shock and anger, it rarely reaches the level anticipated or feared by managers.

Employment-At-Will: Origins and Status

Employment-at-will dates back in American legal precedent to 1884. With the coming of the Industrial Revolution and its booming and transient labor markets, nineteenth century American courts abandoned the English common law doctrine that employment was presumed to be for one year in the absence of an agreement to the contrary.

For most of the next century, employment remained "at will." Unless a specific provision in an employment contract stated an agreed-upon duration of employment, employees could quit and employers could terminate as a matter of their own preference.

Employment-at-will is not a federal issue. The overall concept of employment-at-will has not been addressed by the executive branch, the U.S. Congress, or the Supreme Court.

Employment in the United States generally remains "at will," although the scope of the employment-at-will doctrine has been reduced significantly and is under continuing attack in state courts and in state legislatures. This has been particularly true in the last decade.

The erosion of the employment-at-will doctrine began with the rise of organized labor and the inclusion of grievance and arbitration provisions in labor contracts.

However, the real catalyst for change was government intervention into employment relationships. The enactment of federal statutes that created "protected" activities and classes, originated and perpetuated the legal philosophy that: (1) there are non-contractual exceptions to the employment-at-will doctrine, (2) some employee dismissals are contrary to societal interests as a matter of public policy, and (3) the government, in its various forms and at its various levels, has a legitimate role and appropriate interest in regulating employers and advancing employee rights regarding employment matters.

These initial legislative exceptions to the employment-at-will doctrine set in motion further enactments of federal and state laws that prohibited employer job actions against employees: (1) as discriminatory against a protected group, or (2) as retaliatory for the legitimate exercise of employee rights.

However, a much more widespread, pervasive, and controversial erosion of the employment-at-will doctrine has followed, based on the common law claims of discharged employees. Legal challenges that dismissals are (1) against public policy, (2) in breach of implied contract rights, or (3) in breach of implied covenants of good faith and fair dealing have become increasingly commonplace, costly, and disconcerting for employers across the country. This is especially true in California, where wrongful discharge lawsuits have their strongest and deepest roots.

Express Contract Exceptions

Since its inception, the employment-at-will doctrine has been predicated on the absence of an agreed-upon duration of employment.

■ **Collective Bargaining Agreements** — The success that labor unions have had in organizing employees has created a significant exception to the employment-at-will rule. Collective bargaining agreements are, in fact, labor contracts, that besides addressing wages and benefits, also address terms and conditions of employment. Most often collectively bargained labor contracts specify disciplinary procedures. A unionized employer thus has much less fear regarding employee dismissals. In most cases, unionized employers must anticipate the possibility of facing union grievance and arbitration procedures whenever they dismiss an employee.

■ **Specific Contracts With a Definite Period of Employment** — A relatively small but growing number of employees also are excluded from the "at will" rule by employment under contract. Express employment contracts are more formal, more specific, more inflexible, and more likely to be binding on both parties. They also represent an obvious exception to employment-at-will.

With the growth of wrongful discharge litigation, some employers, particularly in

133

California, have decided to use express employment contracts in an attempt to reduce the risks of litigation and liability for employee dismissals.

Statutory Exceptions

There are numerous legislatively determined "public policy" exceptions to the employment-at-will doctrine (in addition to judicially determined public policy exceptions). These exceptions are anti-discrimination or anti-retaliation in nature and are designed to protect employees from dismissal because they: (1) are in a protected class, or (2) exercise their legitimate rights as employees or as private citizens — rights which should not be compromised by employer intimidation.

It is important to keep in mind that these laws do not prohibit employers from dismissing someone in a protected class (e.g. an employee who is a racial minority) or someone who has exercised protected activities (e.g. filed a complaint with a federal agency), but only from dismissing that employee *because* of such factors.

1. Federal Law

■ **Union Activities** — The National Labor Relations Act (NLRA) prohibits employers from dismissing employees because they are union members or supporters, serve as union leaders, participate in union organizing efforts, or engage in any other "protected concerted activity."

■ **Protected Classes** — Title VII of the Civil Rights Act of 1964 prohibits dismissals — and other forms of discrimination in hiring and employment — that are based on race, sex, color, creed, or national origin.

The Age Discrimination in Employment Act (ADEA) extends the same protections to employees over the age of 40.

The Pregnancy Discrimination Act protects female employees from dismissal because of pregnancy, childbirth, or related medical conditions.

The Vocational Rehabilitation Act of 1973 prohibits recipients of federal dollars from discriminating in employment, including employee discharge, against qualified handicapped persons because of their handicap.

The Vietnam Era Veteran Readjustment Assistance Act takes a more specific but time-limited approach: Employers are prohibited from dismissing a reemployed Vietnam veteran within one year after rehiring, without a showing of "good cause."

■ **Exercise of Employee Rights Under Safety and Health and Other Labor Laws** — Beyond the rights of employees to engage in union activities — and those protections afforded minority, handicapped, veteran, and pregnant employees — various other employee rights are protected under federal law.

The Occupational Safety and Health Act prohibits employers from discharging employees because: (1) they refuse to work in a workplace they reasonably believe to be unsafe, or (2) they exercise their rights under the Act, in regard to employer compliance with safety and health standards — including their right to complain about unsafe or unhealthful working conditions to the Occupational Safety and Health Administration (OSHA) and to cooperate and talk with OSHA inspectors. The Federal Mine Safety and Health Act (MSHA) and the Railroad Safety Act have very similar provisions.

Employees also cannot be discriminated against because of the exercise of their rights in regards to the wage and hour law under the Fair Labor Standards Act, or for exercising their right to obtain benefits under a pension plan covered by the Employee Retirement Income Security Act of 1974.

■ **"Whistle Blower" Protections for Employees Under Federal Energy and Environmental Laws** — The Engery Reorganization Act, the Clean Air Act, and the Federal Water Pollution Control Act all prohibit employers from discharging employees who assist or participate in any proceeding to enforce or assure compliance with these acts. As a matter of public policy, Congress has enacted these provisions to encourage such cooperation as well as to discourage employer interference.

■ **Protections for Employees Facing Personal Indebtedness** — Two federal laws also prevent employers from discharging employees because of their personal finance problems. The Bankruptcy Reform Act of 1978 makes it unlawful to fire an employee because he or she has filed for bankruptcy. Similarly, the Consumer Credit Protection Act prohibits dismissal based on a wage garnishment relating to a single instance of indebtedness.

■ **Job Protection for Federal Jurors** — Finally, federal law also prohibits dismissal of any "permanent" employee because of his or her service on a federal jury.

2. State Laws

State legislatures also have been active in this area. In many instances, states merely have recodified federal protections or extended them to their own broader definitions of protected classes.

However, many states also have granted "new" protections, enacting laws which shield employees from employer interference with activities not protected by federal law.

Primary examples are in the political expression and workers' compensation areas. Employers are prohibited under several state laws from trying to influence employees' political beliefs and involvement. In many more states, employer interference with employees' right to file workers' compensation claims is prohibited. Discrimination on either basis, including employee dismissal, violates these states' laws.

In either case — federal or state prohibitions — exception to the employment-at-will rule is clear. The "at will" rule allows dismissal for *good cause, bad cause,* or *no cause;* those federal and state laws protecting various classes of employees and employee activities are specifically and appropriately intended to disallow *bad cause.*

Common Law Exceptions

Three major common law exceptions to the employment-at-will doctrine have been carved out by the courts: (1) public policy, (2) implied contract rights, and (3) implied covenant of good faith and fair dealing.

1. Public Policy. Just as Congress and various state legislatures have composed public policy limitations on "at will" employment, so have the courts.

The public policy exception to employment-at-will was the first common law exception to be established and remains the most widely applied. The earliest cases involved dismissal of employees for refusing to perform illegal acts (such as committing perjury), or for "whistle blowing" to government officials regarding illegal employer practices (such as price fixing).

Wrongful discharge claims that are based on a public policy exception to employment-at-will are a hybrid of both tort and contract law. The major significance of inclusion of a tort cause of action is the potential recovery. Contract violations are redressed by "make whole" remedies such as back pay and reinstatement, remedies which put the plaintiff in the position he or she would have been in absent the breach of contract. Tort remedies can be far more extensive and can include open-ended punitive and compensatory damages.

Before an employee is terminated, the reasons for dismissal and the conditions of employment should be analyzed to determine if the dismissal contravenes a significant public policy interest in society.

2. Implied Contract Rights. An increasing number of plaintiff actions have been taken by employees who have been dismissed, claiming that an employer's actions, inaction, or statements constituted an express employment contract and that the employee's dismissal is therefore a breach of contract.

This extension by the courts to employees of implied contractual protections against "at will' dismissal has created a mild revolution in personnel policies and practices.

It is important to keep in mind that contracts need not be written to be enforceable. Oral contracts can be just as binding as written contracts.

In numerous cases, dismissed employees have successfully claimed that they relied on employer representations that they had job security, that they would only be laid off for "just cause," and that their jobs were not terminable "at will."

Such representations can include statements made by recruiters or personnel staff during the hiring process, statements contained in employee handbooks or training manuals, supervisor assurances, or the statements made as part of an employee's performance evaluations.

For example, if an employer mentions to a newly hired employee that the employee will have a performance evaluation in one year and that employee is fired after only eight months, the employee may sue under the wrongful discharge theory claiming that there was an implicit promise to continue employment for one year.

Courts also have inferred that an employer's conduct limits its rights to dismiss an employee. An employee's longevity on the job, promotions, commendations, and positive performance evaluations can constitute an implied employment contract or, at the very least, support the legal claim of wrongful discharge if a worker is dismissed.

Thus, personnel policies and manuals which were intended to serve only as guidelines for managers and supervisors have been viewed by the courts as binding contract provisions.

A key to such legal claims is an illustration by the employee that he or she relied on such assurances, or conduct, regarding job security. If a dismissed employee can show that he or she passed up other job opportunities, or left another job and accepted his or her current job with good faith reliance on long-term employment, the case for a wrongful discharge claim is much stronger.

However, the Statute of Frauds may provide a valid employer defense even when an employer gives assurances to terminate only for "just cause." In many states, oral employment contracts are unenforceable if their terms of employment exceed one year. With no contract, there can be no cause of action for breach of contract.

3. Implied Covenant of Good Faith and Fair Dealing. The newest, most creative, and potentially most far-reaching common law exception to the employment-at-will doctrine is the implied-in-law covenant of good faith and fair dealing.

This exception currently is not as widely recognized as the public policy and implied contract exceptions. To date, only six states have recognized the implied covenant of good faith and fair dealing exception to "at will" employment: Alaska, California, Massachusetts, Montana, Nevada, and Oklahoma.

However, while not as widely recognized, the good faith covenant exception represents the most troubling concept because it disallows employee dismissals on the highly subjective basis of fairness. "Fairness" is an imprecise concept, particularly in a legal context, and even more so in the minds of inexperienced jurors.

The legal basis of implied good faith covenants is rooted in insurance law. It is a longstanding and widely accepted insurance law principle that each of the parties must act in good faith not to deprive the other of the benefit of their agreement.

When applied to employment relationships, however, this legal principle directly contradicts the employment-at-will rule and, in its place, imposes on employers, by judicial fiat, a "just cause" requirement for all terminations.

This calls into question every decision to dismiss an employee, and could lead to: (1) an explosive growth in litigation in the already too litigious employment law field, and (2) hesitancy on the part of employers to fire even those employees most deserving of dismissal (to the detriment of the company and its employees.)

Perhaps most troubling is the potential for non-meritorious cases being pursued by plaintiffs as a litigation strategy. In some states, breach of an implied covenant of good faith and fair dealing can provide a cause of action under tort law. Like the public policy exception, this permits damages far in excess of those under contract law.

The ability to seek compensatory and punitive damages, to take the case before a jury instead of a judge, and to argue for recovery, based on such an ill-defined and ephemeral standard as "good faith," effectively encourages legal claims,

Guidelines for Limiting Employer Liability:
What Employers Should Do

■ Review and revise all written company policy statements, job application forms, employee handbooks, training manuals, performance evaluation forms, and the standard form letters offering or terminating employment. Repeat this re-evaluation and revision process periodically and as necessary.

■ Establish a "paper trail." Generate documents and maintain comprehensive personnel files. Include documents regarding hiring and exit interviews, conferences, reprimands, warnings, probationary notices, performance evaluation, absenteeism records, commendations, and any evidence of remedial efforts. Record all oral admonitions. Assume the worst: that disciplinary cases will lead to discharge and that discharge will lead to court.

■ Train and retrain interviewers, recruiters, supervisors, managers, and personnel staff. Make sure they know company policy. Make sure they know what to say, what not to say, and the importance of documentation and employee performance evaluations.

■ Assure that employees are evaluated fairly, accurately, on time, and in accordance with company policy. Make sure supervisors and managers recognize the importance of candid, accurate evaluations.

■ Require employees to sign and date key employment documents, and to acknowledge that they have read and understood the contents and importance of these documents.

■ Consider establishing formal progressive disciplinary procedures. Recognize that progressive discipline can be a two-edged sword — if a company adheres to it effectively, it decreases the likelihood of legal claims and demonstrates fairness to potential juries; if it is enforced inconsistently, it can trigger and sustain legal claims. It also tends to delay the dismissal process by implementing a multi-step process. It is not for all employers. However, progressive discipline which includes educating employees about the company's grounds for discharge, warnings that a lack of improvement will result in termination, and an internal level of appeal or review, can resolve a lot of would-be problems, enhance employee morale, and ultimately save money.

■ Assure consistency of application for all company personnel policies. Even-handed enforcement with the same response taken for all similar cases is more likely to be accepted by employees and sustained by courts.

Guidelines for Limiting Employer Liability: What Employers Should Do (continued)

■ Include appropriate disclaimers on company documents such as job application forms, employee handbooks, and company policy manuals. State explicitly that the information contained in such documents is intended only to inform and provide guidelines; it should not be considered a binding contract, terms and conditions of employment, or a promise or reassurance of continued employment.

■ Consider including statements in these documents that employment is "at will" and can be terminated by either party, at any time, and for any reason. The "plus" is that such language protects employers against all of the common law "wrongful discharge" claims, excluding the public policy exception. The "negative" is that such statements may hurt recruiting efforts.

■ Make sure reliable witnesses, who are able to appear in court if necessary, are present during confrontations regarding incident-driven dismissals. Employee theft, destruction of company property, and sale of contraband are examples of situations where a quick employer response may be necessary and appropriate.

■ Know the law, all of the law, as it pertains to personnel policies and employee dismissals. Keep abreast of legal and legislative developments. Stay current with relevant federal, state, and local laws. Retain outside counsel to periodically review your programs and policies. If it is determined that the company's position is legally vulnerable, then change that position.

■ Consider all the circumstances before dismissing an employee. Look at the total picture to determine how significant the company's legal exposure could be. Be particularly sensitive regarding long-term employees.

discourages settlements and encourages appeal. Given the employer's cost of litigation, the unpredictability of jury decisions in this area, and the ability of plaintiffs to retain attorneys on a contingency basis (with no plaintiff out-of-pocket expense), discharged employees — no matter how deserving of their dismissal — may view the decision to sue as a "can't lose" situation.

With employers at such a disadvantage in handling personnel matters because of the lack of guidance on what legally constitutes "good faith" and "fair dealing," employers must be tremendously circumspect in taking job actions — particularly in the six jurisdictions where good faith covenants have been recognized.

However, employers have reason to be pleased in light of a recent California Supreme Court decision, which narrowed the right of recovery in a wrongful discharge action. The court ruled that such an action could only be based upon a breach of an expressed or implied contract. In such breach-of-contract litigation, a prevailing plaintiff typically receives reinstatement and recovers back pay. In contrast, a recovery under a tort theory of action allows for punitive and emotional damages. As a result of this case, California has closed the door on a runaway trend of wrongful discharge damage payments awarded to former employees.

The rationale for this decision was that the employment relationship is fundamentally contractual; and, therefore, "contractual remedies should remain the sole available relief for breaches of employment context." The need for commercial stability requires that an employer should not be "deprived of discretion to dismiss an employee by the fear that doing so will give rise to potential tort recovery in every case."

What is clear is that employers must evaluate each and every employment decision, and be prepared to justify their actions in court.

The Employment Contract Option

As the threat of wrongful discharge litigation inhibits and alarms employers in their personnel programs and practices, one option which may be considered to limit potential liability is express employment contracts.

Such express employment contracts require specialization to address each particular employment relationship involved. Generally, these agreements specifically state the duration of employment and expressly limit the circumstances upon which employment can be terminated, by either party, prior to a certain date.

Express employment contracts may include provisions that permit dismissal "for cause," invalidate the agreement at the discretion of the employer in the event of a company merger or acquisition, and specifically waive the contracting employee's access to grievance and arbitration procedures available to other employees. Perhaps most importantly, express employment contracts usually limit the remedies available for breach of contract. On the other hand, express employment contracts guarantee employment for a set period, subject to those exceptions which are enumerated.

The disadvantages of express employment contracts are: (1) greater administrative costs, (2) reduced flexibility, (3) inconvenience, (4) a potential "chilling" effect on recruitment, and (5) potential liabilities due to inadvertent omissions or unforeseen developments.

However, as the wave of wrongful discharge claims rise and judges demonstrate an increasing willingness to infer contractual protections for employees, express employment contracts may become a company policy worth pursuing.

Wrongful Discharge

Employers recognize that while employment-at-will is still the law in many jurisdictions and for most employees, the constant erosion of the doctrine, by the creation of pervasive exceptions imposing a "just cause" standard on dismissal decisions, has dramatically changed employers' exposure to employee lawsuits.

Businesses are well advised, therefore, to implement defensive personnel policies in order to counteract wrongful discharge challenges. These policies should assert that employees have a right to their jobs and can only be discharged for "just cause." Typically, the wrongful discharge plaintiff is white, male, non-union, upper or middle management, and without an employment contract.

Wrongful discharge started as—and sometimes continues to be—an add-on claim to other plaintiff employment actions, based upon alleged violations of some of the laws covered by this book, as well as others outside of its scope (such as defamation and invasion of privacy). It also can be joined with criminal charges of assault, battery, and/or false imprisonment as a result of a supervisor's oral notice of dismissal, an exit interview, or a counseling session which becomes antagonistic and results in the exchange of threats or even minor physical contact.

Employers also should recognize that it is not uncommon for employees who are passed over for a promotion, denied a raise, rejected for a training program, or unwillingly transferred, to resign and subsequently sue under a wrongful

---

Personnel Practices to Avoid

■ **Don't** give oral assurances of job security.

■ **Don't** allow recruiters or job placement firms to speak for, or make promises on behalf of, your company.

■ **Don't** promise annual or periodic performance evaluations.

■ **Don't** overstate the signficance of the completion of a "probationary" period.

■ **Don't** allow supervisors or managers to base positive performance evaluations or appraisals on friendship, sympathy, the ability of an employee to qualify for a salary increase, or the hope that an employee's performance will improve.

■ **Don't** allow recruiters, interviewers, or personnel staff to verbally discount or discredit company "at will" statements with such remarks as: "Don't worry about it, it's just a form everyone signs," "Layoffs never really occur," or "Just do your job and you won't be let go."

■ **Don't** state on any document, or at any time, that discharge will only occur for "just cause."

■ **Don't** list in an employee handbook or company manual the reasons or grounds for termination, or if you do, make it clear that it is not an exclusive list — for example, by stating ". . . and for other reasons at the discretion of the company."

■ **Don't** permit staff to discuss dismissals with employees who don't need to know. Such indiscretions could lead to a defamation action.

■ **Don't** allow supervisors to provide inaccurately positive, or laudatory, letters of recommendation, or references, for discharged employees.

■ **Don't** dispense severance pay without first receiving a properly executed release from liability.

---

discharge cause of action. Such plaintiffs claim the denial or transfer constituted a "constructive discharge."

What you don't do in your personnel practicescan be as important as what you do, especially regarding employee dismissals. The following checklist provides some guidance on activity to be discouraged, so as to be better able to defend against wrongful discharge litigation.

WARN — Legislative Purpose

In 1988, Congress passed the Worker Adjustment and Retraining Act (WARN), commonly referred to as the "plant closing" law. This law applies to any type of business, not just a "plant," and the law covers layoffs as well as closings of facilities or businesses.

Coverage

Any employer who has 100 or more employees, excluding part-time employees, or has 100 or more employees who in the aggregate work at least 4,000 hours per week, exclusive of hours of overtime, is subject to the provisions of the law. Multi-site enterprises will be covered even if only one site is involved in a closing or layoff, if the entire enterprise under common control employs 100 or more employees.

A part-time employee is a worker who is employed for an average of fewer than 20 hours per week or who has been employed for fewer than 6 of the 12 months preceding the date on which notice is required.

Closings Requiring Notice

The law defines separate criteria for notification in the event of a business closing and a mass layoff. In the event of a business closing, employers are required to comply if the shutdown results in an employment loss during any 30-day period for 50 or more employees, excluding any part-time employees, at the site of the shutdown.

A closing is defined as the permanent or temporary shutdown of a single site of employment.

In the event of a "mass layoff" that is not a business closing, employers are required to comply if the layoff results in an employment loss at a single site during any 30-day period for at least 33 percent of the employees, but for no fewer than 50 employees (excluding part-time employees.)

If an employer of 101 workers lays off 40 workers, the employer would not be required to provideerage of fewer than 20 hours per week or who has been employed for fewer than 6 of the 12 months preceding the date on which notice is required.

Temporary Employment

No notice is required if the closing is of a temporary facility or if the closing or layoff is the result of the completion of a particular project or undertaking, and the affected employees were hired with the understanding that their employment was limited to the duration of the facility or the project or undertaking.

Employees must clearly understand at the time of hire that their employment is temporary. Should questions arise, the burden of proof lies with the employer to show that the temporary nature of the project of facility was clearly communicated.

Employers in agriculture and construction frequently hire workers for harvesting, processing, or work on a particular building or project. Such work may be seasonal but recurring. Such work falls under the exemption if the workers understood at the time they were hired that their work was temporary. Giving written notice that a project is temporary will not convert permanent employment into temporary work.

Employment Loss

Both the closing and mass layoffs notices are triggered by "employment loss." Employment loss is termination of employment other than a discharge for cause, voluntary departure, or retirement. It is also a layoff exceeding 6 months or a reduction in hours of work of more than 50 percent during each month of any 6-month period.

A layoff of more than 6 months which, at its outset, was announced to be a layoff of 6 months or less, shall be treated as an employment loss. If the extension beyond 6 months is caused by business circumstance (including unforeseeable changes in price or cost) not reasonably foreseeable at the time of the initial layoff, and notice is given at the time it becomes reasonably foreseeable that the extension beyond 6 months will be required, it will not result in liability.

If the closing or layoff is the result of a relocation or consolidation of part or all of the employer's business, and prior to the closing or layoff the employer offers to transfer the employee to a different site of employment within a reasonable commuting distance with no more than a 6-month break in employment, the employee will not be considered to have experienced an employment loss.

Likewise, if the employer offers to transfer the employee to any other site of employment, regardless of distance, with no more than a 6 month break in employment, and the employee accepts within 30 days of the offer of the closing or layoff, whichever is later, the employee will not be considered to have experienced an employment loss.

In the case of a sale of the employer's business, the seller has responsibility for compliance up to the effective date of the sale and buyer thereafter. If the seller is made aware of any definite plans on the part of the buyer to carry out a business closing or mass layoff within 60 days of purchase, the seller may give notice to affected employees as an agent of the buyer, if so empowered. If the seller does not give notice, the buyer is, nevertheless, responsible to give notice. If the seller gives notice as the buyer's agent, the responsibility for notice still remains with the buyer.

It may be prudent for the buyer and seller to determine the impact of the sale on workers, and to arrange between them for advance notice to be given to affected workers if a mass layoff or business closing is planned.

When Notice Must Be Given

With certain exceptions, notice must be given at least 60 calendar days prior to any planned business closing or mass layoff. When all employees are not terminated on the same date, the date of the first individual termination with the statutory 30-day or 90-day period triggers the 60-day requirement. A worker's last day of employment is considered the date of the worker's layoff. The first and each subsequent group of terminees are entitled to a full 60 days notice. In order for an employer to decide whether issuing a notice is required, the employer should:

1. Look ahead 30 days and behind 30 days to determine whether employment actions both taken and planned will, in the aggregate for any 30-day period, reach the minimum numbers for a business closing or a mass layoff and thus trigger the notice requirement; and,

2. Look ahead 90 days and behind 90 days to determine whether employment actions both taken and planned, each of which separately is not of sufficient size to trigger WARN coverage, will, in the aggregate for any 90-day period, reach the minimum numbers for a business closing or mass layoff and thus trigger the notice requirement. An employer is not, however, required to give notice if the employer can demonstrate that the separate employment losses are the result of separate and distinct actions and causes, and are not an attempt to evade the requirements of WARN.

The point in time at which the number of employees is to be measured for the purpose of determining coverage is the date the first notice is required to be given. If this "snapshot" of the number of employees employed on that date is clearly unrepresentative of the ordinary or average employment level, then a more representative number can be used to determine coverage. Examples of unrepresentative employment levels include cases when the level is near the peak or trough of an employment cycle or when large upward or downward shifts in the number of employees occur around the time notice is to be given.

Notice Requirements

An employer cannot order a business closing or mass layoff until the end of the 60-day period beginning with written notice to:

1. The representative of the affected workers. The representative means basically the union representative as determined by federal labor law, or if there is no such representative, to each affected employee;
2. The State's dislocated worker unit; and
3. The chief elected office of the local jurisdiction in which the closing or layoff will occur.

Mailing notice to an employee's last known address or inclusion of the notice in the employee's paycheck will be considered acceptable methods of fulfilling the employer's obligation to provide notice.

Notice may be given conditional upon the

occurrence or nonoccurrence of an event (e.g. the renewal of a major contract), only when the event is definite, and consequences of occurrence or non-occurrence will necessarily, in the normal course of business, lead to a covered business closing or mass layoff less than 60 days after the event.

The information provided in the notice shall be based on the best information available to the employer at the time the notice is served. Errors that occur in the information provided in a notice because events subsequently change, or that are minor, inadvertent errors, are not to be the basis for finding a violation of WARN.

The term "date," for the purposes of notice, refers to a specific date or to a 14-day period during which a separation or separations are expected to occur. If separations are planned according to a schedule, the schedule should indicate the specific dates on which or the beginning date of each 14-day period during which any separations are expected to occur. Where a 14-day period is used, a notice must be given at least 60 days in advance of the first day of the period.

If the notice is given to a representative of employees, it should contain:

■ The name and address of the employment site where the business closing or mass layoff will occur, and the name and telephone number of a company official to contact for further information;

■ A statement as to whether the planned action is expected to be permanent or temporary and, if the entire business is to be closed, a statement to that effect;

■ The expected date of the first separation and the anticipated schedule for making separations; and

■ The job titles of positions to be affected and the names of the workers currently holding affected jobs.

If notice is to be given directly to affected employees, it is to be written in language understandable to the employees and is to contain:

■ A statement as to whether the planned action is expected to be permanent or temporary, and

if the entire business is to be closed, a statement to that effect;

■ The expected date when the business closing or mass layoff will commence and expected date when the individual employee will be discharged.

■ An indication whether or not bumping rights exist; and

■ The name and telephone number of a company official to contact for further information.

The notices separately provided to the State dislocated worker unit and to the chief elected official of the unit of local government are to contain:

■ The name and address of the employment site where the business closing or mass layoff will occur, and the name and telephone number of a company official to contact for further information;

■ A statement as to whether the planned action is expected to be permanent or temporary and, if the entire business is to be closed, a statement to that effect;

■ The anticipated date of the first separation, and the anticipated schedule for making separations;

■ The job titles of positions to be affected, and the number of employees in each job classification;

■ An indication as to whether or not bumping rights exist; and

■ The name of each union representing affected employees and the name and address of the chief elected officer of each union.

Reduction in Notification Period

WARN sets forth three conditions under which the notification period may be reduced to less than 60 days. The employer bears the burden of proof that conditions for the exceptions have been met.

1. Faltering Company Exception

The exception termed "faltering company" applies to business closings but not to mass layoffs.

An employer must have been actively seeking capital or business at the time that the 60-day notice would have been required. That is, the employer must have been seeking financing or refinancing through the arrangement of loans, or the issuance of stocks, bonds, or other methods of internally generated financing; or the employer must have been seeking additional money, credit, or business through any other commercially reasonable method. The employer must be able to identify actions taken to obtain capital or business. There must have been a realistic opportunity to obtain the financing or business sought.

The financing or business sought must have been sufficient, if obtained, to have enabled the employer to avoid or postpone the shutdown. The employer must be able to objectively demonstrate that the amount of capital or volume of new business sought would have enabled the employer to keep the facility open.

The employer reasonably, and in good faith, must have believed that giving the required notice would have precluded the employer from obtaining the needed capital or business. The employer must be able to objectively demonstrate that it reasonably thought that a potential customer or source of financing would have been unwilling to provide the new business or capital if notice were given; that is, if the employees, customers, or the public were aware that the site might have to close. This condition may be satisfied if the employer can show that the financing or business source would not choose to do business with a troubled company or with a company whose workforce would be looking for other jobs.

2. Unforeseeable Business Circumstances Exception

The unforeseeable business circumstances exception applies to business closings and mass layoffs caused by business circumstances that were not reasonably foreseeable at the time that 60-day notice would have been required. An important indicator of a business circumstance that is not reasonably foreseeable is that the circumstance is caused by some sudden, dramatic, and unexpected action or condition outside the employer's control. A principal client's sudden and unexpected termination of a major contract with the employer, or an unanticipated and dramatic major economic downturn, might each be considered as such a business circumstance. The test for determining when business circumstances are not reasonably foreseeable focuses on an employer's business judgment. The employer must exercise such commercially reasonable business judgment as would a similarly situated employer in predicting the demands of its particular market. The employer is not required, however, to accurately predict general economic conditions that also may affect demand for its products or services.

3. Natural Disaster Exception

The "natural disaster" exception applies to business closings and mass layoffs due to any form of a natural disaster. Floods, earthquakes, droughts, storms, tidal waves or tsunamis, and similar effects of nature are natural disasters. To qualify for this exception, an employer must be able to demonstrate that its business closing or mass layoff is a direct result of a natural disaster. While a disaster may preclude full or any advance notice, such notice, as is practical, must still be given. Where a business closing or mass layoff occurs as an indirect result of a natural disaster the exception does not apply, but the "unforeseeable business circumstance" may be applicable.

Sanctions

Employees are permitted to sue an employer for back pay and benefits under WARN. The amounts may be reduced by the courts under certain conditions. The employer may also be liable for a civil penalty for failing to provide notice to the local government.

Polygraph Use

A whole new area of potential employer liability for improper discharge involves the reliance on the results of polygraph examinations. To assist employers in understanding their rights and responsibilities, there is in this and the following sections an expanded explanation of the Employee Polygraph Protection Act. The law prohibits an employer from directly or indirectly requiring, requesting, suggesting, or causing any employee or prospective employee to take or submit to any lie detector test. Similarly, an employer may not inquire about the results of any previous test taken at the direction of someone other than the current or prospective employer. Please note that state laws and collective bargaining agreements that are more restrictive prevail over the federal law. Thus, if state law prohibits polygraph examinations, one need read no further. The state prohibition is operative.

Further, an employer may not discharge, discipline, discriminate against in any manner, deny employment or promotion to, or threaten to take any such action against any employee or prospective employee who refuses, declines, or fails to take or submit to any lie detector test, or on the basis of any lie detector test results.

Every employer must post and maintain a Department of Labor poster in a conspicuous place for the benefit of employees. A pull-out copy of the poster appears at page 171.

Limited Exemption

The law bans the use of the polygraph to pre-screen prospective employees of a private business, except for security firms and firms whose businesses are authorized to deal in controlled substances. Under extremely limited conditions, an employer may request an employee to submit to a polygraph test. A request may be made if:

1. The test is administered in connection with an ongoing investigation involving economic loss or injury to the employer's business, such as theft, embezzlement, misappropriation, or an act of unlawful industrial espionage or sabotage;
2. The employee had access to the property that is the subject of the investigation;
3. The employer has a reasonable suspicion that the employee was involved in the incident or activity under investigation; and

4. The employer executes a statement, provided to the examinee before the test, that —
   a. sets forth with particularity the specific incident or activity being investigated and the basis for testing particular employees,
   b. is signed by the person (other than the polygraph examiner) authorized to legally bind the employer,
   c. is retained by the employer for at least 3 years, and
   d. contains at a minimum —
      i. an identification of the specific economic loss or injury to the business of the employer,
      ii. a statement indicating that the employee had access to the property that is the subject of the investigation, and
      iii. a statement describing the basis of the employer's reasonable suspicion that the employee was involved in the incident or activity under investigation.

Rights and Responsibilities

If a polygraph test is conducted under these special circumstances, the law establishes further restrictions on employers and grants certain rights to the examinee.

The examinee is permitted to terminate the test at any time and may not be asked questions in a manner designed to degrade, or needlessly intrude. The examinee may not be asked any question concerning: religious beliefs or affiliations; beliefs or opinions regarding racial matters; political beliefs or affiliations; any matter relating to sexual behavior; and, beliefs, affiliations, opinions, or lawful activities regarding unions or labor organizations.

The examiner cannot conduct the test if there is sufficient written evidence by a physician that the examinee is suffering from a medical or psychological condition, or undergoing treatment, that might cause abnormal responses during the actual testing phase.

Prior to the test, the employer must provide the examinee with reasonable written notice of the date, time, and location of the test. Also included in the statement must be a disclosure of the examinee's right to obtain and consult with legal counsel or an employee representative before each phase of the test.

The examinee must also be informed, in writing, of the nature and characteristics of the tests; whether other devices, including any device for recording or monitoring the conversation, will be used; or that the employer or the examinee may (with mutual knowledge) make a recording of the entire proceeding.

Further, prior to the test, the examinee must be read, and sign, a written notice informing the examinee: that he or she cannot be required to take the test as a condition for employment; that any statement made during the test may constitute additional supporting evidence for the purposes of an adverse employment action; of limitations imposed under the law for use of the polygraph; and of the legal rights and remedies of the employer under the law.

The examinee must be provided the opportunity to review all questions to be asked during the test and must be informed of the right to terminate the test at any time. During the actual testing phase, the examiner may not ask the examinee any relevant question during the test that was not presented in writing for review to the examinee before the test.

After the test, but before any adverse employment action, the employer must interview the examinee on the basis of the results of the test; and provide the examinee with a written copy of any opinion or conclusion rendered as a result of the test, and a copy of the questions asked during the test along with the corresponding charted responses.

Enforcement

If the employer fails to meet the conditions permitting limited use of the polygraph, the polygraph test used under the limited exemption will be considered in violation of the law. An employee cannot be discharged, disciplined, denied employment or promotion, or otherwise discriminated against in any manner on the basis of the analysis of one or more polygraph test charts or the refusal to take a polygraph test, without additional supporting evidence.

Any employer who violates any provision of the law may be assessed a civil penalty of not more than $10,000. The Secretary of Labor may determine the amount of the penalty and has the authority to issue subpoenas, make investigations and inspections, and require the keeping of records that are necessary and appropriate. The Secretary may bring court cases against employers.

An employee or job applicant may also sue the employer. The suit must be brought within three years of the alleged violation. The employer can be held liable for legal and equitable relief, including employment, reinstatement, promotion, and the payment of lost wages and benefits.

Polygraph Use — Some Advice

The complexity of the law reflects Congress's strong bias against polygraph use in the private sector. The immediate consequences arising out of the law have been a dramatic reduction in the use of polygraph examinations by private sector employers. Employers who resort to using polygraphs, in the opinion of the author, do so at considerable legal peril. At the very least, employers who elect to use the polygraph in states where it is still allowed should take the additional precaution to have legal counsel provide guidance.

Written psychological tests, or "pencil-and-papers," are outside the scope of federal law. These tests inquire into the applicant's attitudes toward personal behavior and work environment. This technique predicts future behavior based on the individual's attitudes and admissions of prior conduct. Pencil and paper integrity tests are formulated on the basis that dishonest and honest people don't think alike. Congress, during the consideration of the Polygraph Protection Act, considered including these tests under the bill's provisions, but this idea was dropped along the way. It is likely, therefore, that there will be continued congressional scrutiny of these integrity tests in the future.

Appendix

Appendix

HANDBOOK FOR EMPLOYEES

ABC Widget Company

I. Introduction

This Employee Handbook is presented to all of our employees because it is important for everyone in the ABC Widget Company to know, in as much detail as possible, the kind of company we are and what we believe in.

I am proud of the reputation and success of our company, and I feel very strongly that these accomplishments were achieved, in large measure, because of the dedication and hard work of our employees. I am grateful for this team effort, and I pledge to do all I can to continue the tradition of excellence.

The company operates with an "open door" policy, and all employees are invited to visit our Personnel Office at any time to seek advice or to obtain information about any company practice.

I hope you will find your association with our company rewarding, and I wish you good luck in your new career.

Sincerely,
John A. Widget
President

ABC WIDGET COMPANY

II. Personnel Policies

Employment

Employment at ABC Widget Company is "at will." Employment can be terminated by either party, at any time, and for any reason. This includes termination with or without cause, and with or without notice.

Any oral statements, promises, or assurances to the contrary are not binding on the employer and should not be relied upon by the employee or job applicant. If you believe such assurances have been made, contact the personnel office for confirmation. The employer is not responsible for, and will not be bound by, any statements that are not reaffirmed in writing by the company's president, vice president, or personnel director.

Statements on the employment application, or in this handbook, training manuals, or other company documents, do not constitute or imply an employment contract and should not be relied upon by the employee or job applicant under any circumstances as assuring continued employment or superseding the company's "at will" employment policy.

Each employee is classified in one of the following categories, based on the conditions under which he or she is employed:

A. **Probationary** — A probationary Employee is one who is hired to fill a regular job but who is on probation for a period of at least six months. If the employee's service is satisfactory after the completion of the probationary period, his or her status is changed to that of a Regular Employee.

B. **Regular** — A Regular Employee is one who has satisfactorily completed a probationary period and is performing the duties of a full-time job in the company.

C. **Temporary** — A Temporary Employee is one who is hired for a specific purpose or job for a period of not more than four months. This temporary employment may be extended for limited periods. The status of a Temporary Employee may be changed to that of a Probationary or Regular Employee providing there is an opening for a full-time job, and he or she is qualified to fill the job. A summer college trainee employed during the summer months is classified as a Temporary Employee.

D. **Part-Time** — An employee who is hired for work which requires part of a day or part of a week, on a regular or irregular schedule, is considered a Part-Time employee.

Promotions

It is an established company policy to fill existing vacancies whenever possible through promotions from within the organization. Employees are selected with due regard for their seniority on the basis of their ability, education, experience, and other qualifications necessary for the position. In this company, an employee's religion, age, sex, national origin, race, or color will not be a consideration in hiring, promotion, pay, or benefits.

Each employee is urged to develop skills in his or her present job and to learn as much as possible about the company, its operations, and its policies to be qualified for promotion when the opportunity presents itself.

As job openings in the organization become available, a formal job posting policy insures that every job opening is advertised on company bulletin boards, and any employee may file an application for the job posted with the Personnel Office.

HANDBOOK FOR EMPLOYEES

Transfers

Employees may be transferred from one department to another, providing an opening is available and such transfer is of mutual advantage to the employee and the company. A request for a transfer should be made to the Supervisor and will be granted upon approval of the department heads concerned and the Personnel Office.

Layoffs

Whenever a layoff of personnel is necessary, those employees affected will be given as much advance notice as possible.

Employees will be chosen for layoff on the basis of their seniority as well as their ability and other qualifications.

Discipline

Discipline shall be for just cause based on a Supervisor's recommendation to the Personnel Office.

Grievance Procedures

A grievance procedure has been established and must be followed by any employee who wishes to bring an issue to the attention of Management.

An employee should discuss with his or her Supervisor any problem about working conditions, fellow employees, alleged unfair treatment, or unsatisfactory job-related situations. If no satisfaction can be obtained from that source or the explanation is believed to be inadequate, the employee should contact his or her Department Head.

If the employee is still dissatisfied, an appeal may be made directly to the Plant Manager — the person ultimately responsible for resolving all grievances.

In addition, the Personnel Office may be contacted at any time for assistance with the grievance or any other problem.

Termination of Employment

If an employee plans to leave the company, he or she is requested to give at least two weeks' notice. If a recommendation is desired, a prospective employer should be referred directly to the Personnel Office.

ABC WIDGET COMPANY

III. Compensation

Wages and Salary Policy

Employees are paid on either an hourly or a salaried basis according to the job being performed. Every job is assigned to a wage classification with a minimum and a maximum rate. Supervisors can provide information concerning wage grades and rates. An employee's rate within a classification is determined by his or her job performance and/or length of service. Adjustments in rate are made periodically on a six-month or annual basis depending on length of service. In addition, adjustments to the wage and salary structure are made whenever dictated by competitive or cost-of-living considerations.

Hours of Work and Workweek

The normal or regular hours of work are eight hours per day or 40 hours per week. The normally scheduled workweek begins on Monday at 12:01 A.M. and terminates on Sunday at 12:00 midnight.

Schedule Workday

The schedule workday is the normal schedule of eight hours' work plus any normal scheduled meal period.

Any premium or allowance, other than the applicable overtime pay, is determined by the number of overtime hours worked prior to, and/or following, the scheduled workday.

Straight Time Pay

The straight time rate of pay is the normal rate of pay, exclusive of shift differentials, for the regular workday of eight hours or the regular workweek of 40 hours.

Paydays

Most hourly employees are paid weekly on Friday. Most salaried employees are paid monthly or semi-monthly. For employees' protection, payments are made by check.

Overtime Pay

If entitled to overtime pay, and an employee has not lost time for unexcused personal reasons, all work performed outside of the regular schedule of eight hours per day or 40 hours per week is considered overtime.

Overtime hours worked during the five scheduled workdays or on the sixth day of the payroll week will be paid at one and one-half times the regular rate of pay. All hours worked on the seventh day of the workweek will be paid at twice the regular rate of pay.

HANDBOOK FOR EMPLOYEES

If an employee is required to work on the seventh day of the workweek and such work continues into the first day of the following workweek, all continuous hours worked up to the start of the regular scheduled hours on the first day will be paid for at twice the regular rate of pay, at which time the rate of pay will revert to the regular straight time rate.

Temporary Rates

When it is necessary to assign an employee to work in a higher classification for a limited period of time which exceeds eight hours, that employee will be paid at a temporary rate.

The temporary rate will be one step higher than the employee's regular base rate or the minimum base rate of the temporary classification, whichever is higher, and will be paid for the hours worked in the temporary classification.

Performance Reviews

Performance reviews are conducted biannually during the employee's first five (5) years of service and on an annual basis thereafter. At these times the Supervisor or Department Head will discuss each employee's job performance since his or her last review.

It is hoped that during these reviews constructive discussions addressing any concerns the employee has about his or her job and the company will take place.

The job performance review is also the basis for merit increases and is the method used to advance pay rates within the guidelines established for each job.

IV. Employee Benefits

Vacations

Vacations with pay will be based on the employee's normal workweek and will be computed as follows:

Employees with 1-9 years of service will receive 2 weeks.

Employees with 10-19 years of service will receive 3 weeks.

Employees with over 20 years of service will receive 4 weeks.

Vacations for part-time employees will be prorated according to length of service.

Vacations are scheduled so as not to interfere with company operations and are usually for one, two, or three week periods.

Vacation time must be taken during the calendar year and is not cumulative.

ABC WIDGET COMPANY

Sick Leave

Each employee has seven sick days per year and may accrue unused sick leave for future use.

Holidays and Holiday Pay

The company observes the following paid holidays each year:
New Year's Day
Memorial Day
July 4th
Labor Day
Thanksgiving Day
Christmas Day
Employees who are required to work on a holiday will be paid at twice their regular rate of pay.

Educational Assistance

All employees are urged to consider obtaining additional education through enrollment in night schools, colleges, or graduate centers which provide courses relative to the employee's present job or promotional opportunities. The company will reimburse any employee up to $750.00 per year for registration fees, tuition, laboratory fees, and books when courses have been approved in advance by the company.

Application forms and information on how this program works are available from the Personnel Office. Successful completion of an educational program is noted in each employee's personnel record and taken into account when promotions are considered.

Leave of Absence

A Leave of Absence, without pay, may be granted for personal reasons.

A request for Leave of Absence must be submitted to the employee's Supervisor, stating the purpose or reason for the request. Each case will be reviewed and must be approved by both the Department Head and the Personnel Office before the leave is authorized. The duration, terms, and conditions of each approval for authorized leave will be based on the circumstances of the individual request.

Death in Immediate Family

Each employee is entitled to up to three (3) days' paid leave in the event of death in the immediate family.

The immediate family includes spouse, father, mother, son, daughter, brother, sister, mother-in-law, or father-in-law.

HANDBOOK FOR EMPLOYEES

Jury Duty

If called for jury duty, an employee will be paid at the base rate of pay (less jury pay) for each scheduled workday which he or she is required to spend at court, up to a maximum of five days.

Military Leave of Absence

If employees have a military obligation to fulfill, leave without pay will be granted without charge to vacation or personal allowances.

V. Group Insurance and Retirement Plan

All of the plans discussed below are set out in detail in a separate Benefits Handbook. For specific questions, employees should contact their Supervisor or the Personnel Office.

Life Insurance is offered to each employee 30 days after the hiring day, and a minimum coverage, equal to the amount of anticipated annual regular earnings, is available at a minimal charge per pay period. The company pays half the cost of this coverage.

Health Insurance is offered to each employee 30 days after the hiring day, and this policy contributes to the cost of doctor visits, hospital charges, and surgery incurred because of accident or illness. A major medical feature covers 80% of most doctor, prescription drug, surgical, and hospital charges not covered under the basic plan up to a lifetime limit of a quarter of a million dollars per employee. The company pays 75% of the entire cost of each employee's health insurance.

Statutory Disability Insurance covers all employees after four consecutive weeks of employment. It provides weekly payments to individuals who become sick or disabled, and coverage extends for a period of six months. The company pays the entire cost of this coverage for its employees.

Long Term Disability Insurance is made available to all employees after 30 days on the job, and the cost is shared 50/50 by the employee and the company. This coverage provides monthly payments after the six-month Statutory Disability Insurance coverage ends.

ABC WIDGET COMPANY

Workers' Compensation Insurance provides statutory benefits for on-the-job injuries. All employees are covered upon reporting for work, and the entire cost of this coverage is paid by the company.

Unemployment Insurance is provided to each employee as required by law, and the cost of this insurance is paid by the company.

The Retirement Plan maintained by the company is a comprehensive program with a variety of features and options and is made available to all employees 21 years of age or older, on each August 1 and February 1, after one full year of service. The basic plan is paid for fully by the company, and a supplemental plan provides for increased retirement benefits paid for by the employee and the company on approximately a 50/50 basis. An employee savings plan is offered as another option for increasing benefits at retirement. The plan conforms to all of the regulations as provided in the Employee Retirement Income Security Act of 1974.

VI. Miscellaneous

Safety Policy

The ABC Widget Company places the highest emphasis on its workers' safety and will continue every effort to make working areas as safe as possible.

Each employee's responsibility is to work safely and do all that is possible to prevent accidents or injuries. Every worker is expected to report unsafe conditions, think before acting, and consciously take care to avoid unnecessary risk.

Smoking restrictions are strictly enforced. Smoking is permitted in certain areas only.

Bulletin Board

Official company bulletin boards have been placed in several locations to inform employees of special company activities, as well as changes within the company. Official notices and communications are displayed on these boards, and no material may be posted unless approved by the Personnel Office.

Employee Acknowledgement

I have read the company Handbook for Employees, I understand its meaning, and I have received a copy.

_____   _____
Employee's Signature   Date

Sample Company Policy Statement — Drug Abuse in the Workplace

[Note: Employers should give job applicants a copy of the company's policy statement at the time of hire and prior to their joining the workforce. It also should be included in employee handbooks and manuals. The signed copy should be retained in the employee's personnel file.]

The [company name] has an obligation to its employees, customers, shareholders, and the public at large to take reasonable and appropriate steps to prevent drug abuse by its employees in or affecting the workplace. This policy is based in substantial part on the company's concern regarding the safety, health, and welfare of its employees, their families, its customers, and the community.

Consistent with this commitment, the company strictly prohibits:

1. The presence of employees on the job while under the influence of intoxicants, drugs, or any other controlled substances;
2. The use, possession, transfer, or trafficking of intoxicants, illegal drugs, or controlled substances in any amount, in any manner, or at any time, either on company premises or while conducting company business;
3. The use of company property, including company vehicles and telephones, or an employee's position within the company to make, transfer, or traffic intoxicants, illegal drugs, or controlled substances; and
4. Any other use, possession, or trafficking of intoxicants, illegal drugs, or controlled substances in a manner which has an adverse impact on the company.

Any employee who is under medication or taking any drug which may affect the employee's ability to perform his or her job in a safe and productive manner must report such use to his or her supervisor. Supervisors, in conjunction with personnel staff, will determine if the employee should remain at work, be restricted in his or her duties, or be sent home.

The company has the right to:

1. Discipline employees, including dismissal, for felony convictions regarding illegal use, possession, or trafficking of drugs;
2. Search, based on reason to believe this policy is being violated, an employee's person, locker, desk, vehicle, work station, briefcase, tool box, wallet, purse, lunch box, pockets, and personal belongings. Entry on company premises constitutes consent to searches and inspections;
3. Test employees, including blood or urine tests, and perform medical examinations for the purpose of determining if the employee has engaged in illegal drug use; and
4. Take disciplinary action against employees who violate this company policy, including refusal to submit to testing, inspection, or searches. Employees also may be suspended pending outcome of an investigation regarding compliance with this policy.

Job applicants may be required to undergo drug testing and medical examination, prior to hire, and be required to agree in writing to permit such tests and examinations and company use of their results. Those job applicants who fail such tests and examinations will not be offered employment.

Notification to law enforcement agencies will be made, at the discretion of the company, regarding violations of this policy as appropriate and/or necessary.

I have read the above company policy statement, understand its meaning, and have received a copy.

_____	_____
Employee's Signature	Date

Sample Company Policy Statement — AIDS in the Workplace

[Note: Employers should give job applicants a copy of the company's policy statement at the time of hire and prior to their joining the workforce. It also should be included in employee handbooks and manuals. The signed copy should be retained in the employee's personnel file.]

The [company name] is committed to maintaining a safe and healthy working environment for all employees.

Consistent with this commitment, Acquired Immune Deficiency Syndrome (AIDS) will be considered and treated on an equal pay basis as any other life-threatening or debilitating disease. This uniform consideration includes the company's personnel policies, and its policies regarding health, life insurance, disability, and other benefit programs.

Employees who are affected by AIDS or any other life-threatening or debilitating disease will be treated in a humane and understanding manner. The company will make every reasonable effort to maintain confidentiality regarding medical information and to preserve the affected employee's right to privacy.

The company recognizes that it is the virtually unanimous medical and scientific consensus, including the views of the Surgeon General of the United States and the Centers for Disease Control of the U.S. Public Health Service, that AIDS is not transmitted in the workplace by normal occupational, professional, or social contacts.

Consistent with this finding, and absent developments based on further medical and scientific research, the company will permit employees with AIDS to continue in the workforce: (1) as long as they are capable of performing the responsibility of their jobs, and (2) as long as their continued employment does not pose a significant risk to themselves or others. Reasonable accommodations will be made to assist employees with AIDS.

Refusals to work by the co-workers of employees with AIDS because of a perceived threat of exposure are without a scientific or medical basis and will be subject to discipline.

Information regarding AIDS, its causes, and its transmission is available in the company's medical and personnel offices. The company encourages all employees to become and stay aware of the facts about AIDS. The company will, as a matter of company policy, make available to employees timely and accurate information about AIDS.

I have read the above company policy statement, understand its meaning, and have received a copy.

_____   _____
Employee's Signature   Date

Sample Company Policy Statement —
Safety and Health in the Workplace

The Occupational Safety and Health Act of 1970 clearly states our common goal of safe and healthful working conditions. The safety and health of our employees continues to be the first consideration in the operation of [Company Name].

Safety and health in our business must be a part of every operation. Without question, it is every employee's responsibility at all levels.

It is the intent of [Company Name] to comply with all laws. To do this we must constantly be aware of conditions in all work areas that can produce injuries. No employee is required to work at a job he or she knows is not safe or healthful. Your cooperation in detecting hazards and, in turn, controlling them is a condition of your employment. Inform your supervisor immediately of any situation beyond your ability or authority to correct.

The personal safety and health of each employee of this company is of primary importance. The prevention of occupationally induced injuries and illnesses is of such consequence that it will be given precedence over operating productivity whenever necessary. To the greatest degree possible, management will provide all mechanical and physical facilities required for personal safety and health in keeping with the highest standards.

We will maintain a safety and health program conforming to the best practices of organizations of this type. To be successful, such a program must embody the proper attitudes toward injury and illness prevention on the part of supervisors and employees. It also requires cooperation in all safety and health matters, not only between supervisor and employee, but also between each employee and his or her co-workers. Only through such a cooperative effort can a safety program in the best interest of all be established and preserved.

Our objective is a safety and health program that will reduce the number of injuries and illnesses to an absolute minimum, not merely in keeping with, but surpassing, the best experience of operations similar to ours. Our goal is zero accidents and injuries.

Our safety and health program will include:

- Providing mechanical and physical safeguards to the maximum extent possible.
- Conducting a program of safety and health inspections to find and eliminate unsafe working conditions or practices, to control health hazards, and to comply fully with the safety and health standards for every job.
- Training all employees in good safety and health practices.
- Providing necessary personal protective equipment and instructions for its use and care.
- Developing and enforcing safety and health rules and requiring that employees cooperate with these rules as a condition of employment.
- Investigating, promptly and thoroughly, every accident to find out what caused it and to correct the problem so that it won't happen again.
- Setting up a system of recognition and awards for outstanding safety service or performance.

We recognize that the responsibilities for safety and health are shared:

- The employer accepts the responsibility for leadership of the safety and health program, for its effectiveness and improvement, and for providing the safeguards required to ensure safe conditions.

(continued)

- Supervisors are responsible for developing the proper attitudes toward safety and health in themselves and in those they supervise, and for ensuring that all operations are performed with the utmost regard for the safety and health of all personnel involved, including themselves.
- Employees are responsible for wholehearted, genuine cooperation with all aspects of the safety and health program, including compliance with all rules and regulations, and for continuously practicing safety while performing their duties.

I have read the above company policy statement, understand its meaning, and have received a copy.

_____   _____
   Employee's Signature   Date

Immigration and Naturalization Service Form I-9

EMPLOYMENT ELIGIBILITY VERIFICATION (Form I-9)

1 EMPLOYEE INFORMATION AND VERIFICATION: (To be completed and signed by employee.)

Name: (Print or Type) Last	First	Middle	Birth Name
Address: Street Name and Number	City	State	ZIP Code
Date of Birth (Month/Day/Year)		Social Security Number	

I attest, under penalty of perjury, that I am (check a box):

☐ 1. A citizen or national of the United States.

☐ 2. An alien lawfully admitted for permanent residence (Alien Number A _____).

☐ 3. An alien authorized by the Immigration and Naturalization Service to work in the United States (Alien Number A _____ .

or Admission Number _____ , expiration of employment authorization, if any _____).

I attest, under penalty of perjury, the documents that I have presented as evidence of identity and employment eligibility are genuine and relate to me. I am aware that federal law provides for imprisonment and/or fine for any false statements or use of false documents in connection with this certificate.

Signature	Date (Month/Day/Year)

PREPARER/TRANSLATOR CERTIFICATION (To be completed if prepared by person other than the employee). I attest, under penalty of perjury, that the above was prepared by me at the request of the named individual and is based on all information of which I have any knowledge.

Signature	Name (Print or Type)		
Address (Street Name and Number)	City	State	Zip Code

2 EMPLOYER REVIEW AND VERIFICATION: (To be completed and signed by employer.)

Instructions:

Examine one document from List A and check the appropriate box. **OR** examine one document from List B **and** one from List C and check the appropriate boxes. Provide the *Document Identification Number* and *Expiration Date* for the document checked.

List A Documents that Establish Identity and Employment Eligibility	List B Documents that Establish Identity	**and**	List C Documents that Establish Employment Eligibility
☐ 1. United States Passport ☐ 2. Certificate of United States Citizenship ☐ 3. Certificate of Naturalization ☐ 4. Unexpired foreign passport with attached Employment Authorization ☐ 5. Alien Registration Card with photograph	☐ 1. A State-issued driver's license or a State-issued I.D. card with a photograph, or information, including name, sex, date of birth, height, weight, and color of eyes. (Specify State)_____) ☐ 2. U.S. Military Card ☐ 3. Other (Specify document and issuing authority) _____		☐ 1. Original Social Security Number Card (other than a card stating it is not valid for employment) ☐ 2. A birth certificate issued by State, county, or municipal authority bearing a seal or other certification ☐ 3. Unexpired INS Employment Authorization Specify form #_____
Document Identification # _____ *Expiration Date (if any)* _____	*Document Identification* # _____ *Expiration Date (if any)* _____		*Document Identification* # _____ *Expiration Date (if any)* _____

CERTIFICATION: I attest, under penalty of perjury, that I have examined the documents presented by the above individual, that they appear to be genuine and to relate to the individual named, and that the individual, to the best of my knowledge, is eligible to work in the United States.

Signature	Name (Print or Type)	Title
Employer Name	Address	Date

Form I-9 (05/07/87)
OMB No. 1115-0136

U.S. Department of Justice
Immigration and Naturalization Service

SOCIAL SECURITY ADMINISTRATION

Request for Earnings and Benefit Estimate Statement

To receive a free statement of your earnings covered by Social Security and your estimated future benefits, all you need to do is fill out this form. Please print or type your answers. When you have completed the form, mail it to us.

1. Name shown on your Social Security card:

   First   Middle Initial   Last

2. Your Social Security number as shown on your card:

   ☐☐☐ - ☐☐ - ☐☐☐☐

3. Your date of birth: _____ _____ _____
                  Month   Day   Year

4. Other Social Security numbers you may have used:

   ☐☐☐ - ☐☐ - ☐☐☐☐

   ☐☐☐ - ☐☐ - ☐☐☐☐

5. Your Sex: ☐ Male   ☐ Female

6. Other names you have used (including a maiden name):

7. Show your actual earnings for last year and your estimated earnings for this year. Include only wages and/or net self-employment income subject to Social Security tax.

   A. Last year's actual earnings:

   $ ☐☐☐,☐☐☐.☐☐
   Dollars only

   B. This year's estimated earnings:

   $ ☐☐☐,☐☐☐.☐☐
   Dollars only

8. Show the age at which you plan to retire: _____

9. Below, show an amount which you think best represents your future average yearly earnings between now and when you plan to retire. The amount should be a yearly average, not your total future lifetime earnings. Only show earnings subject to Social Security tax.

   Most people should enter the same amount as this year's estimated earnings (the amount shown in 7B). The reason for this is that we will show your retirement benefit estimate in today's dollars, but adjusted to account for average wage growth in the national economy.

   However, if you expect to earn significantly more or less in the future than what you currently earn because of promotions, a job change, part-time work, or an absence from the work force, enter the amount in today's dollars that will most closely reflect your future average yearly earnings. Do not add in cost-of-living, performance, or scheduled pay increases or bonuses.

   Your future average yearly earnings:

   $ ☐☐☐,☐☐☐.☐☐
   Dollars only

10. Address where you want us to send the statement:

    Name

    Street Address (Include Apt. No., P.O. Box, or Rural Route)

    City   State   Zip Code

I am asking for information about my own Social Security record or the record of a person I am authorized to represent. I understand that if I deliberately request information under false pretenses I may be guilty of a federal crime and could be fined and/or imprisoned. I authorize you to send the statement of my earnings and benefits estimates to me or my representative through a contractor.

Please sign your name (Do not print)

Date   (Area Code) Daytime Telephone No.

Send to:

Social Security Administration
Wilkes-Barre Data Operations Center
P.O. Box 20
Wilkes-Barre, PA 18703

Model Statement —
Health Insurance Continuation

Very Important Notice

Federal law [Public Law 99-272, Title X] requires that most employers sponsoring group health plans offer employees and their families the opportunity for a temporary extension of health coverage (called "continuation coverage") at group rates in certain instances where coverage under the plan would otherwise end. This notice is intended to inform you, in a summary fashion, of your rights and obligations under the continuation coverage provisions of the law. [Both you and your spouse should take the time to read this notice carefully.]

If you are an employee of [Name of Employer] covered by [Name of Group Health Plan] you have a right to choose this continuation coverage if you lose your group health coverage because of a reduction in your hours of employment or the termination of your employment (for reasons other than gross misconduct on your part). This right to choose continuation coverage also applies to any individual who is in the military reserves and is called up for active duty. (A military health plan does not cut off one's right to continuation coverage.)

If you are the spouse of an employee covered by [Name of Group Health Plan], you have the right to choose continuation coverage for yourself if you lose group health coverage under [Name of Group Health Plan] for *any* of the following reasons:

1. The death of your spouse;
2. A termination of your spouse's employment (for reasons other than gross misconduct) or reduction in your spouse's hours of employment;
3. Divorce or legal separation from your spouse; or
4. Your spouse becomes eligible for Medicare.

In the case of a dependent child of an employee covered by [Name of Group Health Plan], he or she has the right to continuation coverage if group health coverage under [Name of Group Health Plan] is for *any* of the following five reasons:

1. The death of a parent;
2. The termination of a parent's employment (for reasons other than gross misconduct) or reduction in a parent's hours of employment with [Name of Employer];
3. Parents' divorce or legal separation;
4. A parent becomes eligible for Medicare; or
5. The dependent ceases to be a "dependent child" under [Name of Group Health Plan].

Under the law, the employee or a family member has the responsibility to inform [Name of Plan Administrator] of a divorce, legal separation, or a child losing dependent status under [Name of Group Health Plan]. [Name of Employer] has the responsibility to notify [Name of Plan Administrator] of the employee's death, termination of employment, or reduction in hours, or Medicare eligibility.

When [Name of Plan Administrator] is notified that one of these events has happened, [Name of Plan Administrator] will in turn notify you that you have the right to choose continuation coverage. Under the law, you have at least 60 days from the date you would lose coverage because of one of the events described above to inform [Name of Plan Administrator] that you want continuation coverage.

If you do not choose continuation coverage, your group health insurance coverage will end.

If you choose continuation coverage, [Name of Employer] is required to give you coverage which, as of the time coverage is being provided, is identical to the coverage provided under the plan to similarly situated employees or family members. The law requires that you be afforded the opportunity to maintain continuation coverage for 3 years unless you lost group health coverge because of a termination of employment or reduction in hours. In that case, the required continuation coverage period is 18 months. However, the law also provides that your continuation coverage may be cut short for *any* of the following five reasons:

1. [Name of Employer] no longer provides group health coverage to any of its employees;
2. The premium for your continuation coverage is not paid;
3. You become an employee covered under another group health plan (unless that plan excludes or limits coverage of a pre-existing condition the person had);
4. You become eligible for Medicare;
5. You were divorced from a covered employee and subsequently remarry and are covered under your new spouse's group health plan.

You do not have to show that you are insurable to choose continuation coverage. However, under the law, you may have to pay all or part of the premium for your continuation coverage. [The law also says that, at the end of the 18 months or 3-year continuation coverage period, you must be allowed to enroll in an individual conversion health plan provided under [Name of Group Health Plan].]

This law applies to [Name of Group Health Plan] beginning on [applicable date under § 10002(d) of COBRA]. If you have any questions about the law, please contact [Name and Business Address of Plan Administrator]. Also, if you have changed marital status, or you or your spouse have changed addresses, please notify [Name of Plan Administrator] at the above address.

Notice to Employees About the Training Wage

The 1989 Amendments to the Fair Labor Standards Act (FLSA) include a provision permitting covered employers to pay eligible workers at a training wage under certain specified conditions. The law requires that you be furnished with a copy of this written notice.

1. The FLSA generally requires that employees receive at least the minimum wage of $3.80 per hour beginning April 1, 1990, and $4.25 per hour beginning April 1, 1991. Unless an exemption in the law applies to you, you are also entitled to one and one-half times your regular rate of pay for hours worked over 40 in a workweek.

2. If you are under the age of 20, your employer may be eligible to employ you for up to 90 days at a training wage of 85 percent of the FLSA's minimum wage or $3.35 per hour, whichever is greater, under the following conditions:

   a. You are provided this notice.

   b. No other employee has been laid off from the position or a substantially equivalent position.

   c. No other employee has been terminated, or had his or her hours of work or wages, benefits, or employment conditions reduced or changed for the purpose of hiring you or any other individual at the training wage.

   d. You are not a migrant or seasonal agricultural worker or a nonimmigrant agricultural worker admitted to the United States under the H-2A program.

   e. You have not previously been employed at the training wage for 90 days.

   f. You have furnished your employer with proof of your age and a signed statement (or documentation) about the starting and ending dates of your previous employment since January 1, 1990, and the hourly wage(s) you earned or, if none, a signed written statement to that effect.

   g. Your hours of work and the type of work you do are permitted under Federal, State, and local child labor laws.

   h. The total number of hours worked by all employees paid at the training wage in any month does not exceed 25 percent of the total number of hours worked by all employees in the establishment.

3. If you are under the age of 20 and you have been employed for 90 calendar days at the training wage, you may be employed at the training wage for up to an additional 90 calendar days provided all of the conditions above are met and, in addition:

   a. Your employer is *not* an employer who employed you during any portion of the initial 90-day period.

   b. Your employer provides on-the-job training in accordance with regulations issued by the Department of Labor.

   c. Your employer provides you with a copy of the training program, and retains a file copy of the training program.

   d. Your employer posts in the establishment a notice of the types of jobs (including yours) for which on-the-job training is being provided and sends the Department of Labor a copy of the notice annually.

4. Unless your employer follows the above rules, you must be paid the full minimum wage.

5. Violation of the training wage provisions by employers can result in the following:

   a. Any employee (or the Department of Labor on his or her behalf) who is terminated, laid off, or has hours, wages, benefits, or conditions of employment reduced or changed for purposes of employing an individual at the training wage can file a lawsuit for wages lost and an equal amount as liquidated damages, or equitable relief, including employment, reinstatement, or promotion. In addition, the Department of Labor can issue an order disqualifying an employer from employing anyone at the training wage.

   b. Any employee (or the Department of Labor on his or her behalf) who has not received proper minimum or overtime wages (including proper training wages) can file a lawsuit to recover the amount of such wages plus an equal amount as liquidated damages.

   c. The Department of Labor can seek an injunction to restrain violations by employers, including an injunction requiring the payment of proper wages under the FLSA.

   d. Child labor violations and wilful or repeated minimum wage or overtime pay violations by employers can result in the Department of Labor assessing a civil money penalty of up to $1,000 per violation.

   e. In the case of criminal violations by employers, the FLSA provides for penalties of up to $10,000 and, in the case of a second conviction, imprisonment of up to six months, or both.

Index

Pull-Outs of Required Workplace Posters Follow . . .

Federal Minimum Wage
(Department of Labor)

Equal Employment Opportunity is the Law
(Equal Employment Commission)

Job Safety & Health Protection
(Occupational Safety and Health Administration)

Employee Polygraph Protection Act
(Department of Labor)

NOTICE TO EMPLOYEES

Federal Minimum Wage

$3.80 per hour
Effective April 1, 1990

$4.25 per hour
Effective April 1, 1991

Most employees in the United States qualify for both minimum wage and overtime pay under THE FAIR LABOR STANDARDS ACT. Overtime pay may not be less than 1 1/2 times the employee's regular rate of pay for hours worked over 40 in one workweek.

Certain full-time students, student learners, apprentices, and workers with disabilities may be paid less than the minimum wage under special certificates issued by the Department of Labor.

Covered Employees

- Employees engaged in interstate commerce or in the production of goods for interstate commerce (i.e., goods that travel across state lines), regardless of the employer's annual volume of business.
- Employees who work for enterprises that have an annual gross volume of sales made or business done of over $500,000.
- Employees of hospitals, residential facilities that care for those who are physically or mentally ill or disabled, or aged, schools for children who are mentally or physically disabled or gifted, pre-schools, elementary and secondary schools, and institutions of higher education, regardless of the annual volume of business.
- Employees of public agencies.

Child Labor

An employee must be at least 16 years old to work in most non-farm jobs and at least 18 to work in non-farm jobs declared hazardous by the Secretary of Labor. Youths 14 and 15 years old may work outside school hours in various non-manufacturing, non-mining, non-hazardous jobs under the following conditions:
No more than—

3 hours on a school day or 18 hours in a school week;
8 hours on a non-school day or 40 hours in a non-school week.

Also, work may not begin before 7 a.m., or end after 7 p.m., except from June 1 through Labor Day, when evening hours are extended to 9 p.m. Different rules apply in agricultural employment.

Training Wage

A training wage of $3.35 per hour, or 85 percent of the applicable minimum wage, whichever is greater, may be paid to most employees under 20 years of age for up to 90 days under certain conditions. Individuals may be employed at this training wage for a second 90-day period by a different employer if certain additional requirements are met. No individual may be employed at the training wage, in any number of jobs, for more than a total of 180 days. Employers may not displace regular employees in order to hire those eligible for the training wage.

Tipped Employees

A tipped employee is one who regularly receives more than $30 a month in tips. Tips received by such employees may be counted as wages up to a certain percentage of the minimum wage. The minimum cash wage that employers must pay (from their own pockets) to tipped employees is $2.09 an hour effective April 1, 1990. It will rise to $2.13 an hour effective April 1, 1991. If an employee's hourly tip earnings (averaged weekly) added to this hourly wage do not equal the minimum wage, the employer is responsible for paying the balance.

Enforcement

The Department of Labor may recover back wages either administratively or through court action, for the employees that have been underpaid in violation of the law. Violations may result in civil or criminal action.

Civil money penalties of up to $1,000 per violation may be assessed against employers who violate the child labor provisions of the law or who willfully or repeatedly violate the minimum wage or overtime pay provisions. This law *prohibits* discriminating against or discharging workers who file a complaint or participate in any proceedings under the Act.

Note: Certain occupations and establishments are exempt from the minimum wage and/or overtime pay provisions.

Special provisions apply to workers in Puerto Rico and American Samoa.

Where state law requires a higher minimum wage the higher standard applies.

FOR ADDITIONAL INFORMATION CONTACT the Wage and Hour Division office nearest you - - listed in your telephone directory under United States Government, Labor Department.

The law requires employers to display this poster where employees can readily see it.

U.S. Department of Labor
Employment Standards Administration
Wage and Hour Division
Washington D.C. 20210

WH Publication 1088
Revised April 1990

☆U.S.G.P.O. 1990 257-453/00539

Equal Employment Opportunity is the

Private Employment, State and Local Governments, Educational Institutions

Race, Color, Religion, Sex, National Origin:
Title VII of the Civil Rights Act of 1964, as amended, prohibits discrimination in hiring, promotion, discharge, pay, fringe benefits, and other aspects of employment, on the basis of race, color, religion, sex or national origin.

Applicants to and employees of most private employers, state and local governments and public or private educational institutions are protected. Employment agencies, labor unions and apprenticeship programs also are covered.

Age:
The Age Discrimination in Employment Act of 1967, as amended, prohibits age discrimination and protects applicants and employees 40 years of age or older from discrimination on account of age in hiring, promotion, discharge, compensation, terms, conditions, or privileges of employment. The law covers most private employers, state and local governments, educational institutions, employment agencies and labor organizations.

Sex (wages):
In addition to sex discrimination prohibited by Title VII of the Civil Rights Act (see above), the Equal Pay Act of 1963, as amended, prohibits sex discrimination in payment of wages to women and men performing substantially equal work in the same establishment. The law covers most private employers, state and local governments and educational institutions. Labor organizations cannot cause employers to violate the law. Many employers not covered by Title VII, because of size, are covered by the Equal Pay Act.

If you believe that you have been discriminated against under any of the above laws, you immediately should contact:

The U.S. Equal Employment Opportunity Commission
Washington, D.C. 20507
or an EEOC field office by calling toll free 800-USA-EEOC.
(For the hearing impaired, EEOC's TDD number is 202-663-4399.)

Employers holding Federal contracts or subcontracts

Race, Color, Religion, Sex, National Origin:
Executive Order 11246, as amended, prohibits job discrimination on the basis of race, color, religion, sex or national origin, and requires affirmative action to ensure equality of opportunity in all aspects of employment.

Handicap:
Section 503 of the Rehabilitation Act of 1973, as amended, prohibits job discrimination because of handicap and requires affirmative action to employ and advance in employment qualified handicapped individuals who, with reasonable accommodation, can perform the functions of a job.

Vietnam Era and Special Disabled Veterans:
38 U.S.C. 2012 of the Vietnam Era Veterans Readjustment Assistance Act of 1974 prohibits job discrimination and requires

affirmative action to employ and advance in employment qualified Vietnam era veterans and qualified special disabled veterans.

Applicants to and employees of companies with a Federal government contract or subcontract are protected under the authorities above. Any person who believes a contractor has violated its non-discrimination or affirmative action obligations under Executive Order 11246, as amended, Section 503 of the Rehabilitation Act or 38 U.S.C. 2012 of the Vietnam Era Veterans Readjustment Assistance Act should contact immediately:

The Office of Federal Contract Compliance Programs (OFCCP)
Employment Standards Administration, U.S. Department of Labor, 200 Constitution Avenue, N.W., Washington, D.C. 20210 (202) 523-9368, or an OFCCP regional or district office, listed in most telephone directories under U.S. Government, Department of Labor.

Programs or activities receiving Federal financial assistance

Handicap:
Section 504 of the Rehabilitation Act of 1973, as amended, prohibits employment discrimination on the basis of handicap in any program or activity which receives Federal financial assistance. Discrimination is prohibited in all aspects of employment against handicapped persons who, with reasonable accommodation, can perform the essential functions of a job.

Race, Color, National Origin, Sex:
In addition to the protection of Title VII of the Civil Rights Act of 1964, Title VI of the Civil Rights Act prohibits discrimination on the basis of race, color or national origin in programs or activities

receiving Federal financial assistance. Employment discrimination is covered by Title VI if the primary objective of the financial assistance is provision of employment, or where employment discrimination causes or may cause discrimination in providing services under such programs. Title IX of the Education Amendments of 1972 prohibits employment discrimination on the basis of sex in educational programs or activities which receive Federal assistance.

If you believe you have been discriminated against in a program of any institution which receives Federal assistance, you should contact immediately the Federal agency providing such assistance.

10/89

JOB SAFETY & HEALTH PROTECTION

The Occupational Safety and Health Act of 1970 provides job safety and health protection for workers by promoting safe and healthful working conditions throughout the Nation. Provisions of the Act include the following:

Employers

All employers must furnish to employees employment and a place of employment free from recognized hazards that are causing or are likely to cause death or serious harm to employees. Employers must comply with occupational safety and health standards issued under the Act.

Employees

Employees must comply with all occupational safety and health standards, rules, regulations and orders issued under the Act that apply to their own actions and conduct on the job.

The Occupational Safety and Health Administration (OSHA) of the U.S. Department of Labor has the primary responsibility for administering the Act. OSHA issues occupational safety and health standards, and its Compliance Safety and Health Officers conduct jobsite inspections to help ensure compliance with the Act.

Inspection

The Act requires that a representative of the employer and a representative authorized by the employees be given an opportunity to accompany the OSHA inspector for the purpose of aiding the inspection.

Where there is no authorized employee representative, the OSHA Compliance Officer must consult with a reasonable number of employees concerning safety and health conditions in the workplace.

Complaint

Employees or their representatives have the right to file a complaint with the nearest OSHA office requesting an inspection if they believe unsafe or unhealthful conditions exist in their workplace. OSHA will withhold, on request, names of employees complaining.

The Act provides that employees may not be discharged or discriminated against in any way for filing safety and health complaints or for otherwise exercising their rights under the Act.

Employees who believe they have been discriminated against may file a complaint with their nearest OSHA office within 30 days of the alleged discriminatory action.

Citation

If upon inspection OSHA believes an employer has violated the Act, a citation alleging such violations will be issued to the employer. Each citation will specify a time period within which the alleged violation must be corrected.

The OSHA citation must be prominently displayed at or near the place of alleged violation for three days, or until it is corrected, whichever is later, to warn employees of dangers that may exist there.

Proposed Penalty

The Act provides for mandatory penalties against employers of up to $1,000 for each serious violation and for optional penalties of up to $1,000 for each nonserious violation. Penalties of up to $1,000 per day may be proposed for failure to correct violations within the proposed time period. Also, any employer who willfully or repeatedly violates the Act may be assessed penalties of up to $10,000 for each such violation.

There are also provisions for criminal penalties. Any willful violation resulting in death of an employee, upon conviction, is punishable by a fine of up to $250,000 (or $500,000 if the employer is a corporation), or by imprisonment for up to six months, or both. A second conviction of an employer doubles the possible term of imprisonment.

Voluntary Activity

While providing penalties for violations, the Act also encourages efforts by labor and management, before an OSHA inspection, to reduce workplace hazards voluntarily and to develop and improve safety and health programs in all workplaces and industries. OSHA's Voluntary Protection Programs recognize outstanding efforts of this nature.

OSHA has published Safety and Health Program Management Guidelines to assist employers in establishing or perfecting programs to prevent or control employee exposure to workplace hazards. There are many public and private organizations that can provide information and assistance in this effort, if requested. Also, your local OSHA office can provide considerable help and advice on solving safety and health problems or can refer you to other sources for help such as training.

Consultation

Free assistance in identifying and correcting hazards and in improving safety and health management is available to employers, without citation or penalty, through OSHA-supported programs in each State. These programs are usually administered by the State Labor or Health department or a State university.

Posting Instructions

Employers in States operating OSHA approved State Plans should obtain and post the State's equivalent poster.

Under provisions of Title 29, Code of Federal Regulations, Part 1903.2(a)(1) employers must post this notice (or facsimile) in a conspicuous place where notices to employees are customarily posted.

More Information

Additional information and copies of the Act, specific OSHA safety and health standards, and other applicable regulations may be obtained from your employer or from the nearest OSHA Regional Office in the following locations:

Atlanta	(404) 347-3573
Boston	(617) 565-7164
Chicago	(312) 353-2220
Dallas	(214) 767-4731
Denver	(303) 844-3061
Kansas	(816) 426-5861
New York	(212) 337-2325
Philadelphia	(215) 596-1201
San Francisco	(415) 995-5672
Seattle	(206) 442-5930

Elizabeth Dole, Secretary of Labor

U.S. Department of Labor

Occupational Safety and Health Administration

Washington, D.C.
1989 (Revised)
OSHA 2203

U.S. DEPARTMENT OF LABOR

EMPLOYMENT STANDARDS ADMINISTRATION

Wage and Hour Division
Washington, D.C. 20210

NOTICE

EMPLOYEE POLYGRAPH PROTECTION ACT

The Employee Polygraph Protection Act prohibits most private employers from using lie detector tests either for pre-employment screening or during the course of employment.

PROHIBITIONS

Employers are generally prohibited from requiring or requesting any employee or job applicant to take a lie detector test, and from discharging, disciplining, or discriminating against an employee or prospective employee for refusing to take a test or for exercising other rights under the Act.

EXEMPTIONS*

Federal, State and local governments are not affected by the law. Also, the law does not apply to tests given by the Federal Government to certain private individuals engaged in national security-related activities.

The Act permits *polygraph* (a kind of lie detector) tests to be administered in the private sector, subject to restrictions, to certain prospective employees of security service firms (armored car, alarm, and guard), and of pharmaceutical manufacturers, distributors and dispensers.

The Act also permits polygraph testing, subject to restrictions, of certain employees of private firms who are reasonably suspected of involvement in a workplace incident (theft, embezzlement, etc.) that resulted in economic loss to the employer.

EXAMINEE RIGHTS

Where polygraph tests are permitted, they are subject to numerous strict standards concerning the conduct and length of the test. Examinees have a number of specific rights, including the right to a written notice before testing, the right to refuse or discontinue a test, and the right not to have test results disclosed to unauthorized persons.

ENFORCEMENT

The Secretary of Labor may bring court actions to restrain violations and assess civil penalties up to $10,000 against violators. Employees or job applicants may also bring their own court actions.

ADDITIONAL INFORMATION

Additional information may be obtained, and complaints of violations may be filed, at local offices of the Wage and Hour Division, which are listed in the telephone directory under U.S. Government, Department of Labor, Employment Standards Administration.

THE LAW REQUIRES EMPLOYERS TO DISPLAY THIS POSTER WHERE EMPLOYEES AND JOB APPLICANTS CAN READILY SEE IT.

The law does not preempt any provision of any State or local law or any collective bargaining agreement which is more restrictive with respect to lie detector tests.

U.S. DEPARTMENT OF LABOR
EMPLOYMENT STANDARDS ADMINISTRATION

Wage and Hour Division
Washington, D.C. 20210

*U.S. GPO: 1989—(247-870)

WH Publication 1462
September 1988